IMAGES
of America

WAYNE COUNTY

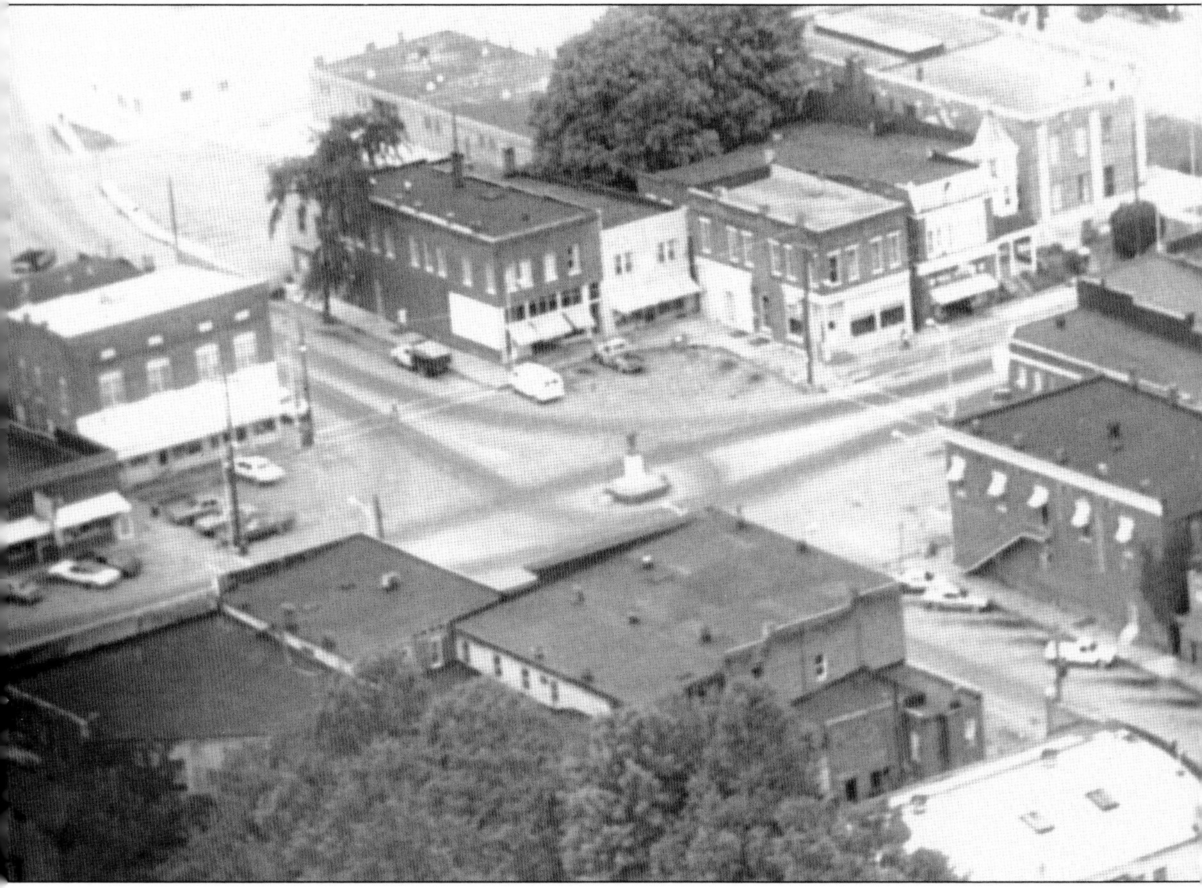

Physical landmarks illustrate and document the history of a community. While some only see man-made buildings or natural structures, others see the human toil and effort that was exerted to tame the natural surroundings and construct those buildings. The town square of Monticello, the seat of Wayne County, speaks volumes about the dedication and determination of its citizens. Three courthouses stood in the center of the square where the political and judicial life of the community took place. When the courthouse site was changed, a monument to World War I soldiers was placed in that spot. The businesses that lined the square declared that their owners possessed certain skills and knowledge to operate them. The places of entertainment were there because people in the community enjoyed the arts and cultural events. All these characteristics make Wayne County one of the most desirable places in south-central Kentucky to live and work. (Wayne County Museum.)

On the Cover: Strong determination motivated the first men and women who moved to the Kentucky wilderness. They were looking for the opportunity to develop the land and provide a home for their families. Determination alone would not accomplish that dream. With a strong work ethic, they did whatever they had to do to achieve their goals. Their descendants inherited these character traits, and they continued to work. The cover photograph provided by William Roberts, a direct descendant of Wayne County pioneers, depicts the tremendous effort these brave men and women put forth to make Wayne County, Kentucky, one of the greatest places in the nation to live and raise a family. In using this image as the cover for this publication, we pay tribute to them. (William Roberts.)

IMAGES
of America

WAYNE COUNTY

Wayne County Museum

ARCADIA
PUBLISHING

ISBN 978-0-7385-8696-0

Published by Arcadia Publishing
Charleston, South Carolina

Printed in the United States of America

Library of Congress Control Number: 2010931196

For all general information, please contact Arcadia Publishing:
Telephone 843-853-2070
Fax 843-853-0044
E-mail sales@arcadiapublishing.com
For customer service and orders:
Toll-Free 1-888-313-2665

Visit us on the Internet at www.arcadiapublishing.com

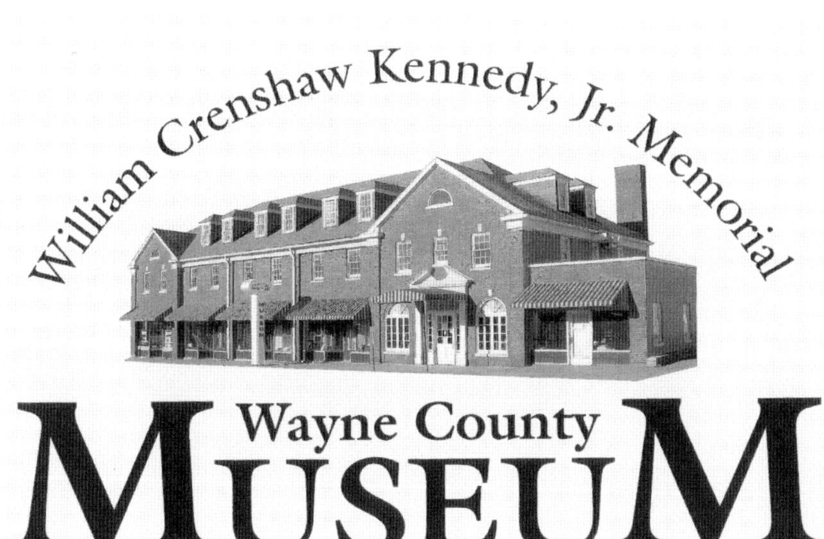

The people of Wayne County have embraced the purpose and mission of the Wayne County Museum in its efforts to collect, interpret, preserve, and display historical artifacts that tell the story of the county. It is their support and interest that make it possible for the museum to exist. They are the ones who tell the stories, provide the photographs, and donate the precious artifacts that will "give our past a future." It is with sincere appreciation to each of them that this publication is dedicated. (Wayne County Museum.)

Contents

ACKNOWLEDGMENTS

This compilation of pictures and text was created to provide a glimpse into Wayne County history. Simply stated, this book is the result of a group effort, involving the entire staff of the Wayne County Museum. Harlan Ogle, Juanita Coffey, Anna Lee Cross, and Margie Williams have given much time and effort to the project. Staff members of the Wayne County Historical Society Library have also helped, particularly Sue Wright, Karen Burnett, and Charlotte Johnson. Special thanks are extended to Joyce Munsey for generously permitting us to draw from the library's treasure trove of pictures. Thanks are also due to the many people who answered our questions and to those who brought their pictures to the museum and supplied the information we needed. Drexell Anderson, Kenneth Coffey, Sue Woolums, Lyle Breeding, Nora Hickam, J. D. Rogers, Joan Abbott, Sula Margaret Gregory, Bill Fred Twyford, and Jane Dalton have been especially helpful.

Information for the text has been gleaned from many places. The files of both the Wayne County Museum and the Wayne County Historical Society Library have been excellent sources. The books of B. G. Edwards, Dorcas Catron, Garnett Walker, Ira Bell, and Robert M. Rennick have also been good reference materials. Old issues of the *Wayne County Outlook* have yielded many dates and facts, and Augustua Phillips Johnson's *A Century of Wayne County* provided additional information we needed.

For the staff of the Wayne County Museum, the development of this project has been an interesting journey through the past. Many thanks to all who helped make the book the best that it could be.

INTRODUCTION

The history of Wayne County began in 1800. On December 13 of that year, the Kentucky Legislature voted to create the new county, and on March 16, 1801, the justices of the peace held their first meeting at the home of Henry Garner. We know, however, that the 210 years in which Wayne County has been a political entity is only a small space on a timeline that shows how long human beings have walked the hills and hollows of this bit of earth that Wayne Countians cherish as home. Paleo-Indian people lived here as much as 9,000 to 12,000 years ago. Following them, group after group of prehistoric people lived here. They hunted, gathered food, and farmed this land, then vanished, leaving behind only hints of their existence. Tools, graves, and pottery representing many layers of human habitation have been discovered in Hines Cave in the Mill Springs community. This major archaeological find is documented in *Ancient Life in Kentucky*.

Many pages closer to modern times, European explorers were followed in 1770 by the Long Hunters, a group of some 22 hunters from Virginia who got their name after uniting for an extended hunting expedition (about three years) into what is now south-central Kentucky. By then, the area that would later be known as Wayne County was the hunting ground and sometimes the battlefield of Native American nations such as the Creek, Catawba, Shawnee, Wyandotte, Delaware, and Iroquois. Most notably, though, this was the territory of the Cherokee, who had roamed and hunted the rich, well-watered acres for centuries. The last Cherokee chief, Chief Doublehead, is a major figure in local history. Many people trace their ancestry to him.

The Long Hunters returned to their homes in Virginia and North Carolina with glowing reports of the abundant and beautiful virgin land lying unclaimed beyond the mountains. The excitement stirred by these reports helped launch the tide of migration that soon followed. Michael Stoner and Daniel Boone came this way in 1774. Their mission was to warn settlers and surveyors to return home until a Native American uprising could be settled. Stoner later returned and spent the rest of his life here. Other settlers, explorers, surveyors, and adventurers arrived. In 1775, Benjamin Price and Nathaniel Buchhannon came down the Cumberland River and left their canoe at the mouth of Meadow Creek. A short distance away was a knoll where they built what was probably the first cabin in the area that would become Wayne County. Later, they built Price's Station, a fort which withstood the 1777 onslaught of Native American attacks aimed at driving white settlers from Kentucky. By the summer of 1779, the area was peaceful enough that Price grew a crop of corn in the nearby meadow. For about 25 years, Price's Station served as a rest stop and supply station for adventurers and settlers traveling up and down the Cumberland. Settlers continued to arrive in ever-increasing numbers. Men who saw service in the Revolutionary War were rewarded with military land grants. At least 46 of those men came to Wayne County. In 1810, Wayne County's population was 5,430.

Settlers at both Mill Springs and Parmleysville built substantial early communities, and both wanted the county seat. A 13-acre piece of land near the halfway point between the two was a compromise location. Only four families lived on this 13-acre plot, which was named Monticello for Thomas Jefferson's mansion. The 1810 census showed 37 people living within the city limits.

During its first century, Monticello grew slowly. In 1815, the town consisted of 50 inelegant hewn-log dwelling houses, a rude courthouse, a place of public worship, four stores, three taverns, three blacksmith shops, and at least one school. By 1890, the population had grown to 413, but tremendous changes would come around the beginning of the 20th century, thanks to an oil boom. Between 1890 and 1910, Wayne County produced more oil than all other Kentucky counties. Commerce thrived during that period, and new buildings went up all over town. All but one of the lots on the public square and on the first block of North Main Street had new buildings constructed on them. Nearly all of those buildings still stand, a lasting testimony to the oil boom. In 1910, Monticello's population was 1,338. This beautiful little town is still, in the year 2010, the only town in Wayne County, but its population is now about 6,000.

Wayne County, like every county in the nation, has been plagued by a multitude of hardships: The Civil War pitted brother against brother, devastated the countryside, and nearly stopped all functions of government. A series of three huge fires in 30 years burned large sections of Monticello. Both tornadoes and floods have wreaked havoc, and the Great Depression hit Wayne County hard. From the vantage point of the present, it is gratifying to look back and see how these hardships have helped shape the county, because after each disaster, county citizens always pulled together to rebuild. As a result, the community became stronger.

The 43rd county created in Kentucky, Wayne County has undergone a number of boundary alterations since its early days. At present its area is 478 square miles. Wayne Countians of 200 years ago could never have imagined the multitude of changes that have taken place, but the county is still unbelievably picturesque. From Shinbone Cliff on the north side of the Cumberland to Bald Rock and Parker Mountain on the Tennessee line, the rolling hills and beautiful valleys are laced with a network of sparkling streams. These streams flow from the hills in the south and the east toward the beautiful lake that forms most of the county's northern border. Lake Cumberland, one of the largest man-made lakes in the country, is fairly new: In 1950, Wolf Creek Dam was completed, and a huge section of the mighty Cumberland River became a lake, which profoundly affected Wayne County.

Today Wayne County is home to about 21,000 people. More than 100 churches dot the landscape. A sign on the edge of town declares Wayne County to be the Houseboat Manufacturing Capital of the World. With numerous civic clubs, businesses of all kinds, good schools, an award-winning local history museum, and beautiful scenery in every direction, the Wayne County of today is an ideal place in which to live. It is also a place steeped in history, and the preservation of that history needs to be the passion and work of at least a few people in every generation.

Pictures are powerful things because they bring hidden snippets of history to light. We hope that all who pick up this book will find that its contents slice through time to give a clearer view of the history of Wayne County, for that is the purpose of the words and pictures offered here. Few of the pictures found in this volume have been printed in earlier publications; therefore, it is quite certain that these images and their captions will flesh out the reader's knowledge of the history of the county and that the book will help pass along the proud heritage of Wayne County to future generations.

One

Early Times

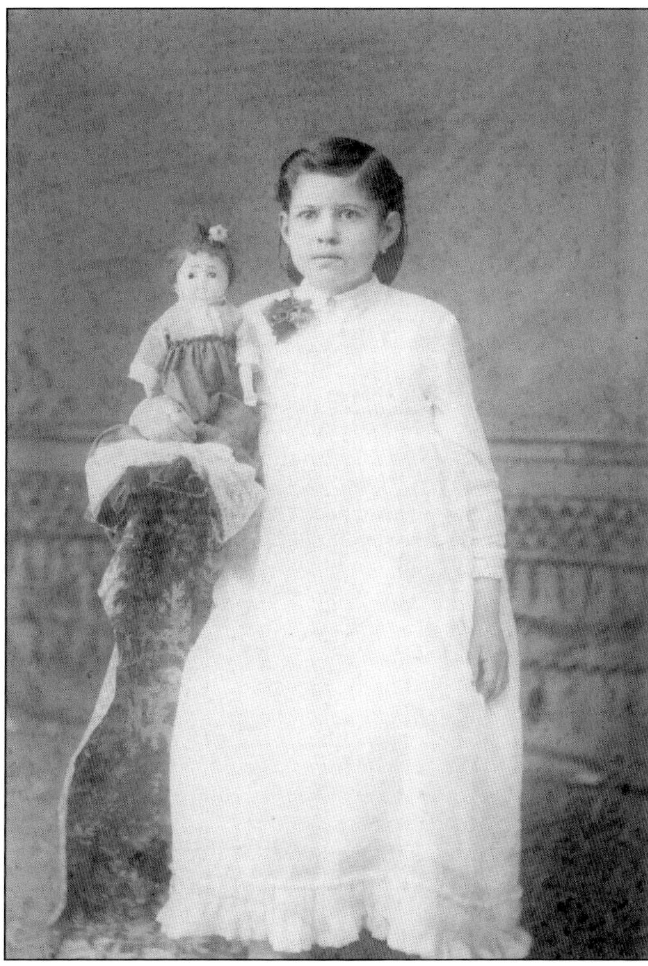

Dr. Avington Simpson Cook (1840–1918) practiced medicine in Wayne and adjacent counties for 57 years. Cook was married three times and was the father of nine children, only three of whom survived him. This beautiful daughter, Franchan Cook, died as a young girl. (Wayne County Historical Society.)

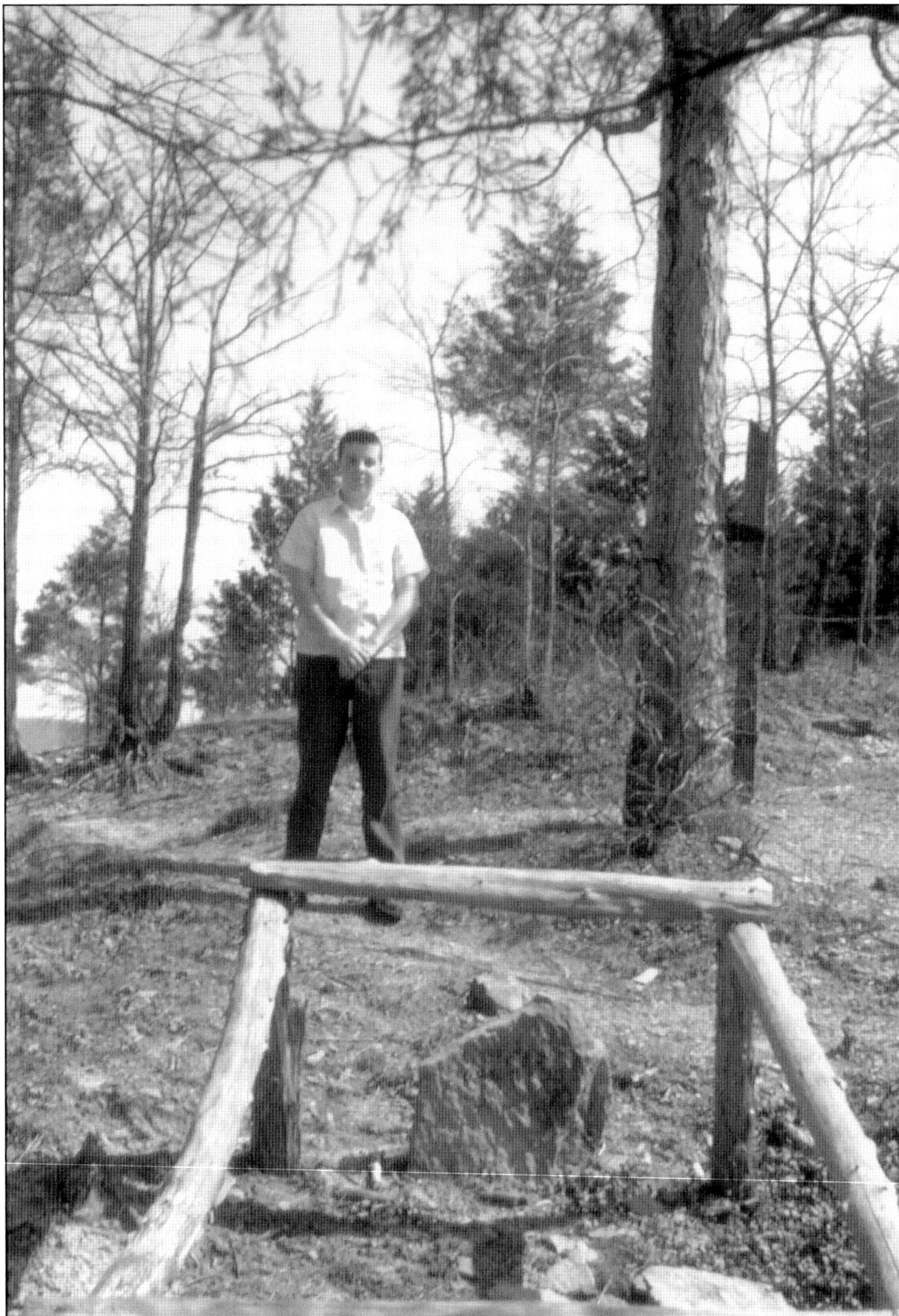

Chief Doublehead was the last great Cherokee chieftain along the Cumberland River, and many Wayne County people claim him as an ancestor. For several years, this simple memorial in the Kidder community of Wayne County honored his memory. In 1978, the marker was replaced by a beautiful memorial stone that is set on a plot nicely enclosed by a white picket fence. (Garnet Walker.)

LONG LOST GOLD MINE

By Odell Campbell

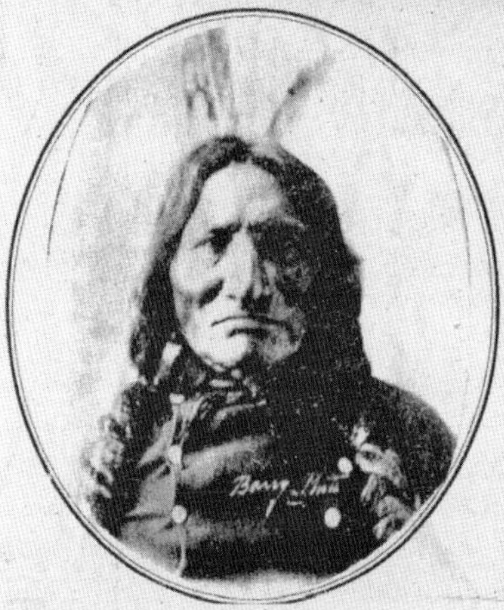

"There's gold in these hills" is a story handed down by Cherokee Indian relatives on the Little South Fork of the Cumberland River in Wayne County Kentucky. The Cherokee tribe was banished from the South Fork Country in 1805 but their white kinfolks were permitted to remain and populate the area. For many years the Cherokees returned to visit and help their kinfolks on the South Fork, find gold mines and treasure they had left behind.

Many stories have been handed down by the Smith, Blevins and Sandusky families about the Cherokee Indian treasure hunts. The most recent and detailed story is related by Elmer Hurt of Cooper, Kentucky, a distant relative of the Cherokees as told to him by his grandparents, Henry Hurt and Mary (Sandusky) Hurt.

About the year 1870, the chief of the Cherokee Indian Tribe of the North Carolina Reservation visited a relative Mary and Henry Hurt at Mount Pisgah, Kentucky. The chief brought along an old Indian map to aid him and his friends in finding the hidden treasure described as being twenty bushels of gold trinkets of Indian design.

The map located the treasure as being within the boundary of an equilateral triangle between Little South Fork and Langham Fork beginning at the Father of Rocks (Big Pilot Mount) extending South to the Mount on top of a Mount (Chimney Rock) then North West to Bridge Cliff (Wolf Cliff) and then back to Big Pilot Mount. The chief attempted to get a clue from top of the Father of Rocks which is known today as Big Pilot Mountain but failed. After searching a month for the treasure, the chief returned home.

People around Mount Pisgah today will tell you they believe there is an Indian treasure near there. Everyone hopes he may be the lucky one to find it. Only the picturesque mountains of the South Fork Country hold the secret.

Stories of lost gold and silver mines abound in Wayne County. Many of these stories have to do with Chief Doublehead and his lost silver mine. There are those who can even provide "authentic" maps that give general directions to the treasure. Odell Campbell related one of these stories that tell about a lost gold mine in the Mount Pisgah area. (Wayne County Museum.)

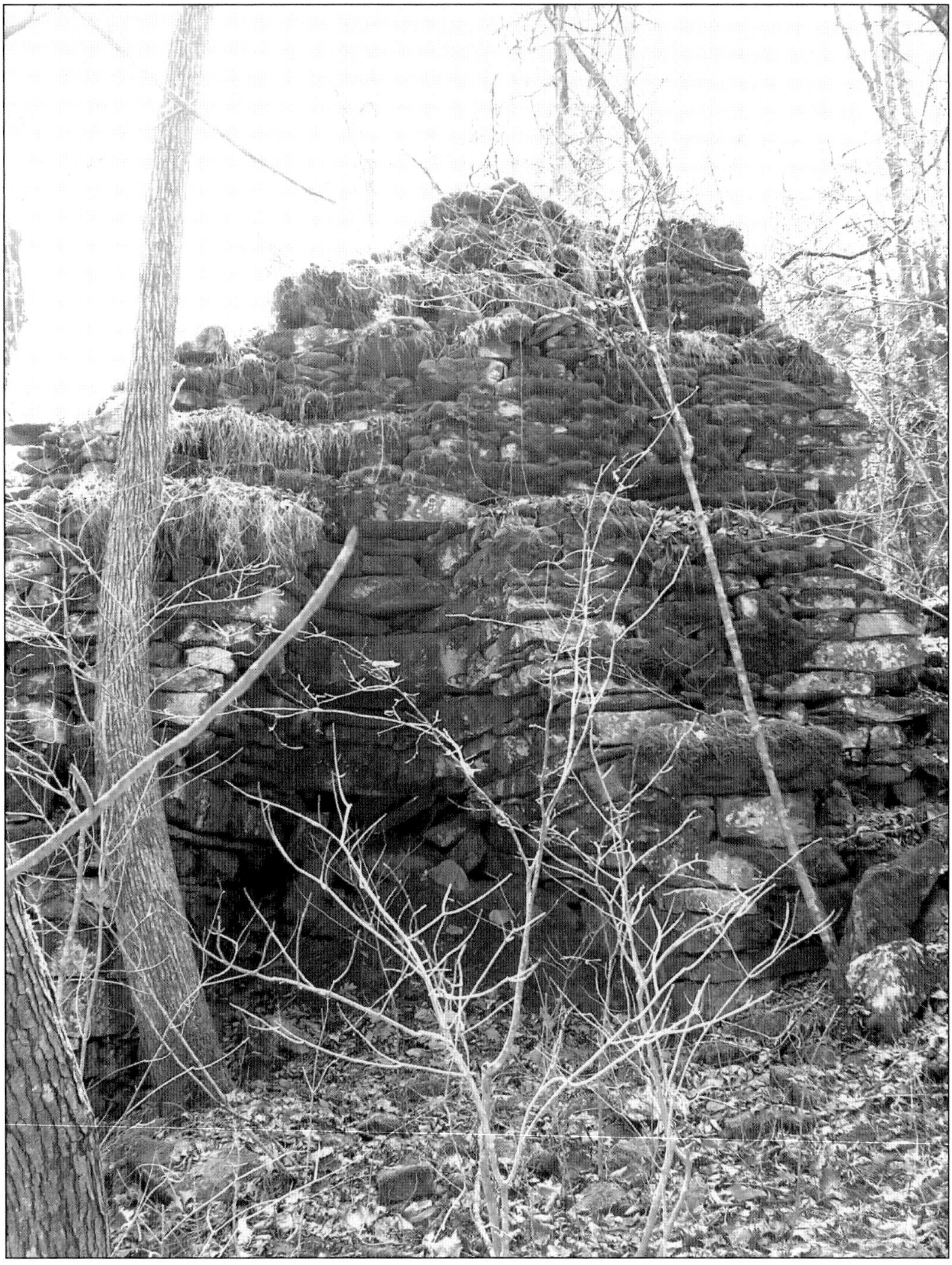

The ruins of the Joshua Jones bloomery stand at the foot of Furnace Mountain near the Jack Duncan house. Jones, a surveyor from Virginia, came to Kentucky in the 1790s to help solve boundary problems of newly claimed lands. Jones set up this furnace and produced more than enough pig iron for the area's needs. The excess pig iron was shipped to Burnside. (Wayne County Museum.)

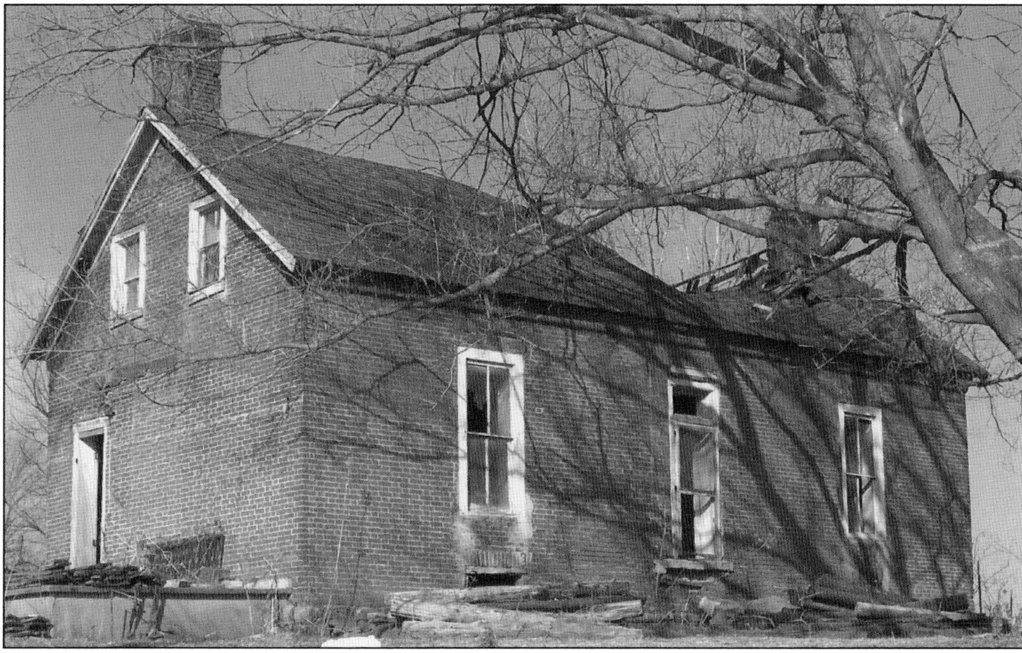

Jack Duncan grew up in this home built before 1843 by John Hutchison Rankin and Corinthia Garth Rankin. Before his death a few years ago, Duncan deeded this historical home, with its 8-inch-thick brick walls and sills made of full-size logs, to a nonprofit organization that will work to restore it to its original condition. Remarkable stories, including Civil War tales, are connected to this house, which stands just outside Monticello on Highway 200. (Wayne County Museum.)

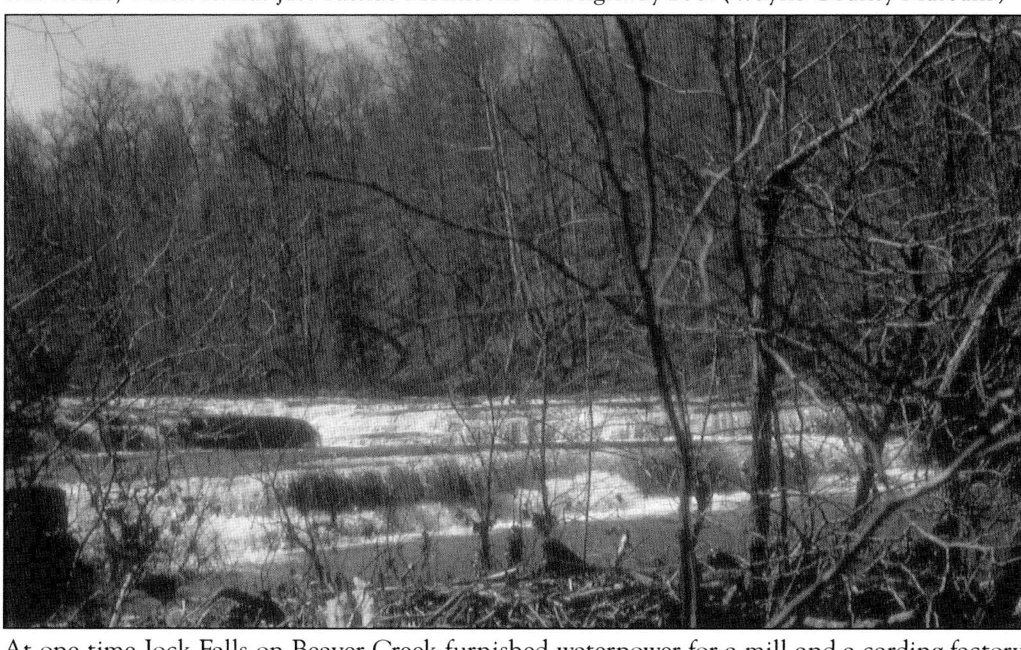

At one time Jock Falls on Beaver Creek furnished waterpower for a mill and a carding factory. John W. Rankin, who was familiarly called "Jock," was the son of John Hutchison Rankin and Corinthia Garth Rankin. Jock farmed, ran a mill, and lived his entire life in the Rankin house near the falls, so it seems safe to assume that the falls were named for him. (Garnett Walker.)

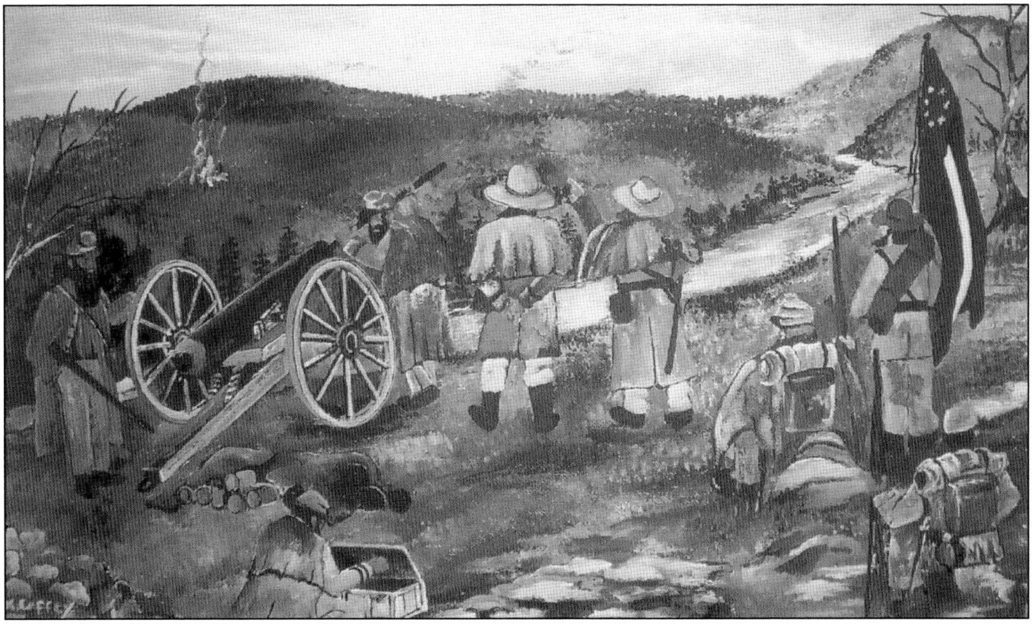

The Battle of Mill Springs was the first significant Union victory of the Civil War. On the cold and stormy night of January 19, 1862, Confederate troops left their winter quarters at Beech Grove near Mill Springs and, for about six hours, sloshed along through rain, sleet, and mud to make a surprise attack against the Union forces camped in Pulaski County. It was a bloody battle. According to the Mill Springs Battlefield Association, the total number of casualties numbered more than 700. Local artist Kenneth Coffey catches the mood of that terrible battle in a painting he calls "Confederate Gun Position at Mill Springs." (Kenneth Coffey.)

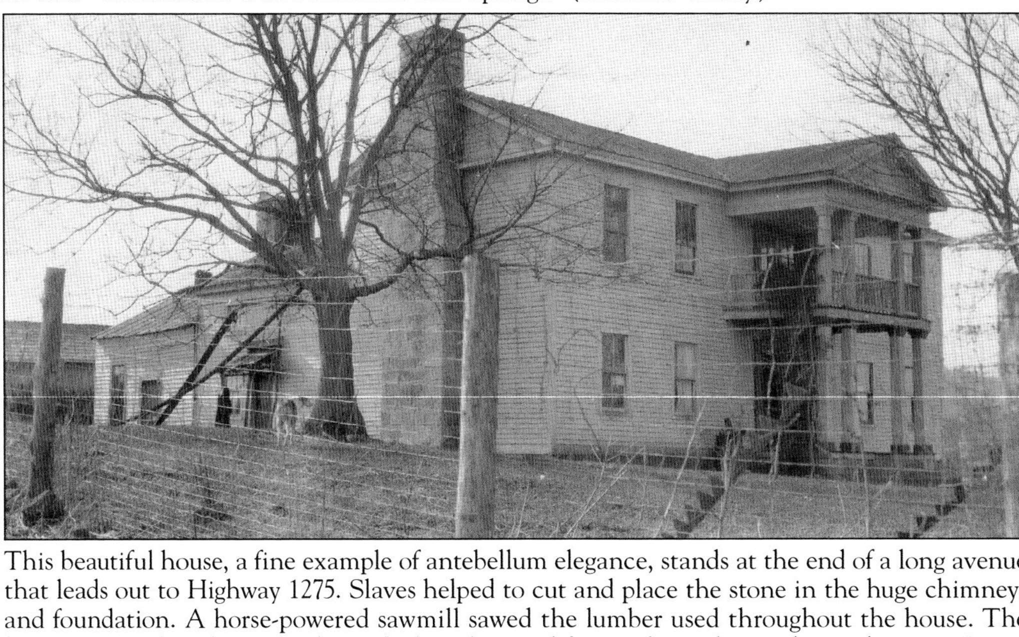

This beautiful house, a fine example of antebellum elegance, stands at the end of a long avenue that leads out to Highway 1275. Slaves helped to cut and place the stone in the huge chimneys and foundation. A horse-powered sawmill sawed the lumber used throughout the house. The large structural timbers were hewn by broad ax and fastened together with wooden pins. It was built in 1858 and was purchased shortly thereafter by plantation owner William J. Kendrick for his oldest son, John Kendrick. (Wayne County Historical Society.)

Two

Around Monticello

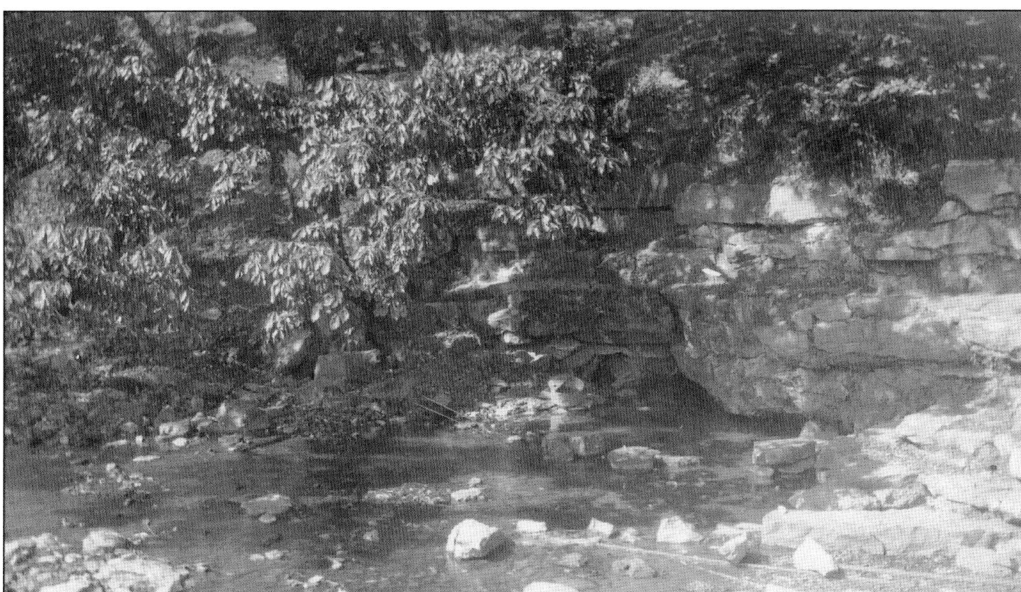

For years, the town spring in the Frog Bottom section of Monticello served as the chief source of water for local residents. Many of the stores and houses south of the public square had ropes rigged up so they could get water from the spring without going down the hill. As time went by, people depended more and more upon wells and cisterns for water, but it was not until 1930 that the first community water system was installed. (Mollie Shearer.)

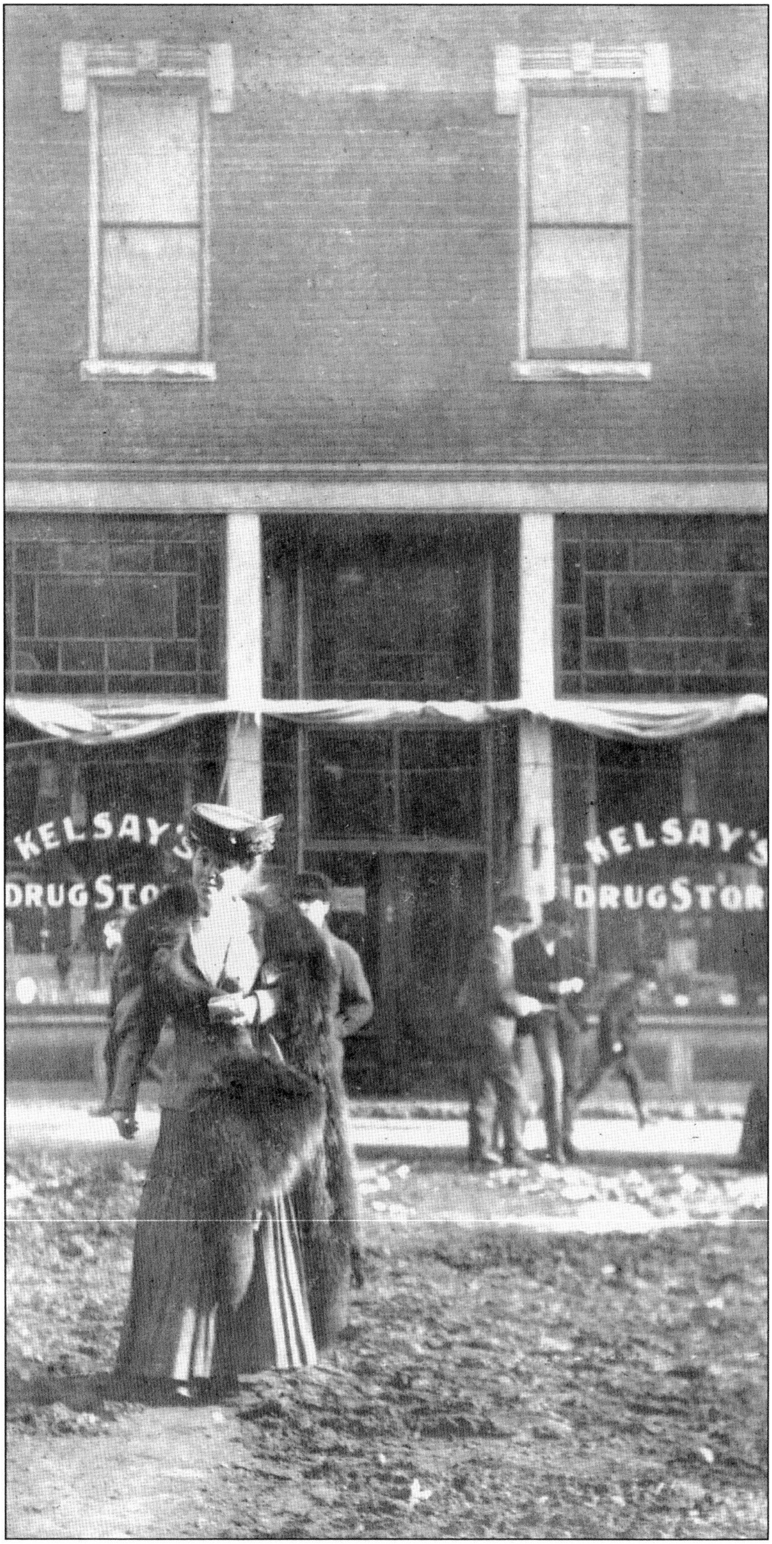

This photograph certainly takes us back to another time. Monticello's streets are not yet paved, a drugstore owned by J. P. Kelsay appears to be a thriving establishment, and an unknown woman dressed to the nines wends her way along a dirt path. Her destination? It is most likely the elegant Hotel Ramsey, which at that time stood across the street from the drugstore. (Wayne County Museumn.)

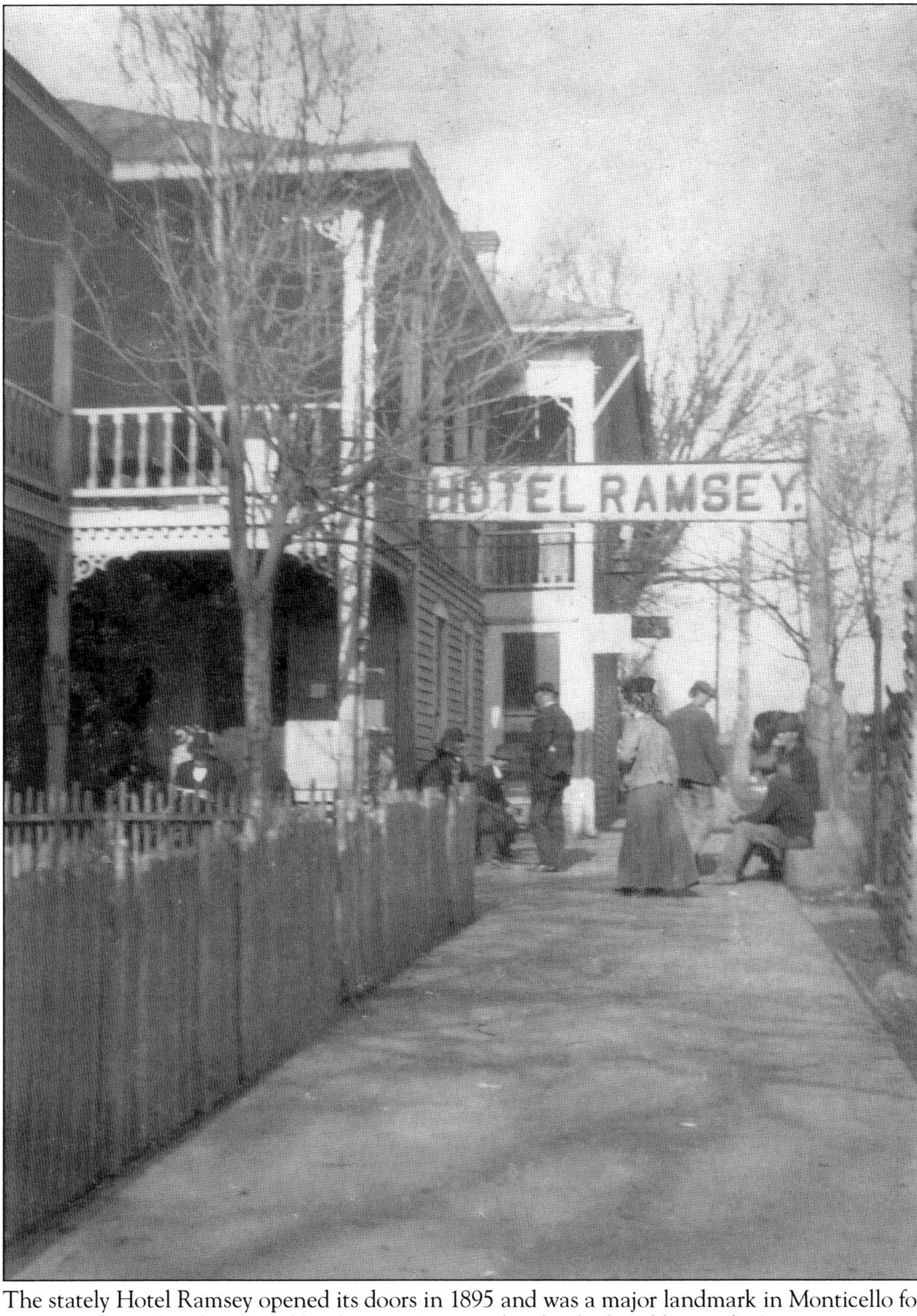

The stately Hotel Ramsey opened its doors in 1895 and was a major landmark in Monticello for 34 years. Owned and operated by the I. C. Ramsey family, the hotel boasted 45 guest rooms and four sample rooms. On February 21, 1929, it was destroyed by the huge fire that swept through Monticello's finest business district. (Wayne County Museum.)

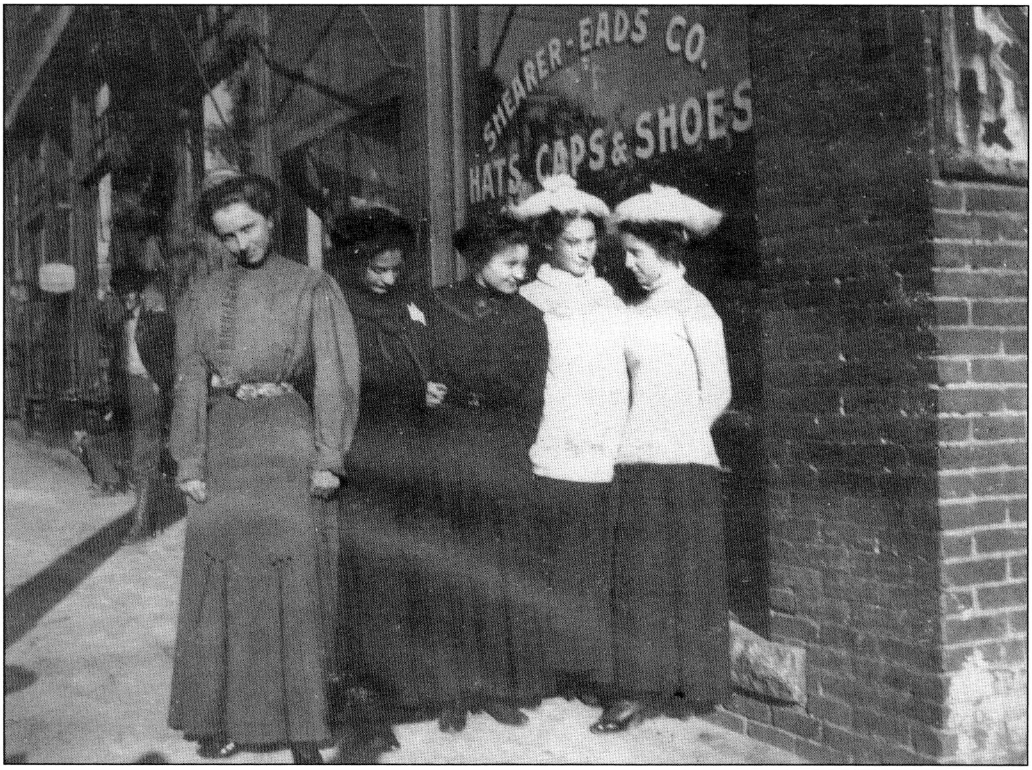

These fashionable young women have probably been shopping at Shearer-Eads General Store, which was, for many years, one of the best stores in Monticello. This business was located on the lot where, in 2010, the F and H Drugstore stands. For a 1908 sale, Shearer-Eads promoted the following items: Royal sewing machines, Victor phonographs, toys, storybooks, carpeting, cloaks, fur sets, overcoats, cravenettes, sweaters, corsets, flannel night shirts, Whip-saw tobacco, and pencil tablets. (Wayne County Museum.)

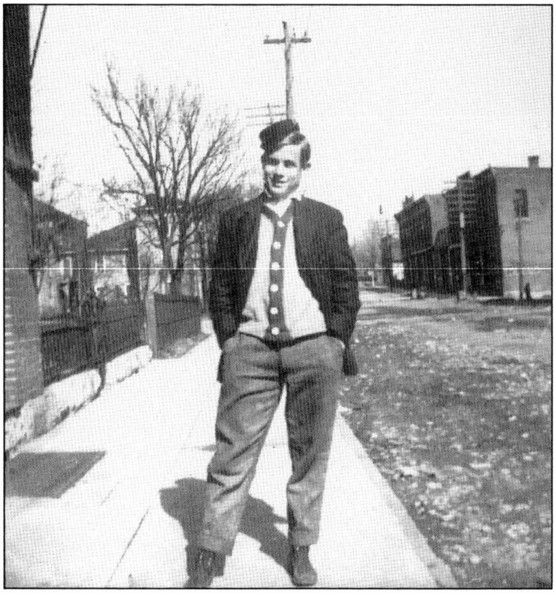

On a long ago day in the early 1900s, sometime before Main Street was paved, a young man posed for a picture on a wide sidewalk of Monticello. The large frame building in the left background was Hotel Ramsey. In the right background, Michigan Avenue (earlier called Cat Street) leads off just this side of the two-story brick building. Next up the street, the one-story building was Monticello Billiard Parlor. The second two-story brick building was the J. H. Shearer Hardware. (Mollie Shearer.)

In the early 1900s, the largest hardware store between Danville, Kentucky, and Knoxville, Tennessee, stood on North Main Street in Monticello. The J. H. Shearer and Company Hardware, both a wholesale and a retail business, became Shearer and Casteel in 1919 when Abram Casteel, son-in-law of Shearer, came into the business. J. H. Shearer is shown in this photograph. (Sue Johnson Woolums.)

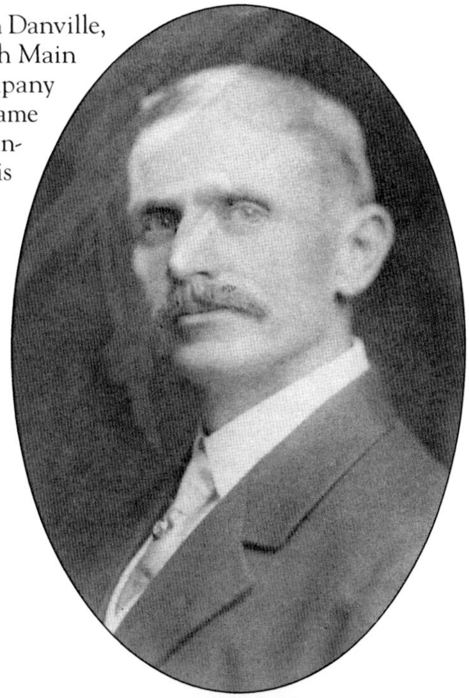

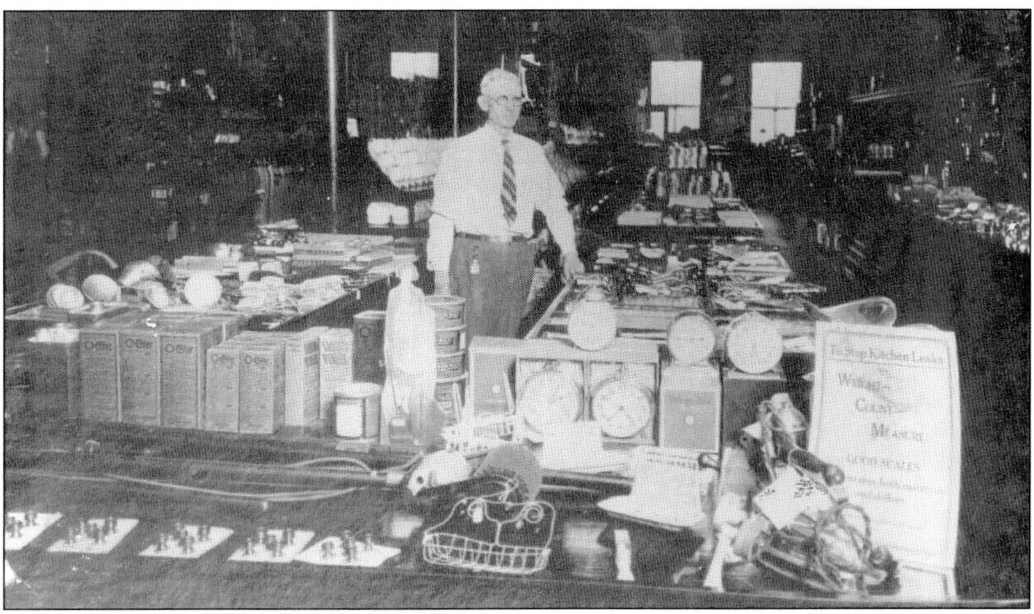

Abram Casteel is shown above inside the J. H. Shearer and Company Hardware store. The big hardware store that contained everything from furniture to oil well supplies burned in the fire of 1929. After the fire, the firm was rebuilt, but the building that housed it was smaller. From the time the first building was built until sometime in the 1990s, when the second building was purchased and torn down by First Southern Bank, descendants of J. H. Shearer had a part, at most times the major part, in its ownership and management. Many Wayne County people remember the 1944–1976 period when this business was known as Correll and Johnson Hardware. (Sue Johnson Woolums.)

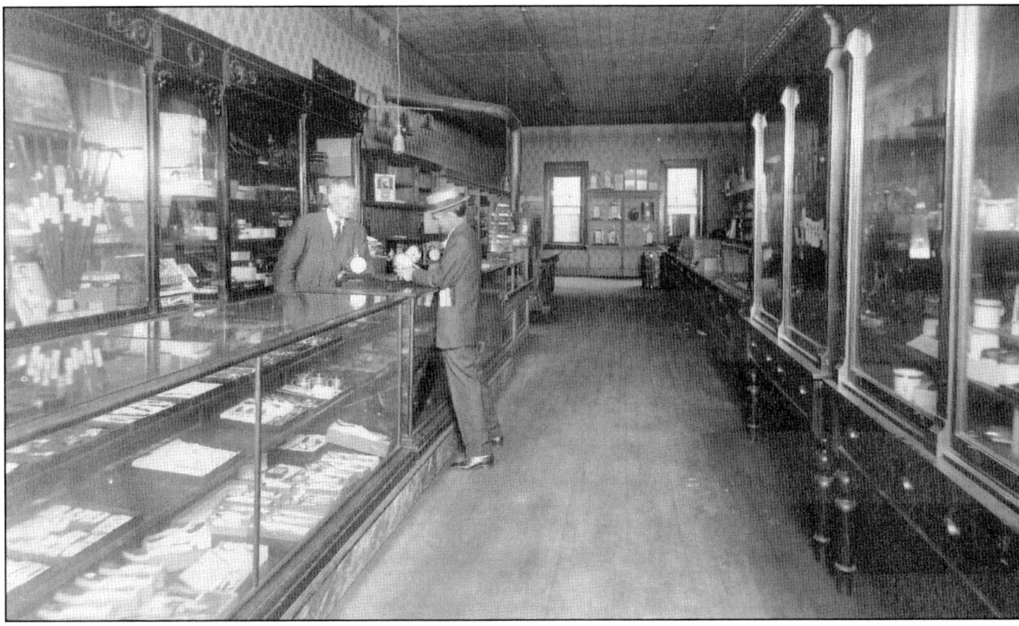

Wilburn F. Fairchild (1861–1931) stands behind the counter of his store on the public square of downtown Monticello. His customer is Dr. Lewis Tuttle, father of Dr. Bill Tuttle. According to Fairchild's business letterhead, he dealt in general merchandise, jewelry, watches, clocks, notions, and musical instruments. (Marsh family.)

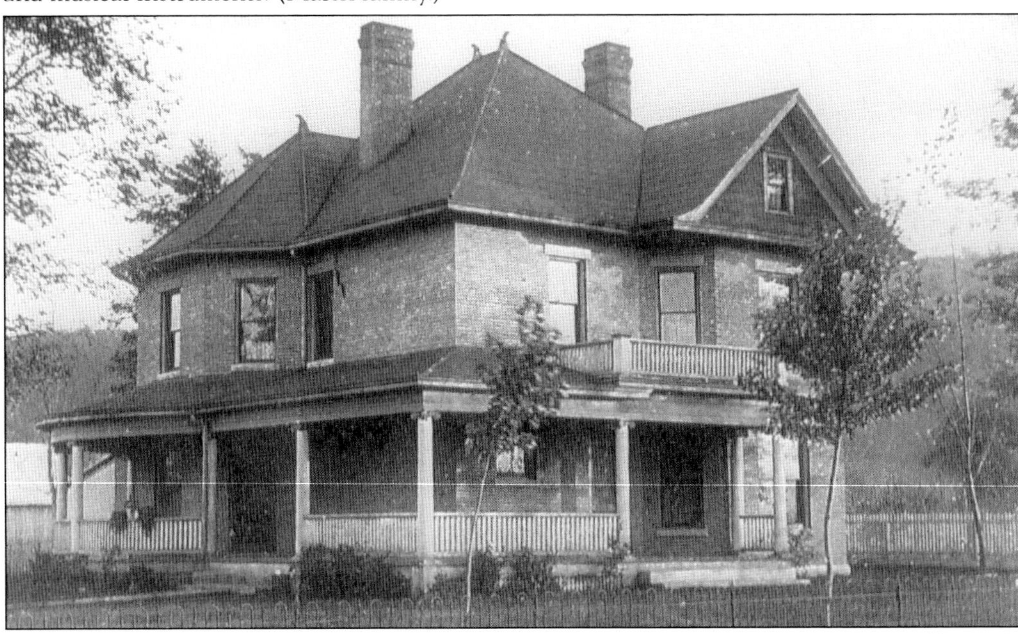

The Fairchild house was built by Wilburn Fairchild for his bride, Nannie Frisbie, and still presides over South Main Street. It is said that this was the first house in Wayne County to be designed by professional architects. Historian Garnett Walker described the house as "tall, many windowed, and bedecked with porches, as any proper Victorian house should be." The house, a Monticello landmark since 1906, has been carefully restored and now operates as Fairchild House Bed and Breakfast. (Marsh family.)

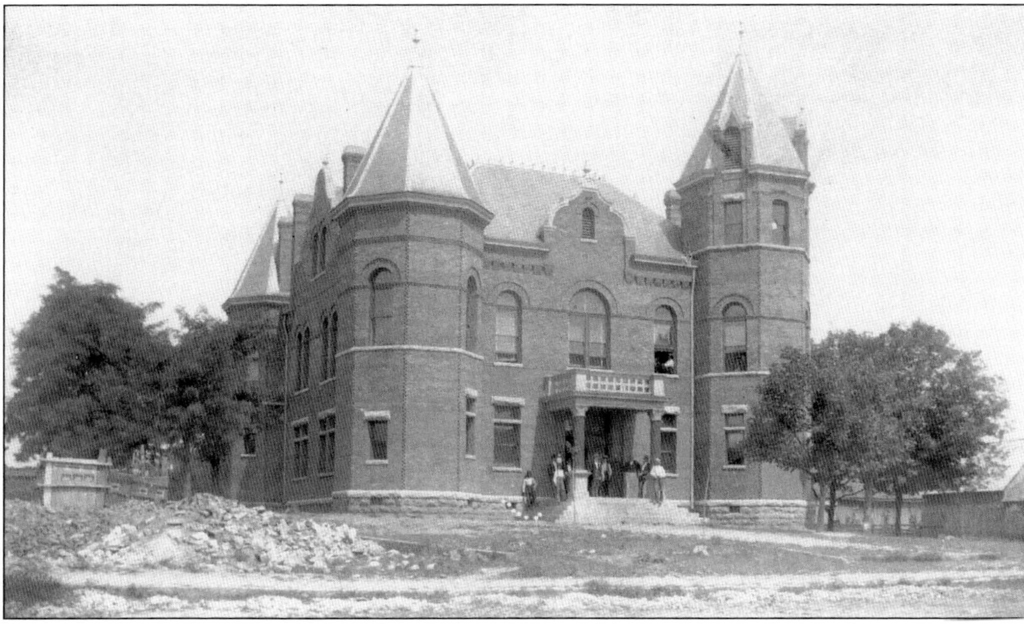

Wayne County's fifth courthouse, built in 1898, was demolished in 1949 to make way for the present structure, which stands on the same site. The photograph here shows the handsome building soon after it was constructed. At that time, the courthouse functioned not only as a center for government, but also served a multitude of other purposes. Social and entertainment events, school activities, revival meetings, and "speakings" of various kinds held at the courthouse were advertised in the *Wayne County Outlook*. Of the four towers at the corners of this building, the northeast tower was taller and more elaborate than the others. This was the bell tower from which the great bronze bell called the people to attend each session of court. (Wayne County Historical Society.)

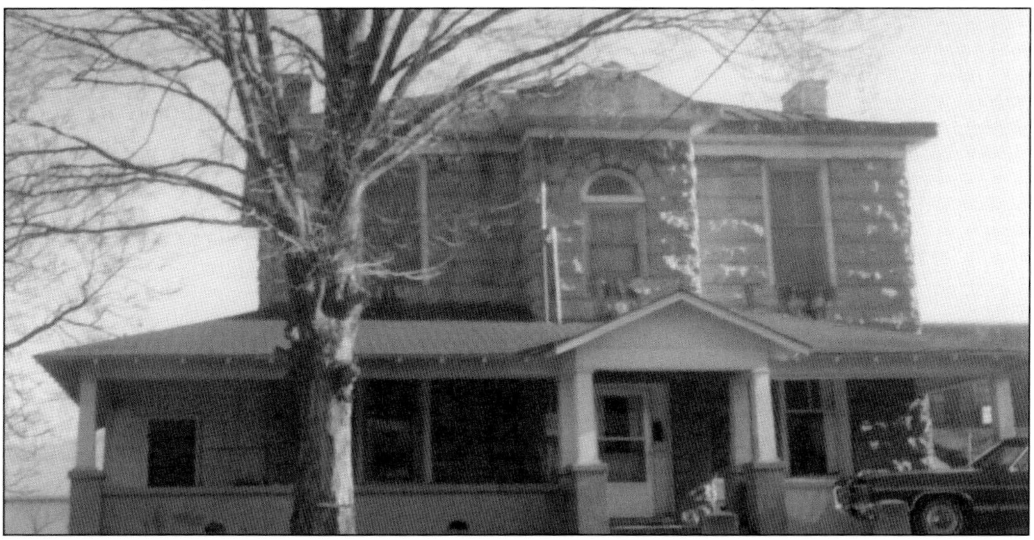

This Wayne County Jail, located on the northern side of West Columbia Avenue, was completed in 1893 at a cost of $10,000. Its stone was quarried on Dr. Jonathan Frisbie's land. When this picture was taken, the tower originally on the building had been removed and porches had been added. The building featured living quarters for the jailer and his family in front and cells for prisoners in the back. Torn down about 1987, it was replaced by another jail. (Katy Lou Rector.)

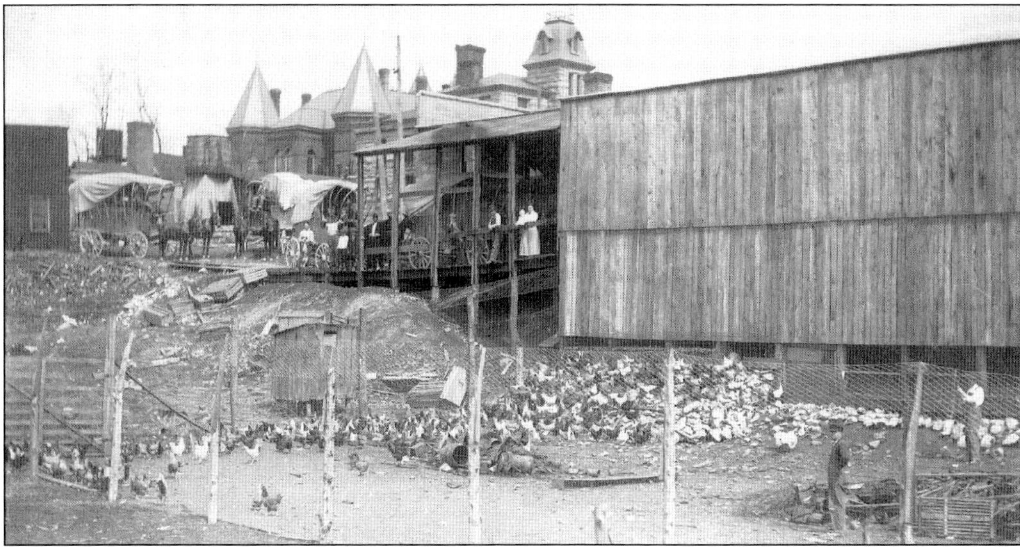

The Shearer Freight House once did a thriving business on Columbia Avenue in Monticello. This c. 1890 photograph shows the freight house, with the 1898–1949 Wayne County Courthouse and the 1893 Wayne County Jail in the background. Owned by Ellis and Emmett Shearer, the business served the community for many years. The owners delivered hay, horse and mule feed, special dairy feed, wheat bran, corn, oats, and tankage anywhere within the city limits. They bought cream, in large or small quantities, for Armour's Creameries. They also bought chickens and rabbits. The rabbits had to be presented according to the specific instructions given in the newspaper and brought to the freight house on Thursday or Friday. (Wayne County Museum.)

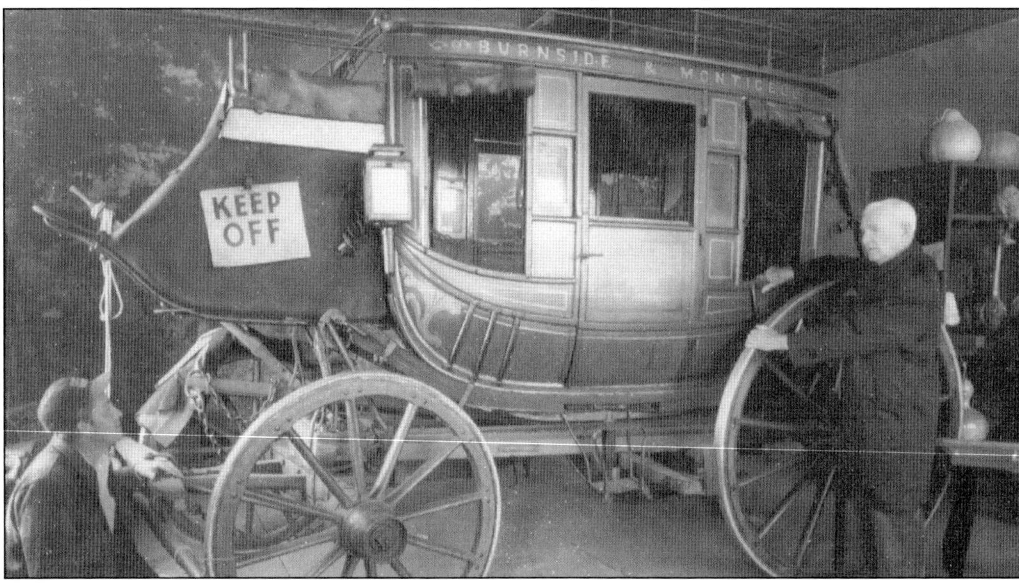

Possessing a strong sense of history, the Burton family of Monticello went to extreme efforts to make sure future generations could have access to the area's deep roots and rich heritage. Charles Burton owned the Burton Stage Line that ran between Monticello and Burnside. Upon his death, the effort was assumed by his son, John Burton. Both were always willing to show the stagecoach they were preserving for history. In this photograph, Charles Burton is showing the stagecoach to a visitor in his "museum," located on North Main Street in Monticello. (Wayne County Museum.)

For more than half of Monticello's history, horse travel was the most common means of transportation, and livery stables were a necessity. Shell Ragan's Livery Stable stood down the street from the *Wayne County Outlook* office on the corner of Short Street (now East Columbia Avenue) and Church Street. The building was destroyed by fire in the 1930s. (Mildred Dalton.)

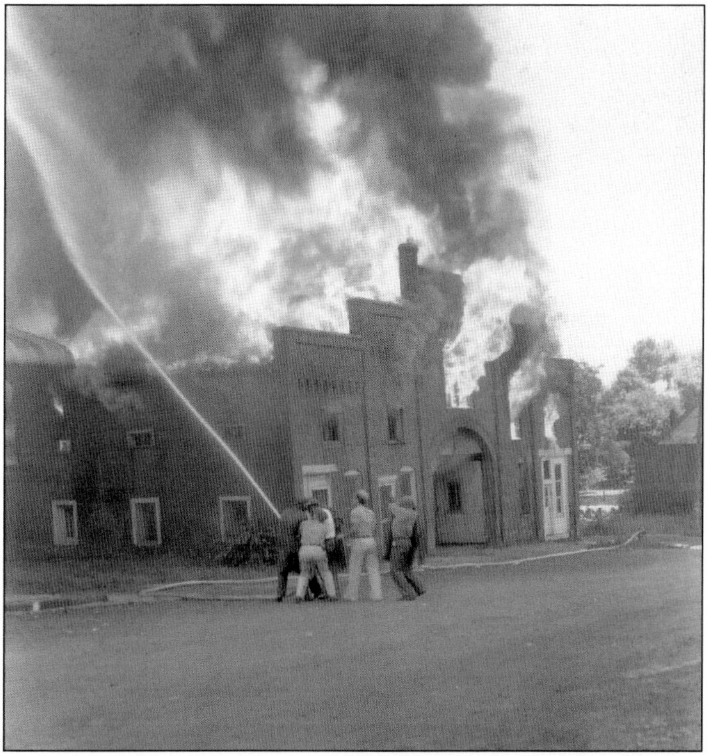

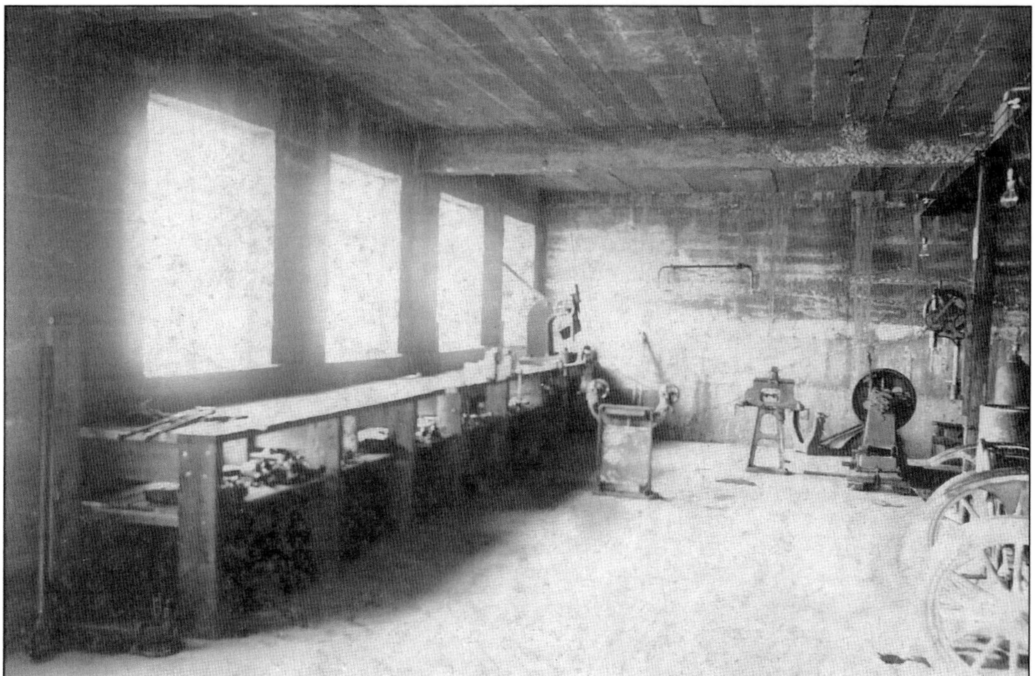

The second floor of the livery stable served as storage space for feed and for the coffins and caskets that Shell Ragan sold. It was also used as a repair shop for harnesses and buggies. This picture shows a portion of the second-floor part of the business. (Katy Lou Rector.)

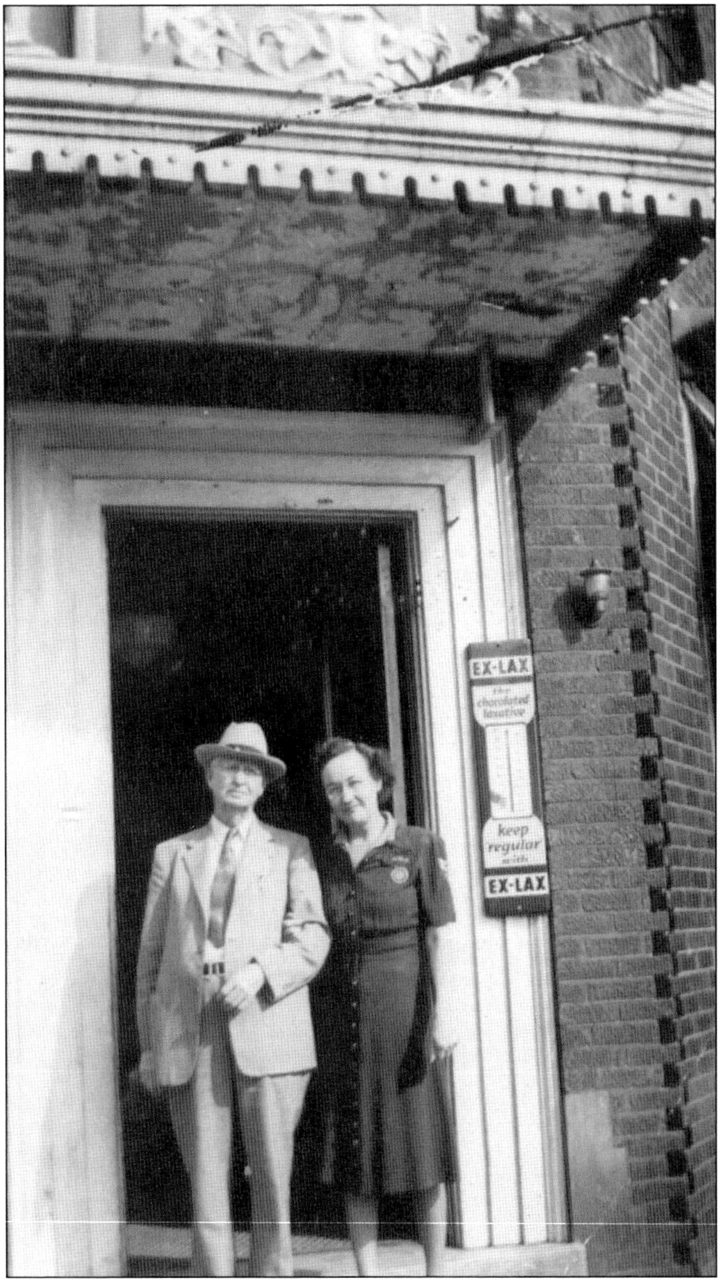

Friends Dr. Claude B. Rankin and Florence Gamblin pose in front of Rankin Drugstore on the northeast corner of the public square in Monticello. Dr. Rankin graduated from the University of Louisville School of Medicine in 1898 and from the New York Polyclinic Hospital in New York City in 1918. He had a long and active career in his profession, serving the people of Wayne County for more than 50 years. The buggy in which he made countless house calls now stands in a place of honor in the Wayne County Museum. In 1930, Dr. Rankin built the Rankin Drugstore for his son, Carl Rankin, who was a pharmacist. For decades, Florence Gamblin was the mainstay in the business next door to the drugstore—Ann's Store. Florence was the wife of Charlie Gamblin and the mother of Mary Sue Gamblin West. (Bob Lee.)

When this picture was taken in 1938, Dalton's Grocery and Market operated in the Fairchild-Kennedy building on the public square of Monticello. Prince Albert Tobacco and lard were sold with no thought of risks to health. Pride in a neat, well-stocked store underpinned many privately owned businesses, including this one. Wendell and Mildred Dalton ran this store for about 10 years. (Mildred Dalton.)

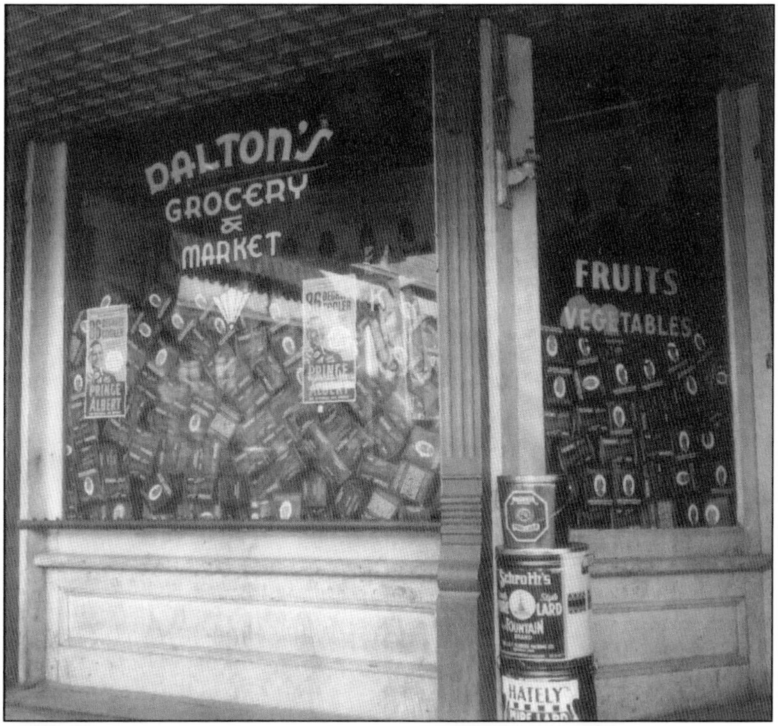

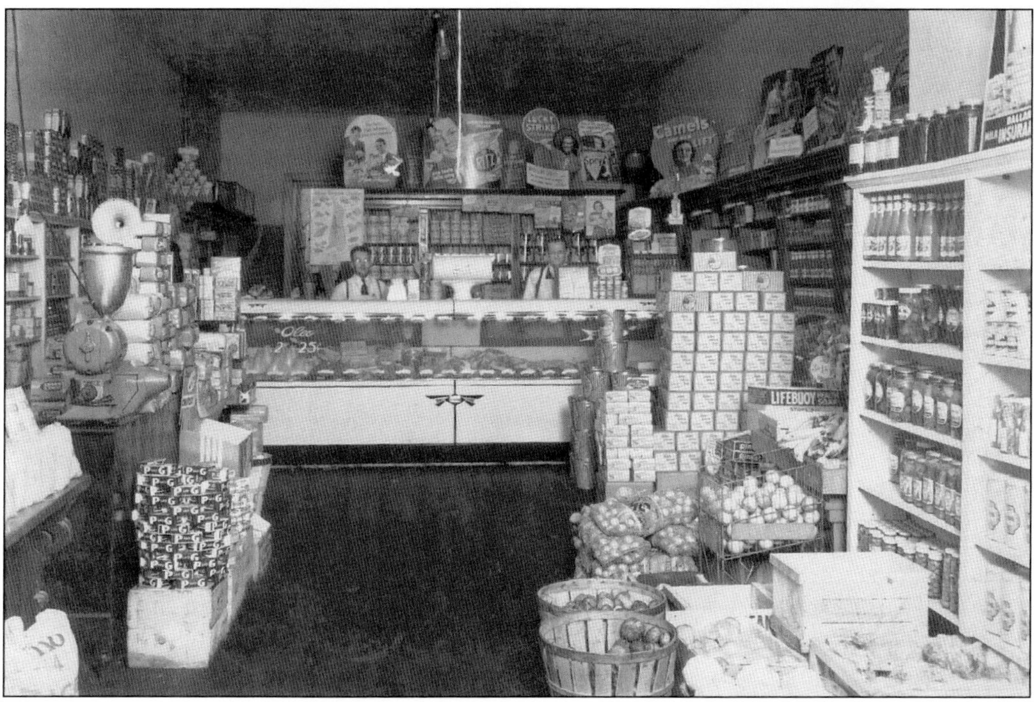

Inside Dalton's Grocery and Market, Wendell Dalton is shown at left behind the meat counter with an unidentified employee. Always with his wife, Mildred, by his side, Wendell was a driving force in the local business community. The Dalton family made tremendous contributions to the growth and development of Monticello. (Mildred Dalton.)

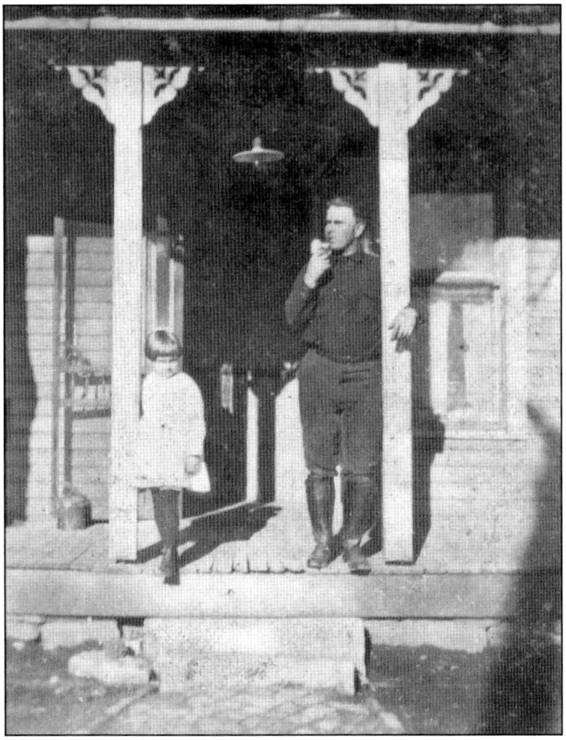

Electronics genius Larry Smith built his first radio in 1920. From his home on Cave Street, he operated a radio station with the call letters W10XAF. His equipment was used around town at public events, such as the Wayne County Fair and at another radio station that operated from W. W. Kendrick's Garage on North Main Street. Smith worked endlessly toward the problem of eliminating static in broadcasting. His experiments contributed to the "static-free" voice of FM radio and television. Although he was self-taught, Smith was engaged to teach radio for the Signal Corps of the U.S. Army. In this 1922 picture he is shown with his daughter, Mildred. (Mildred Dalton.)

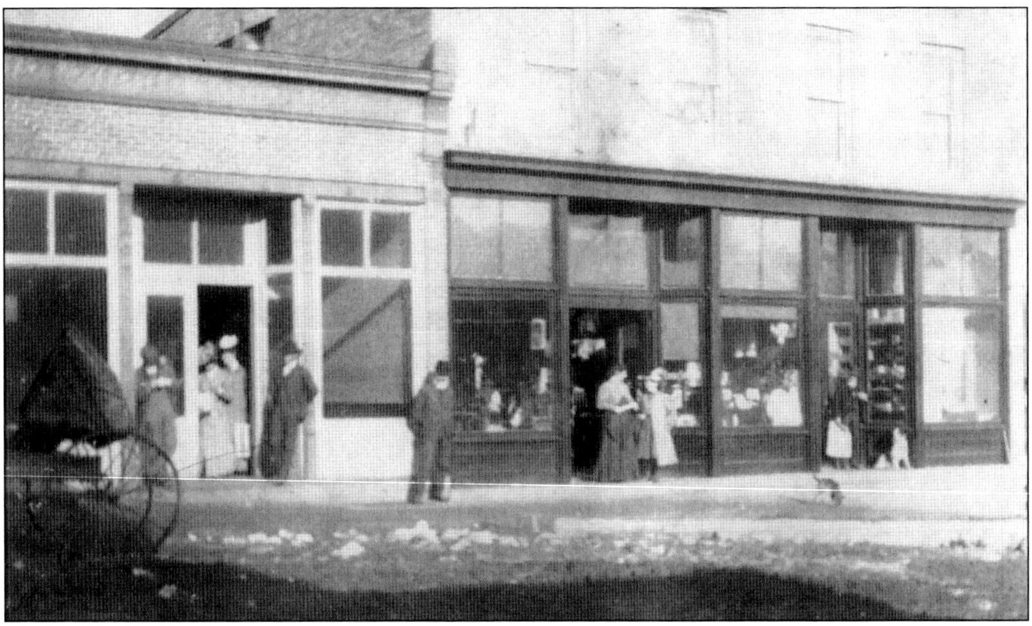

In the early 1900s, Short Street was a busy place. The one-story building at left in this photograph housed the post office. Emma Simpson ran a dress shop next door, and the *Wayne County Outlook*, a weekly newspaper, was composed and printed in the unit on the right. The post office, after a time, moved to another location. The dress shop operated for many years, but it too is gone. After more than 100 years, the *Wayne County Outlook* is still going strong, and the building on Short Street (now East Columbia Avenue) is still its home. (Wayne County Museum.)

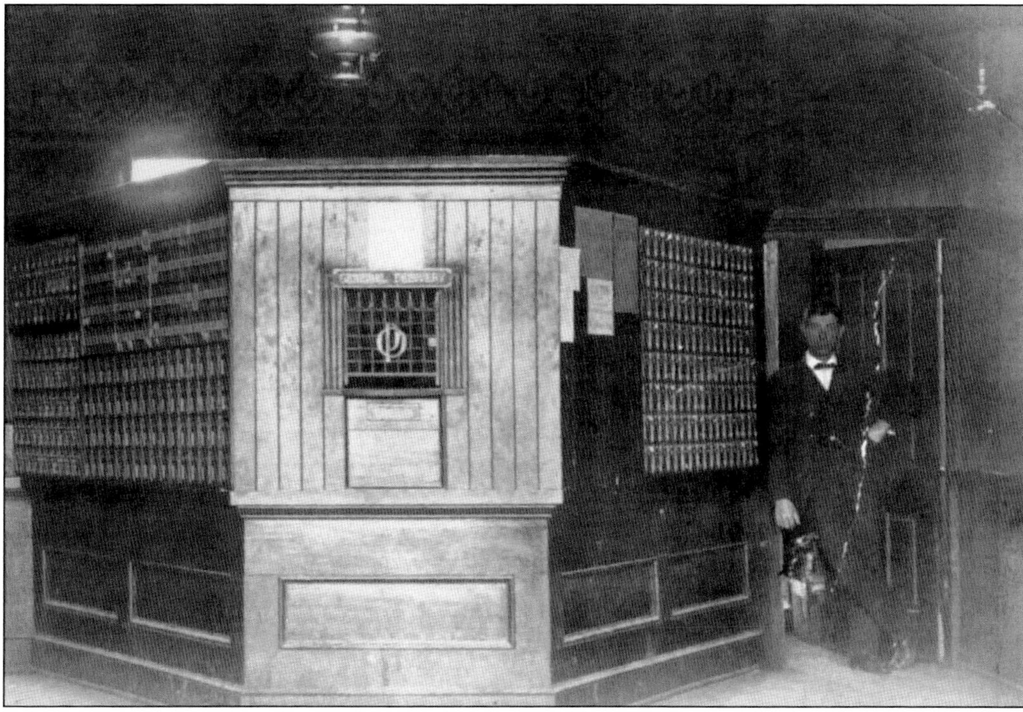

When the Monticello Post Office was on Short Street (now East Columbia Avenue), the building that housed it was privately owned. John M. Kennedy, shown in the interior, owned the building when he served as postmaster from 1901 until 1910. After his tenure as postmaster, Kennedy served eight years as county attorney and later became commonwealth attorney of the 28th Judicial District. (Bonnie Tate Carr.)

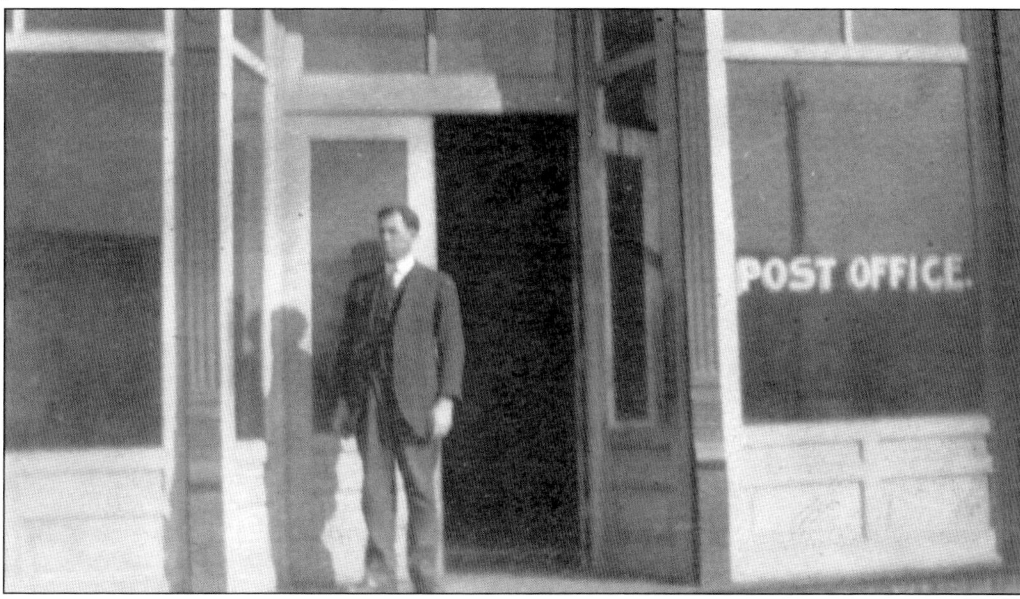

J. Schuyler Sandusky, shown at the entrance of the Monticello Post Office on Short Street, bought the building when he became the postmaster following John M. Kennedy. Sandusky had previously served as Wayne County clerk. Later he became Wayne County judge. (Bonnie Tate Carr.)

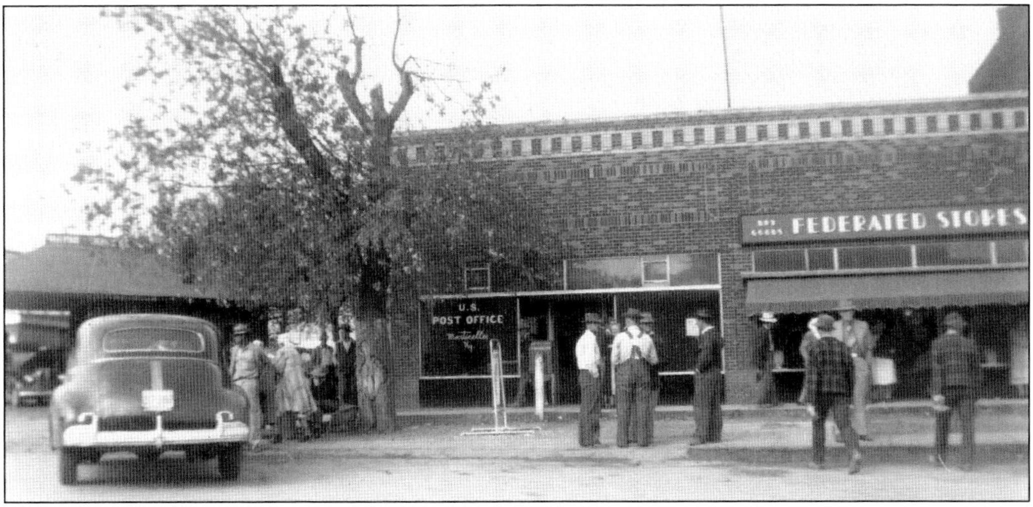

The Monticello Post Office has been housed in so many different buildings that one might say it has circled the town. In this 1940s photograph, it shares a building on the southwest corner of the public square with the Federated Store, which was operated by Jim Duncan. It is flanked on the left by a service station operated by Fred Crouch. (Wayne County Museum.)

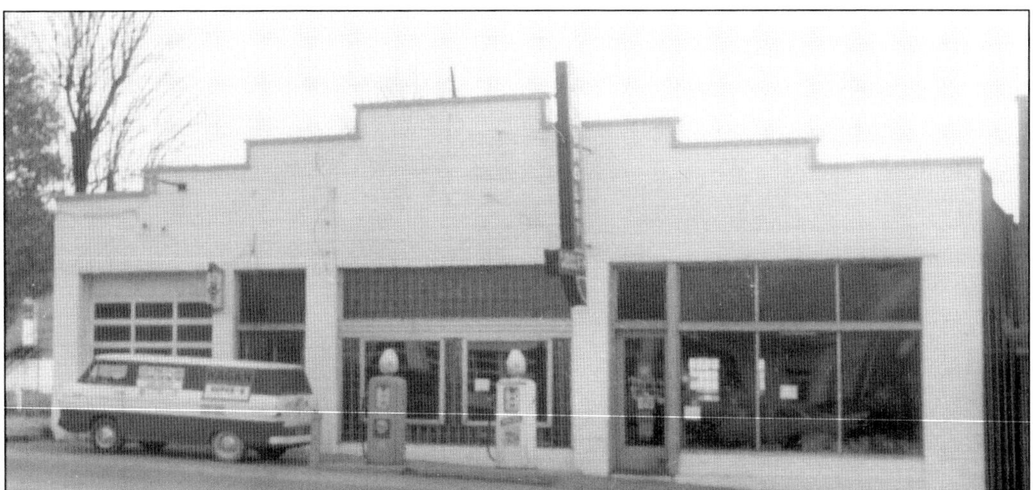

When this picture was taken, the Chevrolet Garage was a major business establishment on North Main Street in Monticello. Later, Peoples State Bank acquired the building and remodeled it, and a new chapter in its history began. In 1970, Peoples State Bank, which from its beginning more than 30 years earlier had been housed in the southern unit of Hotel Breeding, moved up the street and into what appeared to be a completely new facility. Over the years, the name of the bank has changed, first to City and County Bank, then to First State Bank, and last of all, to First Southern National Bank, its present name. (Dr. Robert B. Breeding.)

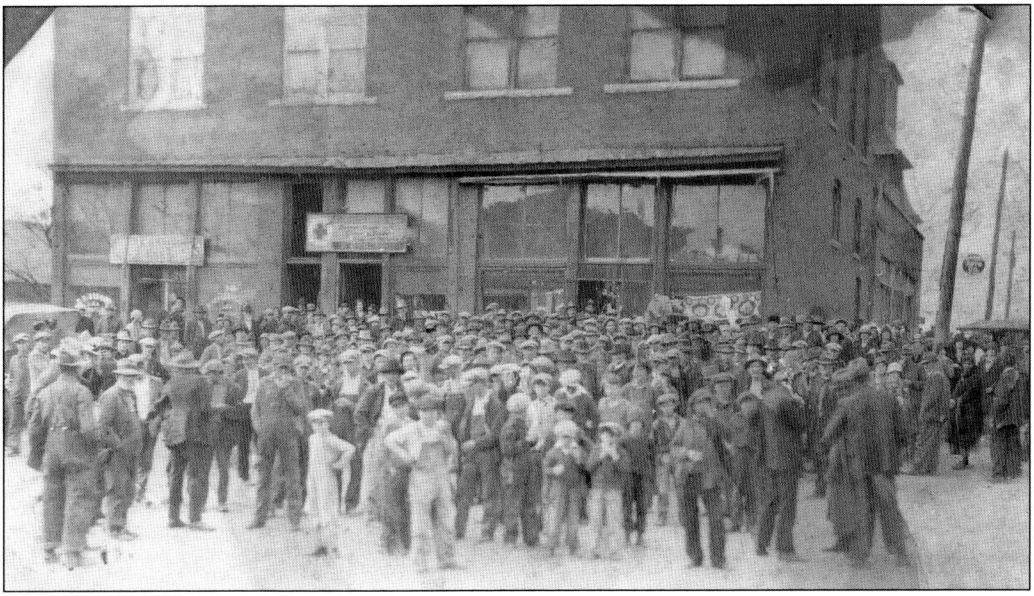

Until the development of shopping centers, the public square of Monticello was, since pioneer days, the town's business and social center and, at times, the political center of Wayne County. The purpose of this gathering on the square in front of the old Masonic Lodge building is unknown. The structure was built in 1905 by W. S. Stone for commercial space. He leased the second story to Masonic Lodge No. 431, which in subsequent years purchased the building. The right edge of the picture shows a bit of West Columbia Avenue and the Church of Christ bell tower. Since the Church of Christ building was constructed in 1918, this picture must have been taken after that time. (Katy Lou Rector.)

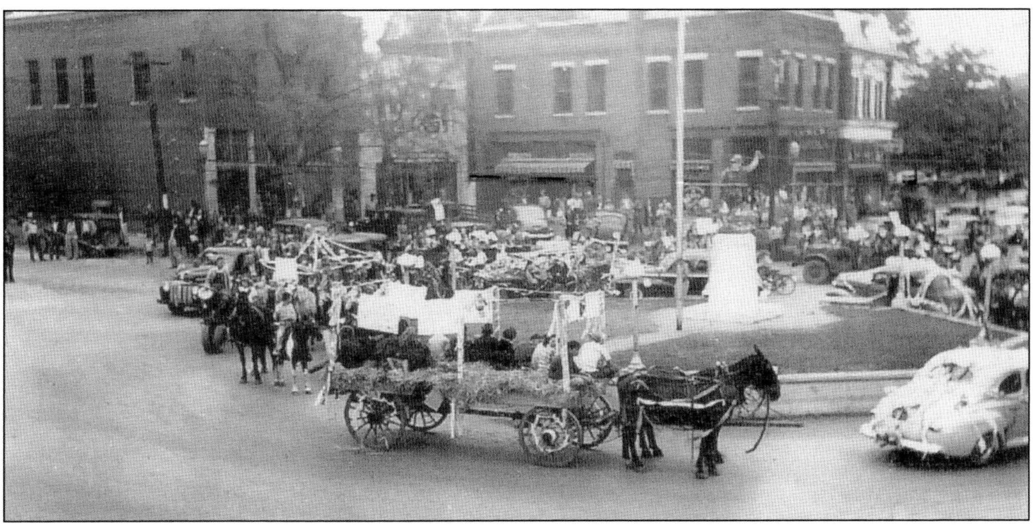

In 1801, Joshua Jones surveyed the 13 acres that would become the site for Monticello and laid out the public square. At that time, he never envisioned the many parades that would come down Main Street and into the square over the years. This parade might have been a 4-H event, or it might have been the beginning of one of the school fairs. Those fairs, held in the 1940s and 1950s, began with a parade that terminated on the grounds of the old Wayne County High School. Children and teachers from both school systems participated. (Maymie Dunagan.)

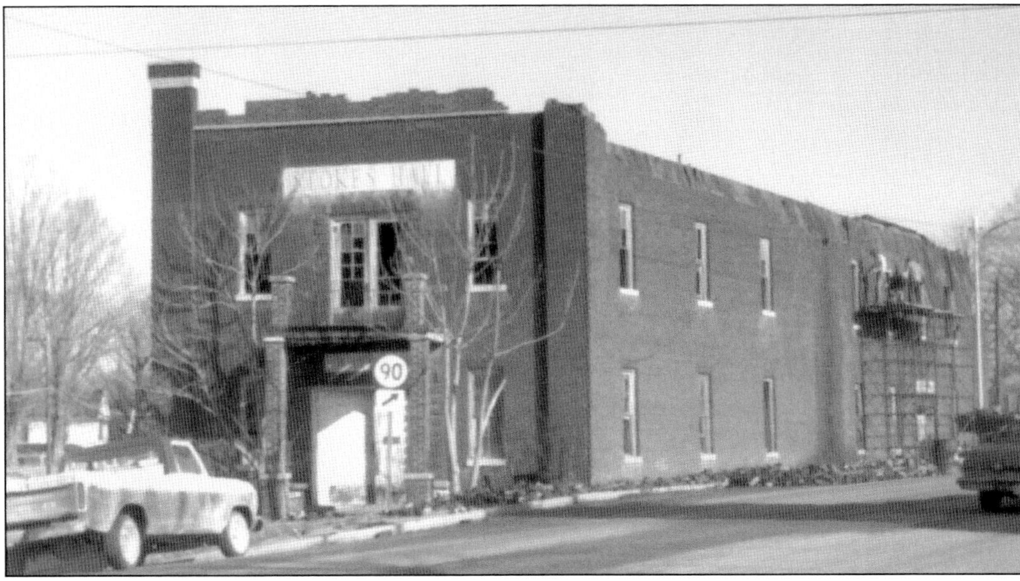

Stokes Hall, built at the juncture of Kendrick Avenue and North Main Street in Monticello, served as a National Guard armory from the time of its dedication on May 25, 1928, until 1964. After standing vacant for several years, the old building that had been both the armory and a community center was torn down. The picture above shows the beginning of that process. Countless Wayne County residents remember the armory as a place that welcomed musical events, religious gatherings, reunion groups, and perhaps most importantly, boys who liked to play basketball. The building was named for Capt. J. L. Stokes. (Dr. Robert B. Breeding.)

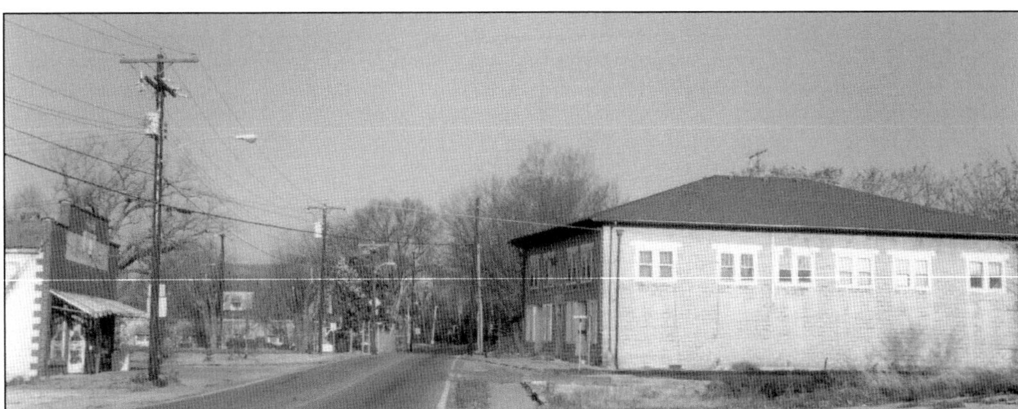

This photograph, taken before the fairly recent street-widening project on West Columbia Avenue, shows Daffron Fruit Market on the left. Ira Bell built the large concrete block building. For many years Bell's hardware store, called Wayne County Cash Store, occupied one unit of that building. Other units of the building were rented. During the years prior to the formation of Lake Cumberland, the second floor was rented to the Land Acquisitions Office of the U.S. Army Corps of Engineers. (Johnny Gibson.)

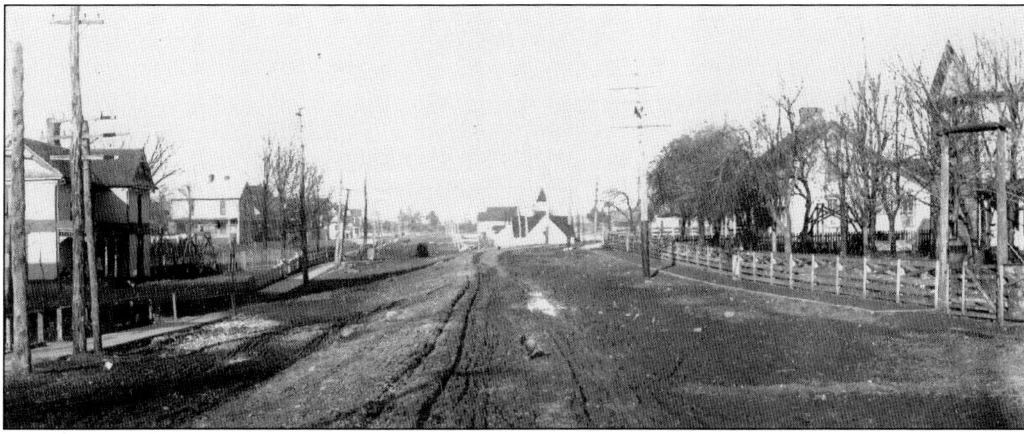

In this 1907 view of North Main Street, the second house on the right is located where the Monticello Motel stands in 2010. For many years Fred and Lillian Ragan lived in that house, and the office for Southern Telephone Company occupied the front room. James W. Simpson is thought to have been the first telephone operator who worked there. In this picture, the white building with a steeple that stands at the juncture of North Main Street and Kendrick Avenue was actually a stable. (Wayne County Museum.)

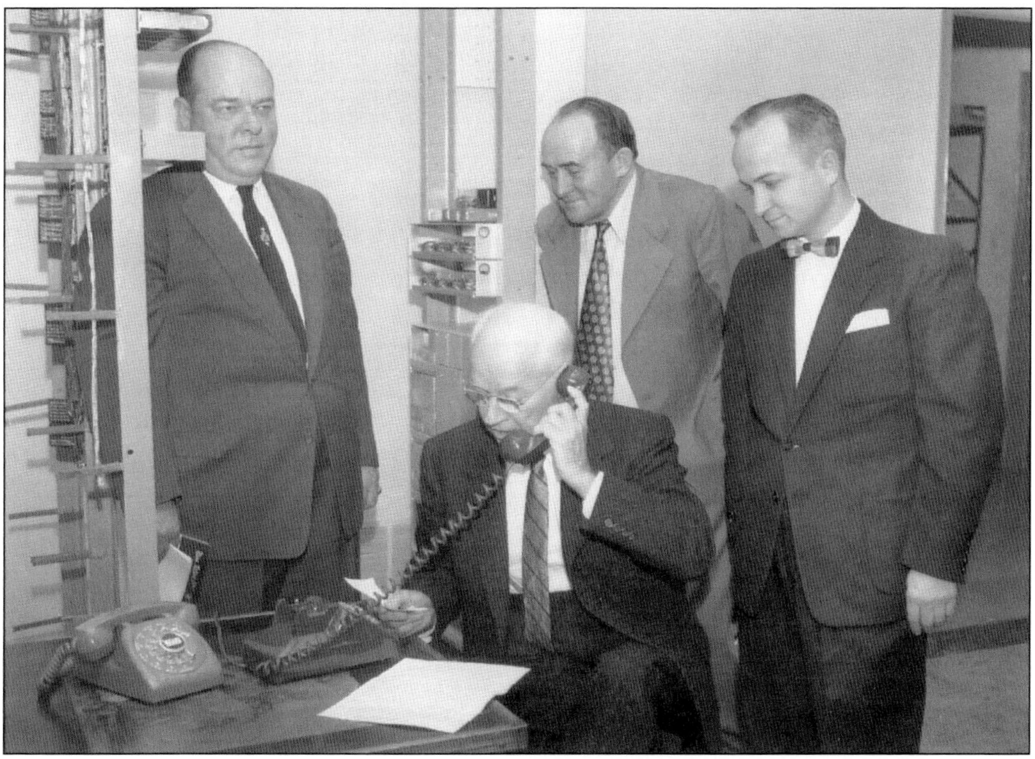

From left to right, a Mr. Heather, Capt. J. L. Stokes, and Bill Breeding watched as Mayor R. G. Breeding (seated) made the first telephone call using newly installed automated equipment owned by General Telephone Company. It was November 15, 1957, the beginning of a new era for the use of the telephone in Wayne County. No more would Wayne County people pick up the telephone and speak to an operator who not only had the local numbers memorized, but also knew where most people could be located. (Dr. Robert B. Breeding.)

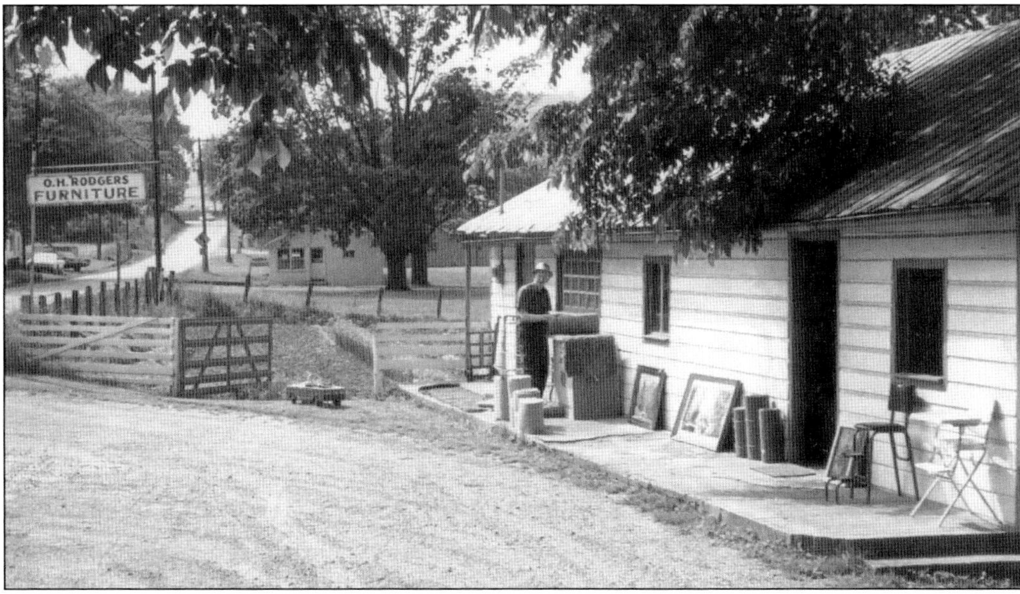

Haskel Rogers ran a gristmill in this small building on Michigan Avenue. Most of his customers dropped off a "turn" (sack) of corn at the mill in the morning and, after a day in town, returned and picked up their sack of freshly ground meal. A "toll" (portion) of the customer's corn paid the bill. In 1955, Rogers sold the milling equipment, and he ran a furniture store at this location for the next 25 years. (J. D. Rogers.)

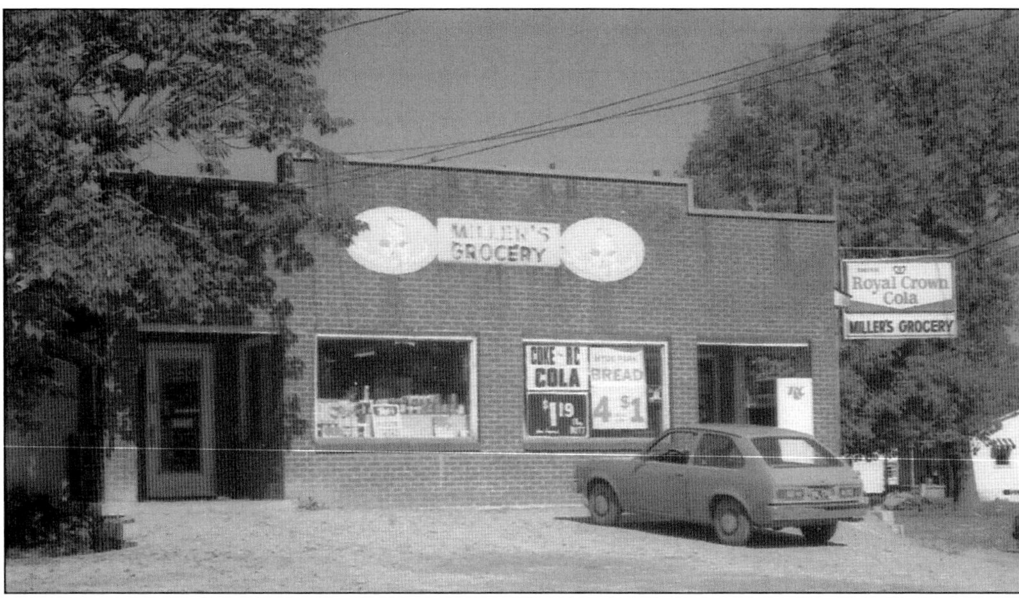

This photograph of Miller's Grocery at 315 Ridgewood Avenue in Monticello was taken at a time when the Gene Miller family, living two doors down, owned and operated the business. The building was constructed about 1959 by Rolland Jones (Miller's father-in-law), as Jones Grocery, and the store, which became something of a gathering place for longtime residents of the neighborhood, was run by one or the other of the families until 1984. Miller's Grocery was a great place to get a cold sandwich and offered free home delivery of groceries. (J. D. Rogers.)

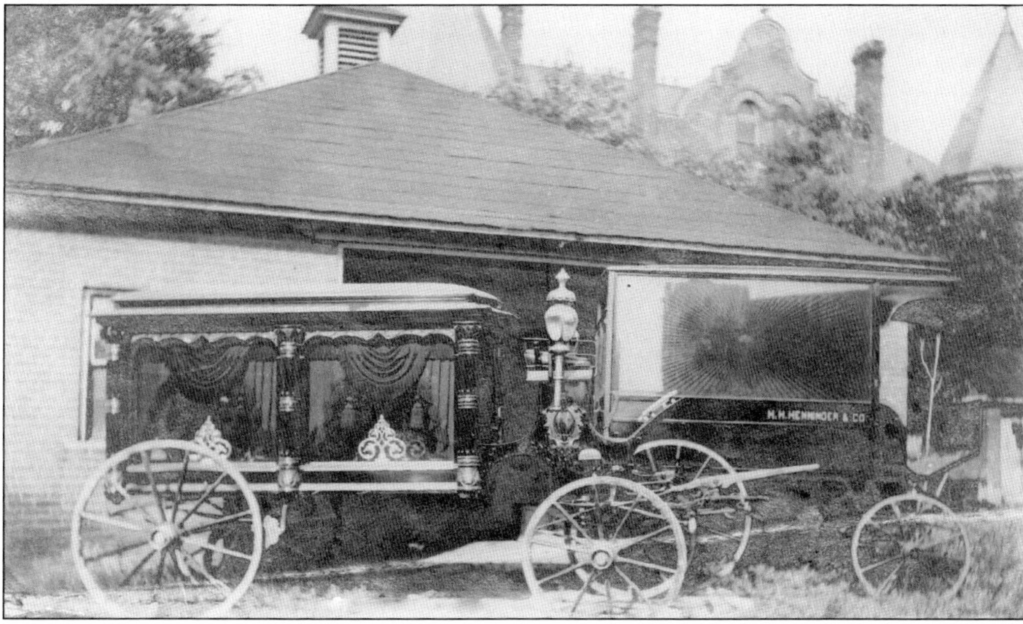

With Wayne County's fifth courthouse in the background and a new-looking hearse and ambulance parked in front, the little brick building shown here was an undertaking parlor. Initially, it was the business of H. H. Henninger. Later, it was owned and operated by Joseph Lewis Shadoan and Ed Lee. In 2010, with Wayne County's sixth courthouse nearby, the building still stands. Its lengthy history includes many years as an office for attorneys. Both Elza Bertram and his son, Randall Bertram, practiced law there. W. C. Dabney, the last attorney to make the little building his office, retired in 1972. (Wayne County Museum.)

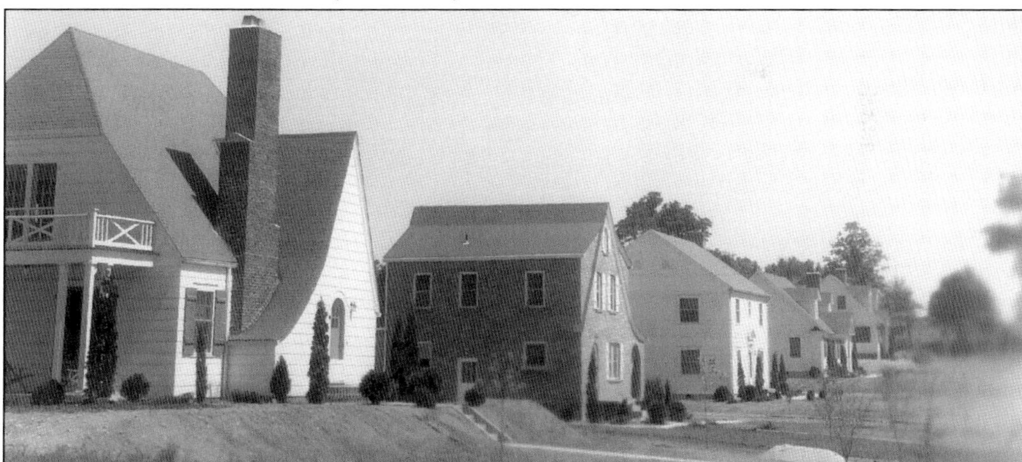

This row of five houses, all built about 1938, stretches along the western side of Kendrick Avenue from Evelyn Avenue to Homestead Lane. When the houses were new, the people who lived in them had an interesting view—across the street a big sawmill sprawled from one end of the block to the other. The first house on the left was ordered from Sears and Roebuck by Everett Roberts. The second house was built by Kay Huddleston and later became the home of Proctor and Tillie Rankin. The third house was the Dr. McClain house, and the fourth was the Jim Duncan house. The fifth house first belonged to Prof. R. F. Peters and later became the residence of Dr. Frank Duncan and his wife, Elizabeth. (Mildred Dalton.)

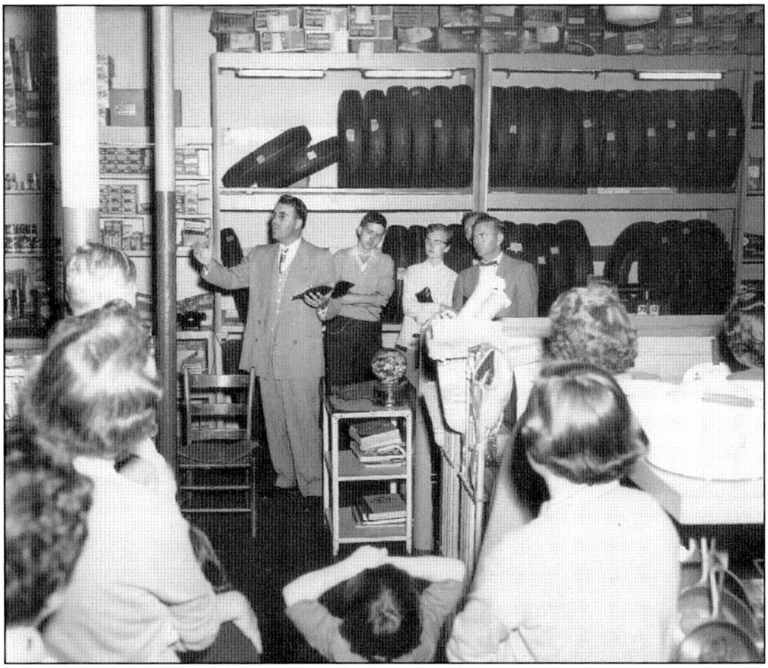

During a revival meeting in the 1950s, when Bro. Charles Secrest was minister at First Christian Church, this evangelist did a bit of preaching while he visited around town. Here he speaks to customers at the Firestone store. Buddy Roberts (left) and Susie Secrest stand in the background. Wendell and Mildred Dalton operated this business, located on the public square of Monticello. (Mildred Dalton.)

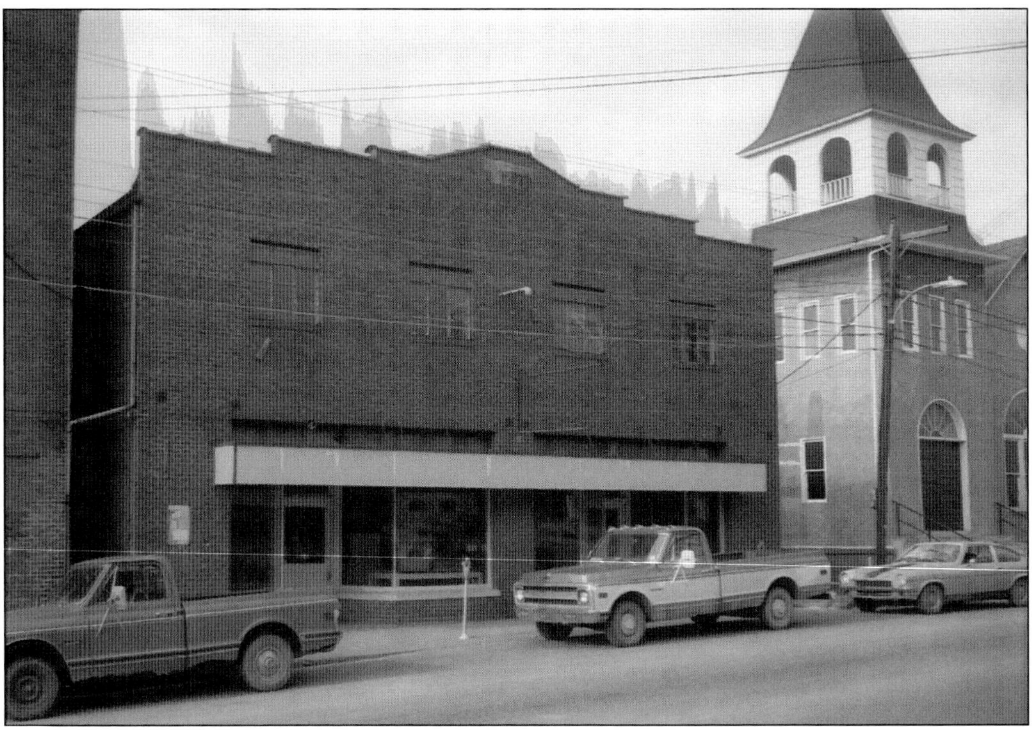

Constructed about 1920 to house the Dodge agency and a service garage, this building stood on Columbia Avenue in Monticello, directly behind the Masonic Lodge building, which faced the public square. Over the years it housed the Green Lantern Restaurant, a dry-cleaning business, the Monticello Hatchery, and a paint store. It burned in 1983 in the same fire that destroyed the Church of Christ building on the adjacent lot. It is pictured here in 1976. (J. D. Rogers.)

During the time that Charles Burton had a stage line between Monticello and Burnside, Charles; his wife, Anna Tate Burton (pictured); and their children, Carrie and John, lived in a large white house on North Main Street in Monticello. (Dr. Robert G. Breeding.)

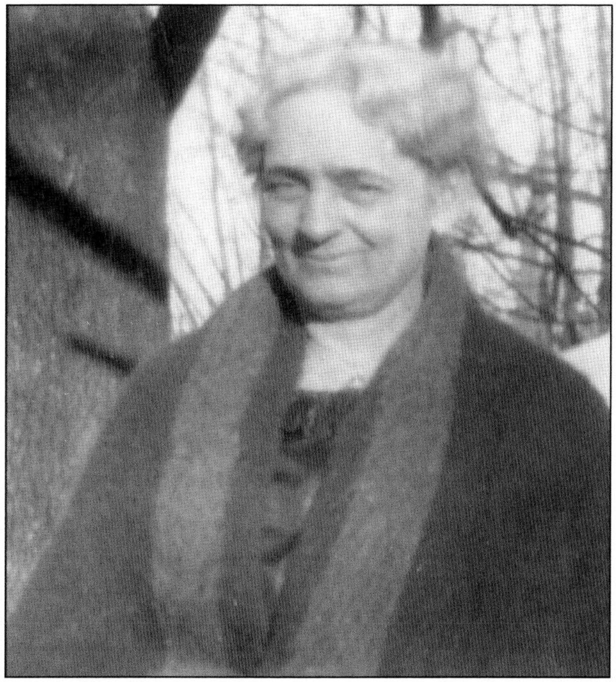

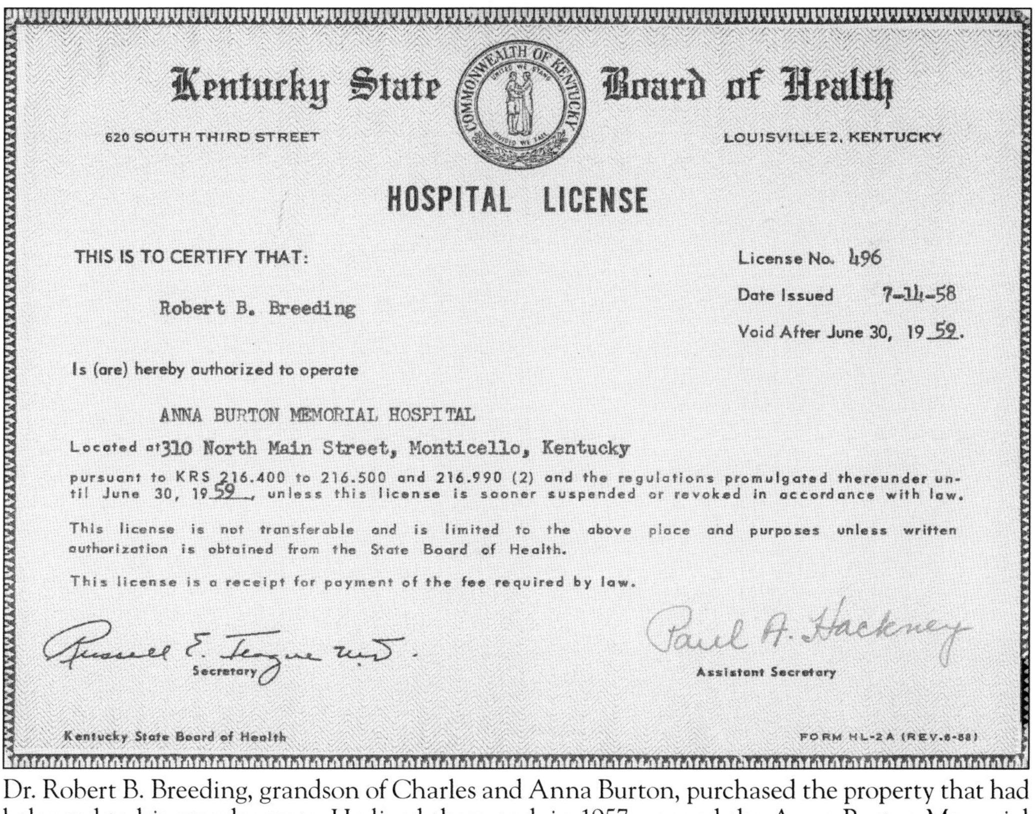

Kentucky State Board of Health

COMMONWEALTH OF KENTUCKY — UNITED WE STAND — DIVIDED WE FALL

620 SOUTH THIRD STREET — LOUISVILLE 2, KENTUCKY

HOSPITAL LICENSE

THIS IS TO CERTIFY THAT:

Robert B. Breeding

License No. 496

Date Issued 7-14-58

Void After June 30, 1959.

Is (are) hereby authorized to operate

ANNA BURTON MEMORIAL HOSPITAL

Located at 310 North Main Street, Monticello, Kentucky

pursuant to KRS 216.400 to 216.500 and 216.990 (2) and the regulations promulgated thereunder until June 30, 1959, unless this license is sooner suspended or revoked in accordance with law.

This license is not transferable and is limited to the above place and purposes unless written authorization is obtained from the State Board of Health.

This license is a receipt for payment of the fee required by law.

Russell E. Teague M.D.
Secretary

Paul A. Hackney
Assistant Secretary

Kentucky State Board of Health — FORM HL-2A (REV.6-58)

Dr. Robert B. Breeding, grandson of Charles and Anna Burton, purchased the property that had belonged to his grandparents. He lived there and, in 1957, opened the Anna Burton Memorial Hospital on the second floor. (Dr. Robert G. Breeding.)

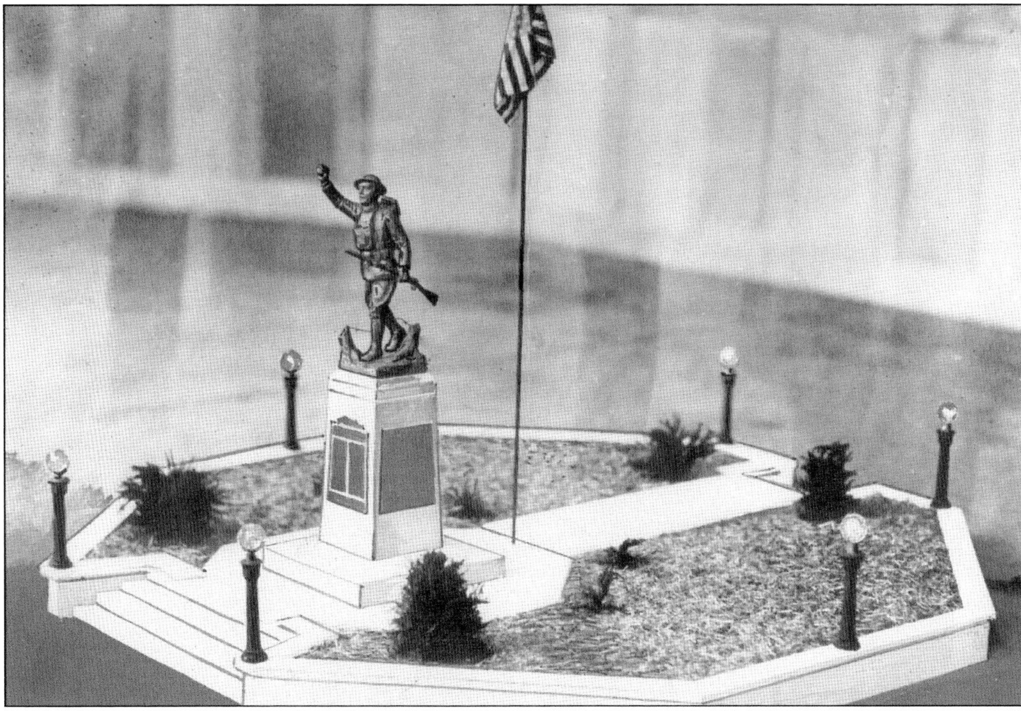

Three military memorials stand in Monticello to honor the men from Wayne County who have faced the horrors of war and have given their lives in the service of their country. The Doughboy statue, dedicated in 1923, stands in the center of the public square to honor the men who served in World War I. On its base is attached a plaque with the names of the 23 Wayne County men who died in that war. The sketch above shows the original Memorial Park before it was reduced in size. (Katy Lou Rector.)

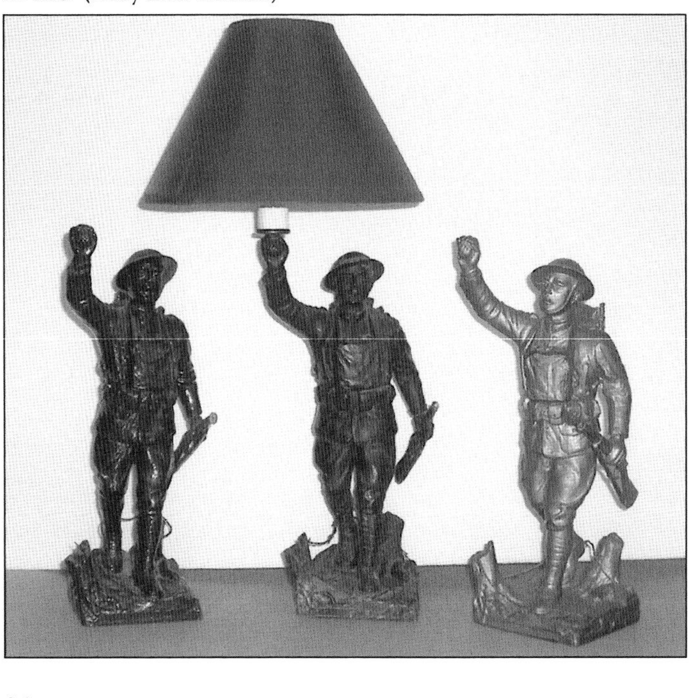

In 1922, the local American Legion post decided to erect a monument in honor and memory of the Wayne County soldiers who had served in World War I. They selected a statue named *The Spirit of the American Doughboy* that had been sculpted by Ernest Moore Viquesney. On April 8, 1923, the statue was placed in the public square. The Wayne County Museum houses an extensive collection of other works by Viquesney. (Wayne County Museum.)

A war memorial stands on the lawn of the Wayne County Courthouse. Plaques on the monument give the names of local men who died in the conflicts of World War II, Korea, and Vietnam. This monument was dedicated in 1955. (Wayne County Museum.)

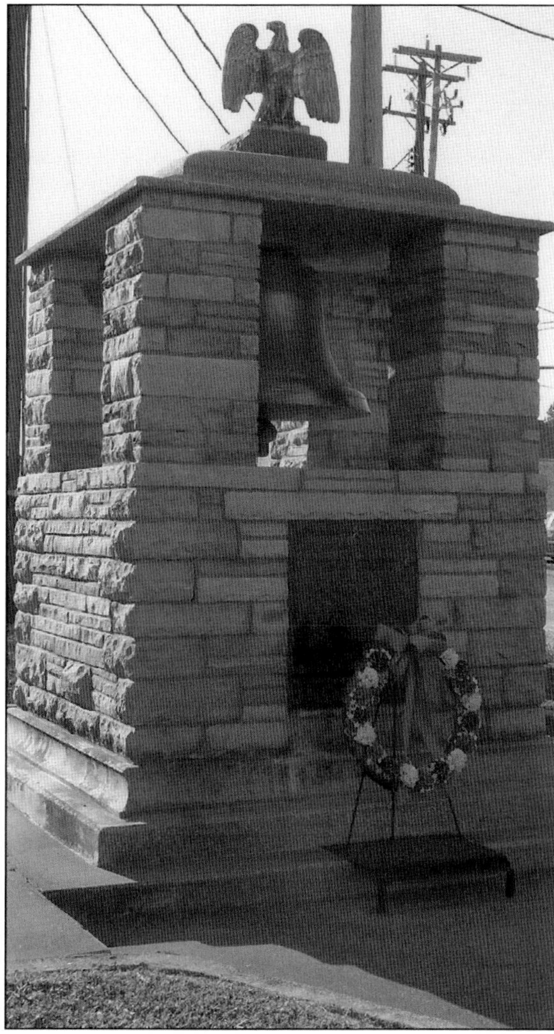

The newest Wayne County War Memorial is located on the lawn of the Wayne County Judicial Center on Columbia Avenue. This beautiful memorial includes the names of all Wayne County men who have died in the service of their country. (Wayne County Museum.)

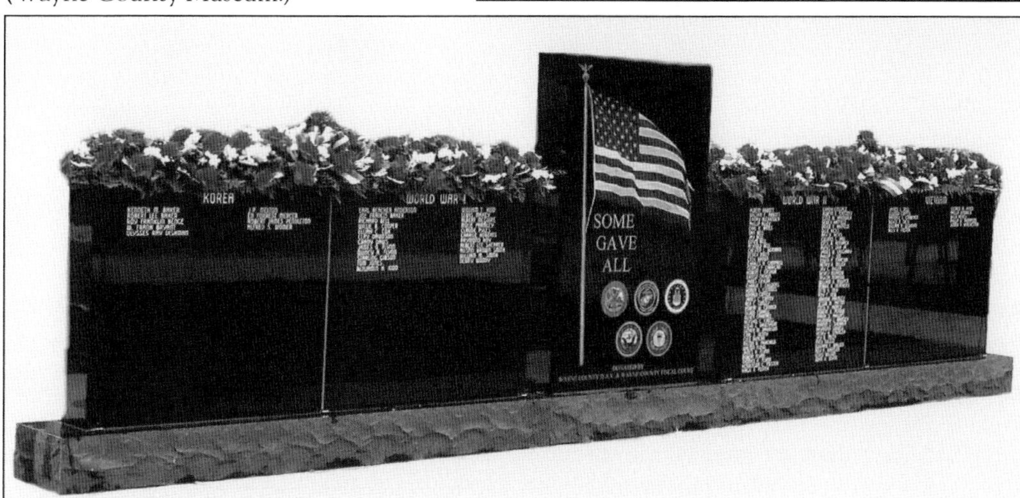

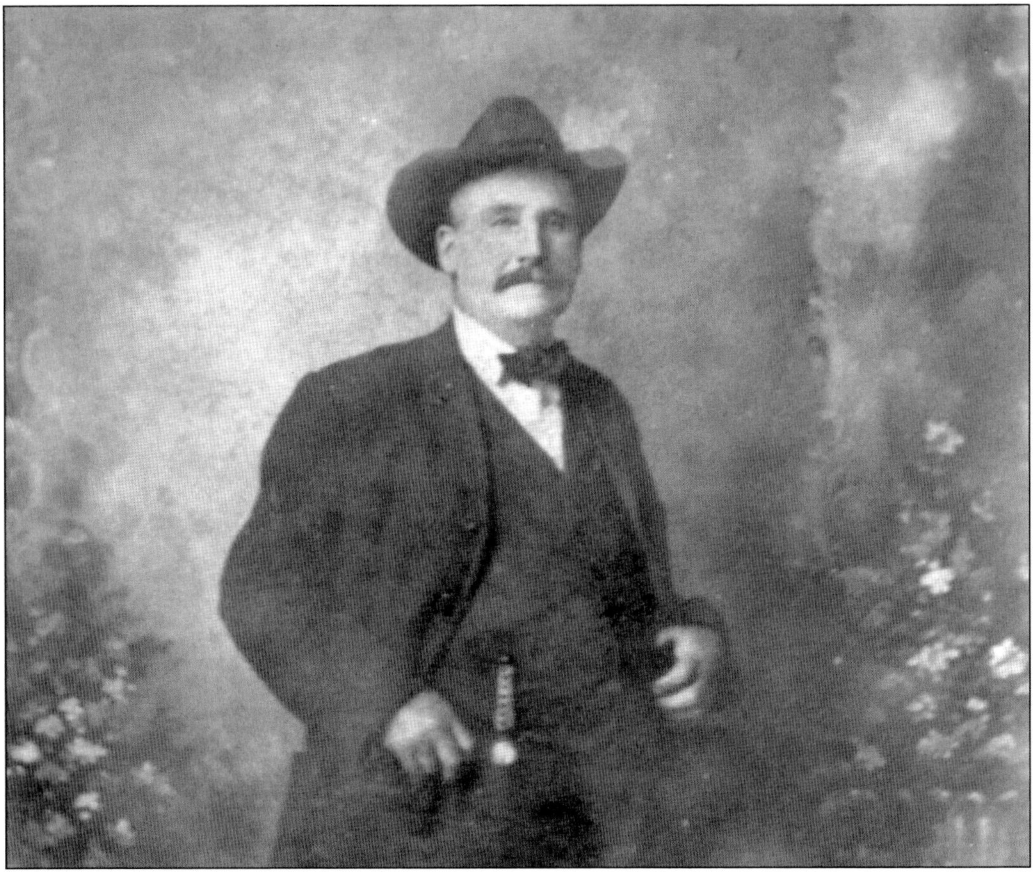

Shell Ragan (1851–1930) owned the livery stable that stood next to the Wayne County Outlook Building on Short Street (now East Columbia Avenue). He was the husband of "Aunt Set" and the father of Tom Ragan and Dora Ragan Cooper-Stockman. (Wayne County Historical Society.)

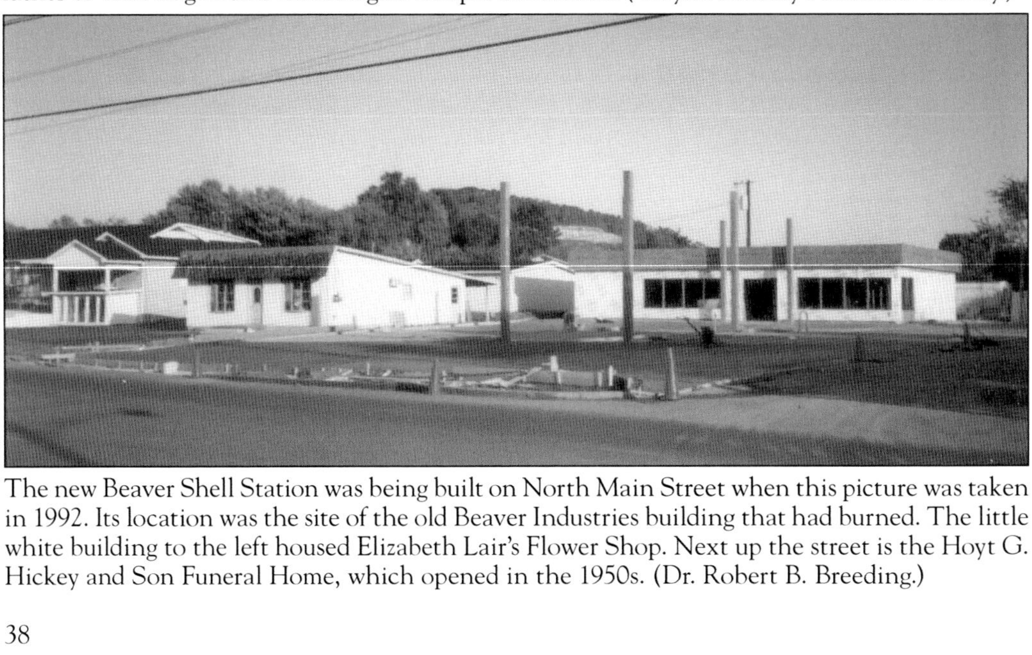

The new Beaver Shell Station was being built on North Main Street when this picture was taken in 1992. Its location was the site of the old Beaver Industries building that had burned. The little white building to the left housed Elizabeth Lair's Flower Shop. Next up the street is the Hoyt G. Hickey and Son Funeral Home, which opened in the 1950s. (Dr. Robert B. Breeding.)

Three

Around Wayne County

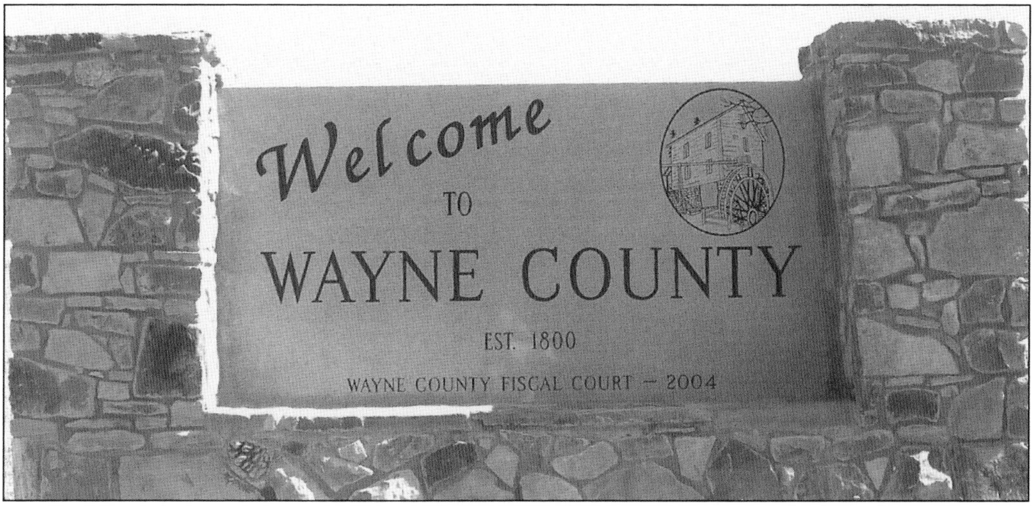

This sign on Highway 90 is, of course, only a welcome sign. It looks much like other welcome signs seen all over the country, their purpose being to greet both home folk and visitors as they enter special places. It is hoped that visitors to Wayne County will quickly learn what local people already know: Wayne County is indeed a special place. (Wayne County Museum.)

Wayne Taxi Company Schedule.

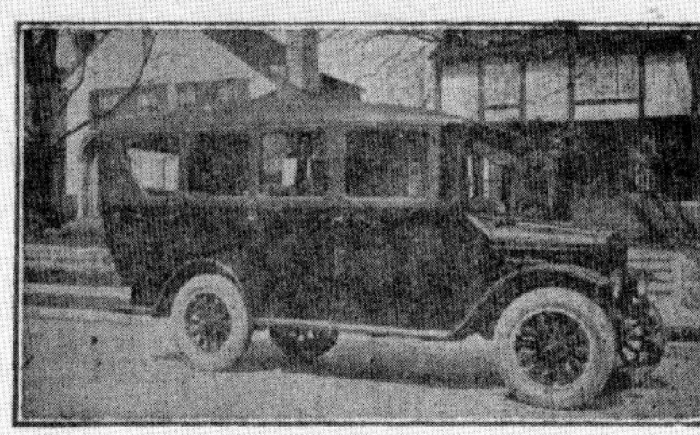

Monticello and Burnside Bus Line

MORNING SCHEDULE.

Bus for early morning train leaves at **3:15** to meet No. 28 at **5:04**, returning off No. 15 at **12:54** p. m.

Bus leaves Monticello at **8:45** to meet No. 16 at **10:30** a. m., returning on the arrival of No. 97 at **2:24**.

AFTERNOON SCHEDULE.

Bus leaves Monticello at **2:30** o'clock to meet No. 4 at **4:14** and returning off No. 27 at **12:05** a. m.

Fares:- To Burnside, $1.10. To Somerset over Colyer Bros. Bus line $1.50, by train $1.37, to and from intermediate points in proportion.

Special Accommodations not given by any other known Bus Line:—Passengers taken to any part of the city. We go to your residence or business house for you when you want to leave. We wake you thirty minutes before leaving time for the early morning train and call for you when time to leave. When you come in on the night train the driver knows what room at the Hotels to take you to. We secure you taxies for country trips, or do any other thing in reason to accommodate our customers. We are truly yours to command.

THE WAYNE TAXI COMPANY

INCORPORATE

KNOX FRAZER, Manager

When this 1927 advertisement appeared in the *Wayne County Outlook*, the time had not yet arrived when every family owned at least one vehicle. Taxis, buses, and the train that ran through Burnside were important means of transportation. (*Wayne County Outlook*.)

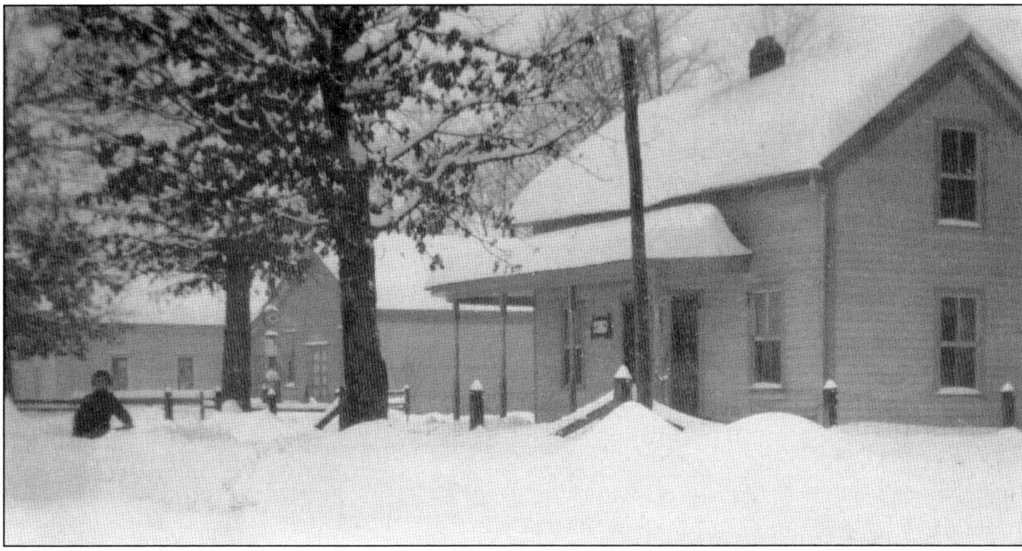

Like many country stores, Murl Store had a gasoline pump—a visible pump—out front. A hand pump brought the amount of gasoline requested by a customer into a glass cylinder near the top. The gasoline was then released by a hose and nozzle into the tank of the automobile. The house was the home of T. R. and Ida Shearer Guffey at the time this photograph was taken, and the wall beyond the store was part of Rector's Flat Baptist Church, which still stands today. (Vera Garner.)

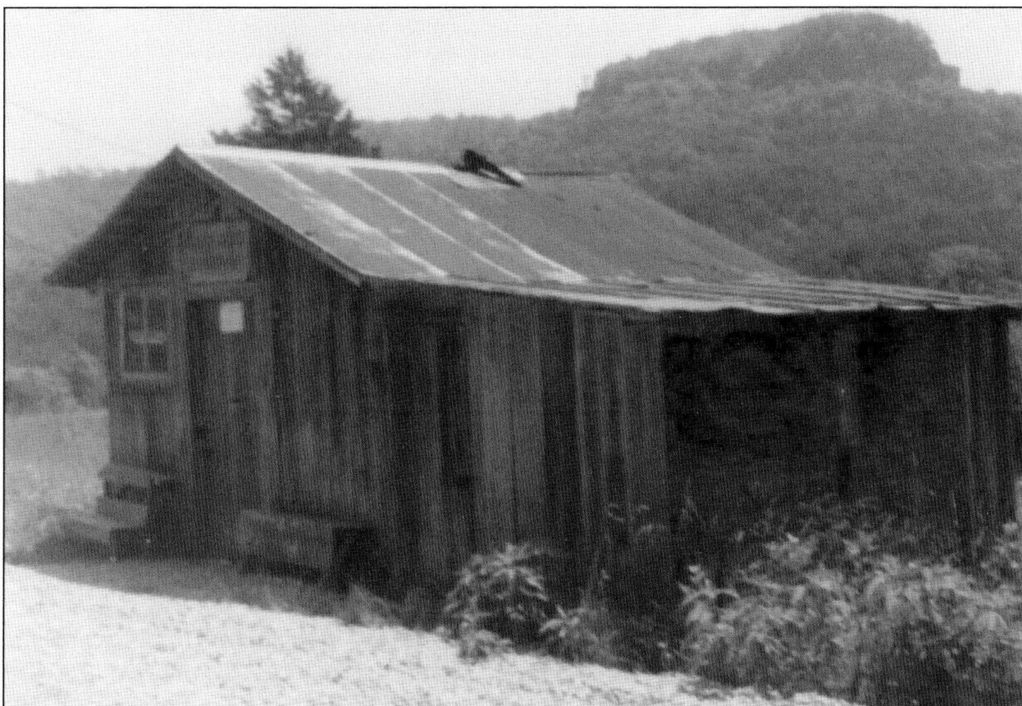

Schuyler Denney operated this store and post office in the Denney community from the early 1930s until the building burned in 1958. After the fire, Schuyler built a smaller structure where he kept the post office for several years. In addition to his business, Schuyler cultivated the family farm. His wife, Fannie Eads Denney, taught in the Wayne County School System. (Carol Campbell Foster.)

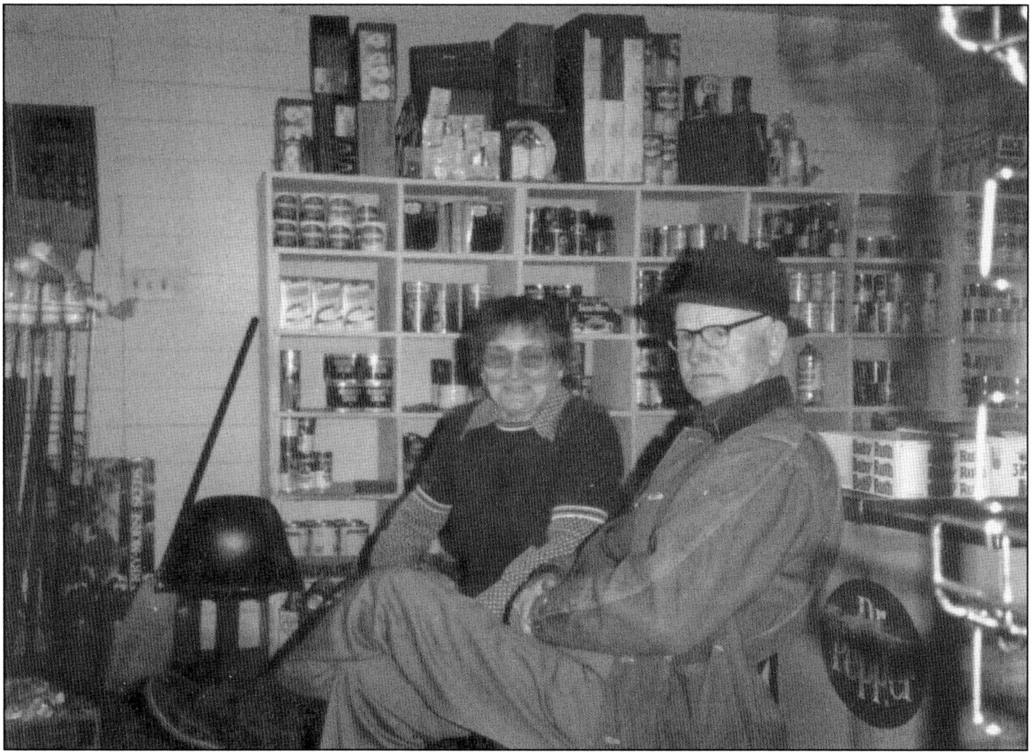

Virgil and Lillie Bell are pictured inside the store they operated in the Coopersville community. (Bell family.)

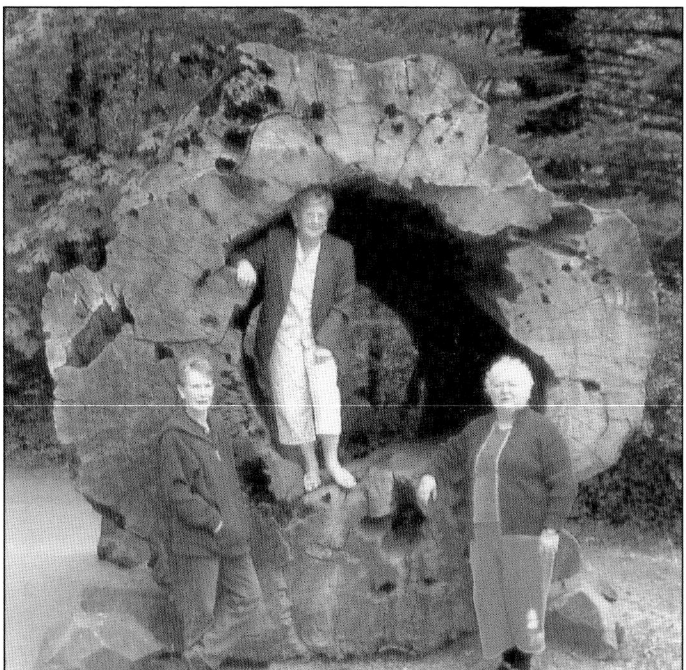

Virgil and Lillie Bell always urged their three daughters to go to college and become teachers. They lived to see all three retire from the Wayne County School System with what must be some kind of a family record: The combined total of teaching time for the sisters was 97 years. From left to right, Shane Bell, Rina Kay Pyles, and Karen Burnett are pictured in 2008 as they vacation together in California. (Bell family.)

As recently as a generation ago, a trip to Monticello on Saturday for shopping and socializing was a part of each week's activities for many Wayne County families. On this particular Saturday, however, a trip to the Burfield Store apparently sufficed for the people seen in this picture. Pictured here are Kenneth Melvin Baker and his sister, Shirley Baker (Abbott). Ralph Baker (left) and Harrison Marcum stand in the background. (Wayne County Museum.)

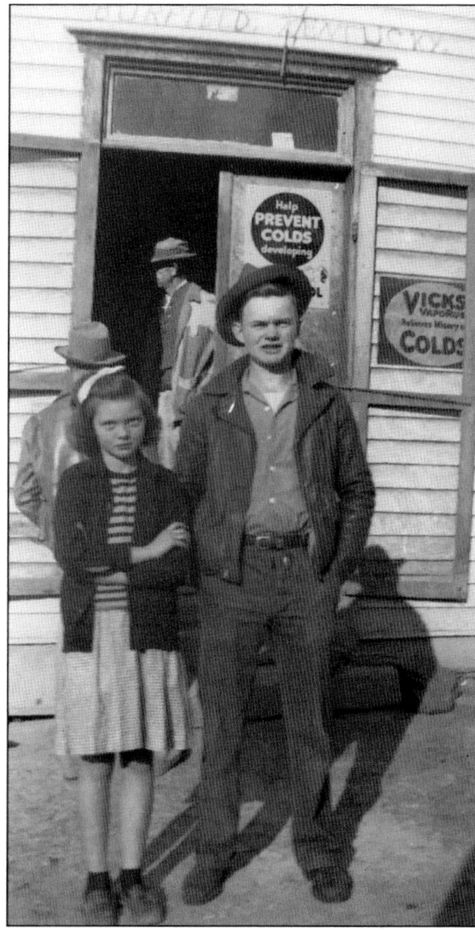

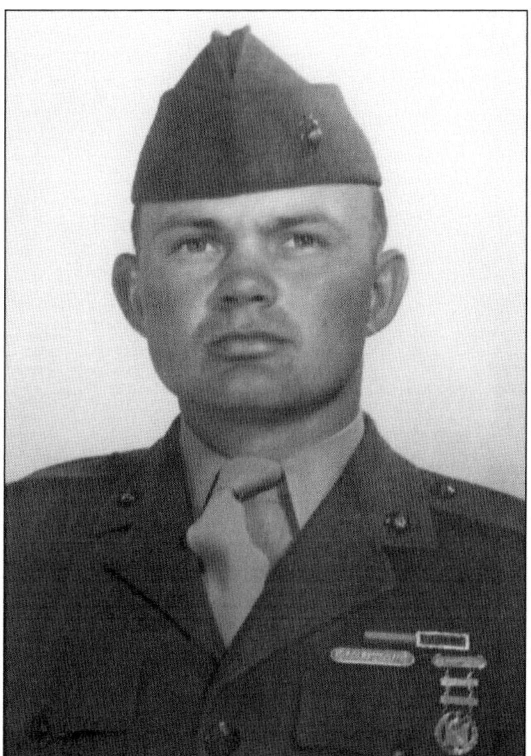

Kenneth Melvin Baker was a carpenter and a farmer in the Burfield Community of Wayne County. He is shown here after joining the Marines during the Korean War. Unfortunately, he drowned in a training camp in California. (John and Alta Baker West.)

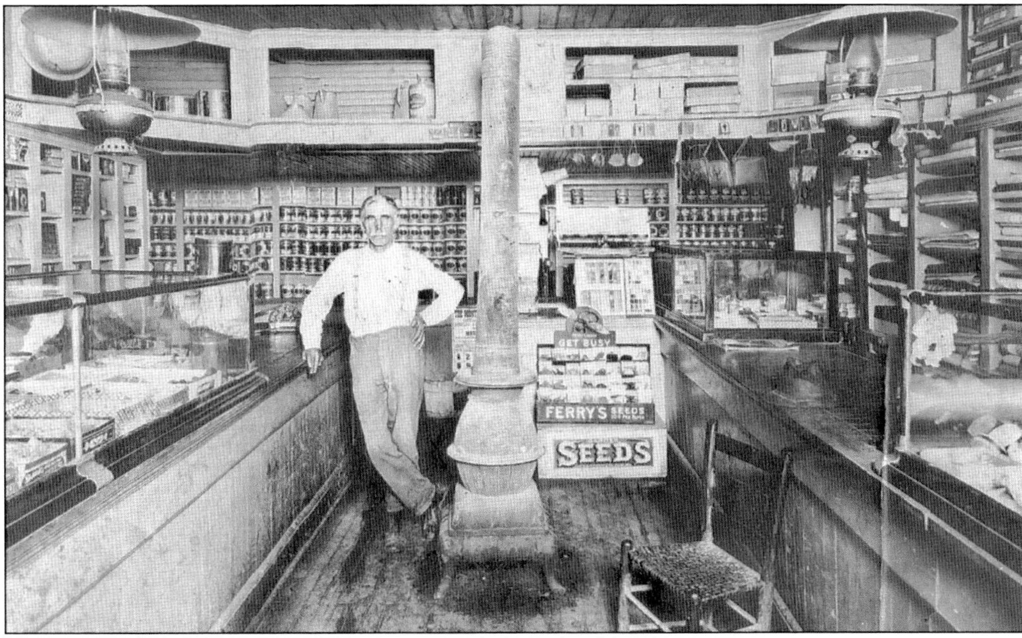

Ayers Alexander built this general store near his home on Cooper Road. He ran it for about 20 years before he passed away in 1932. A grandson, Wade McKechnie, continued operating the business as long as his grandmother, Molly Thornton Alexander, lived. The showcase on the left was a special place to the Alexander grandchildren. This was where candy and chewing gum were kept, and they had free access to it. (Wayne County Museum.)

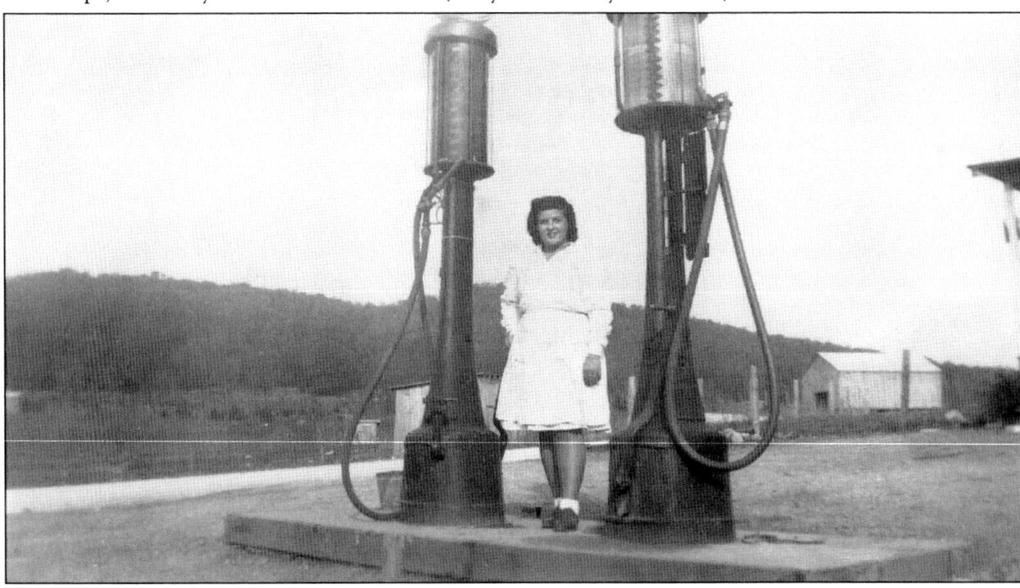

Nadine Abbott (McCune) is one of 10 children of Rupert and Cordie Abbott, who ran a general store in Elk Spring Valley. Nadine worked as a clerk from the time she was small. In 1942, with a feed-sack apron covering her dress (for she had been stocking shelves), Nadine is pictured standing between the gasoline pumps in front of the store. When her father began buying gasoline to resell, he bought it from George Coffey, who distilled gasoline at a little plant in the Gibson Hollow. Later he bought gasoline from Standard Oil. (Abbott family.)

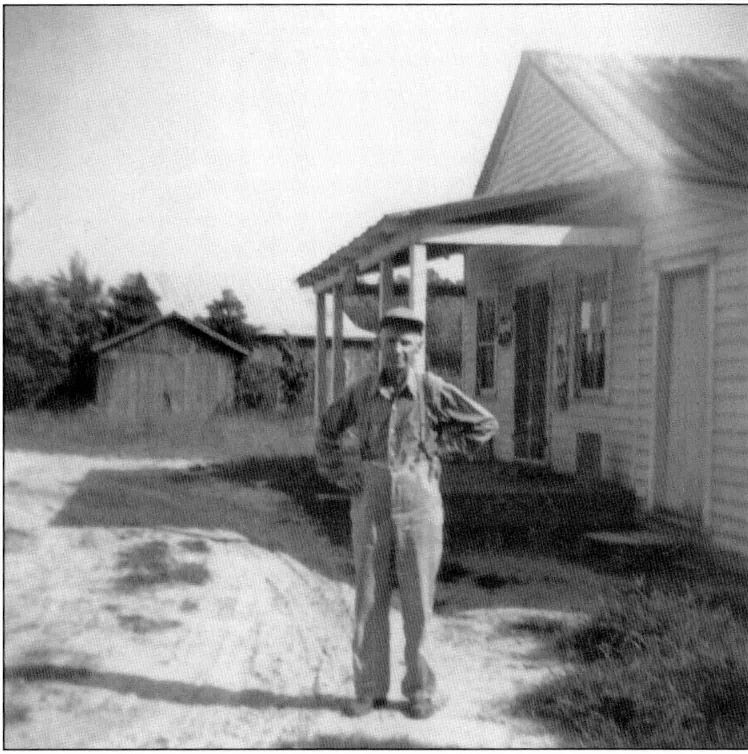

Even though the Campbell Grocery Store was only a small establishment, it played a large role in the Rogers Grove community. Beginning in the mid-1930s, two generations of the Campbell family operated the store until it closed in the late 1950s. When this photograph was taken, Haskell (pictured) and Sallie Campbell operated the business. With their children, they made their home in a side room of the store. (Carol Campbell Foster.)

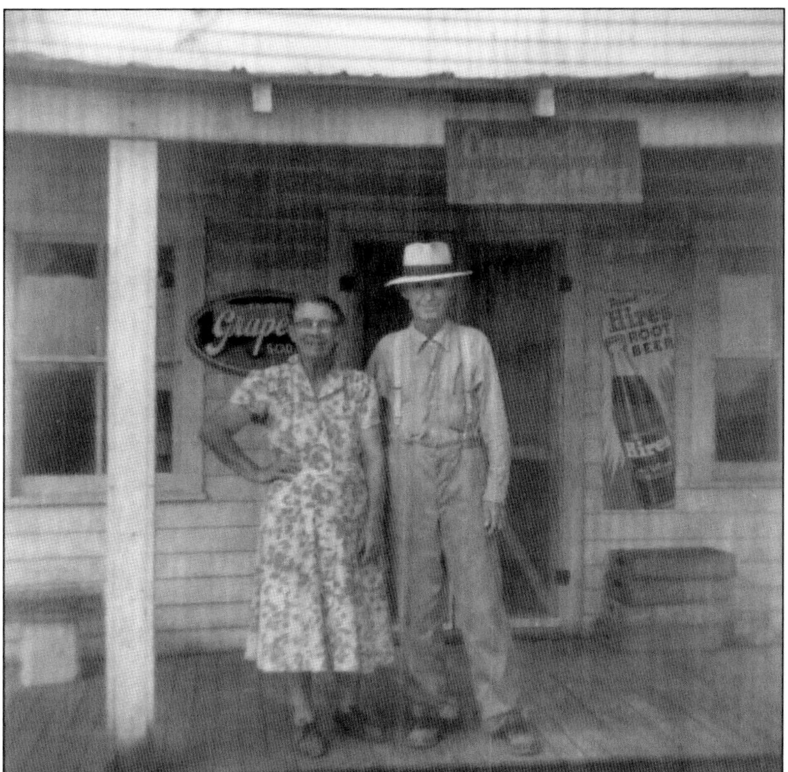

Albert and Minnie Campbell, parents of Haskell Campbell, stand on the front porch of the store they operated for many years. Women of the community appreciated the fact that the Campbell women were knowledgeable about sewing and always kept a good supply of brightly colored bolts of dress material on the shelves. (Carol Campbell Foster.)

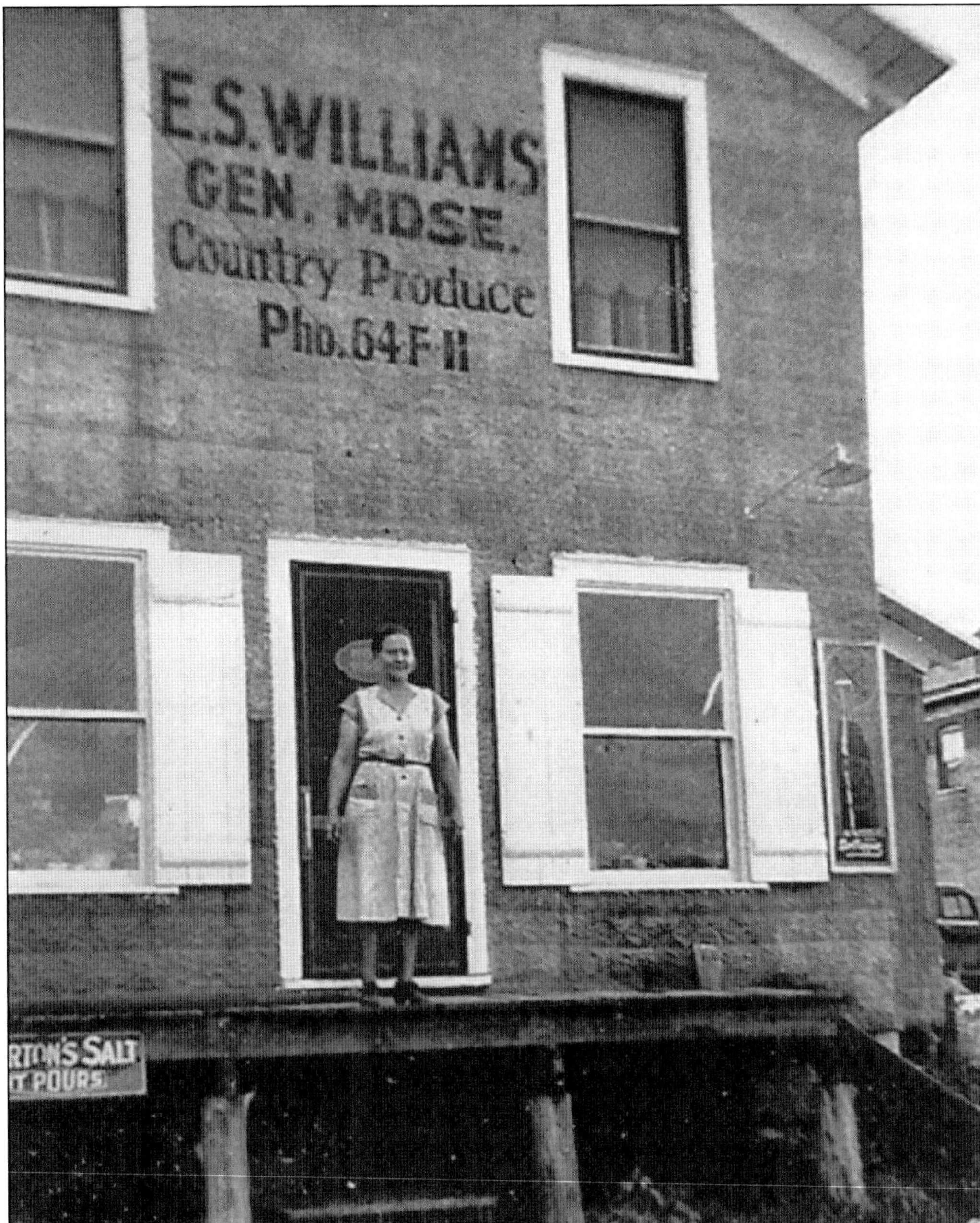

The E. S. Williams General Store, located at Crossroads, was a major shopping place for people in the Touristville community. Lexie Williams is pictured in the 1940s on the porch of the store. (Charlene Duncan.)

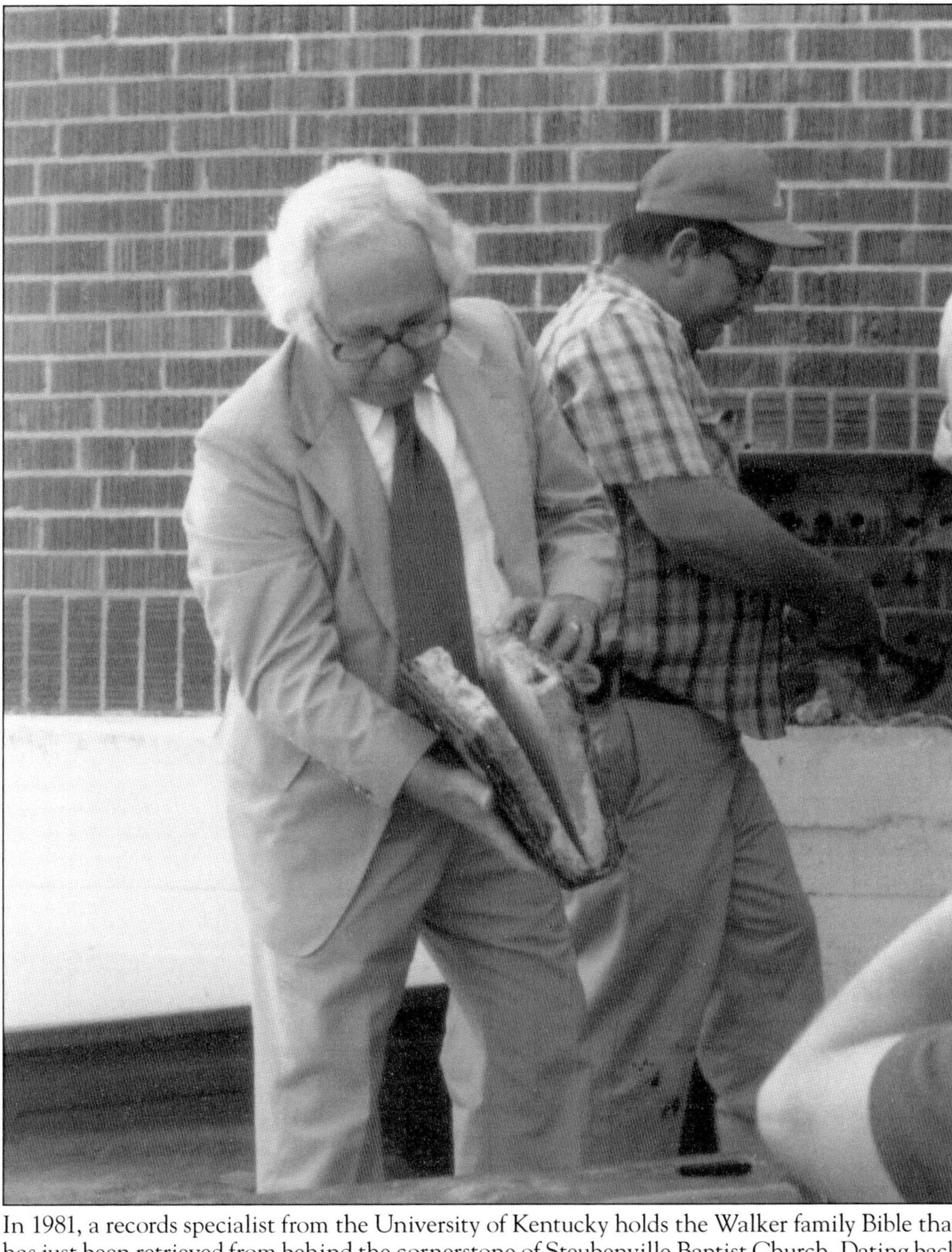

In 1981, a records specialist from the University of Kentucky holds the Walker family Bible that has just been retrieved from behind the cornerstone of Steubenville Baptist Church. Dating back to the 1880s, the Bible had been placed behind the cornerstone in 1947. Unfortunately it was so waterlogged and full of insects that it had to be sent to a document conservation center. It is back at Steubenville Baptist Church today in the best possible condition that could be achieved using modern preservation techniques. (Wayne County Museum.)

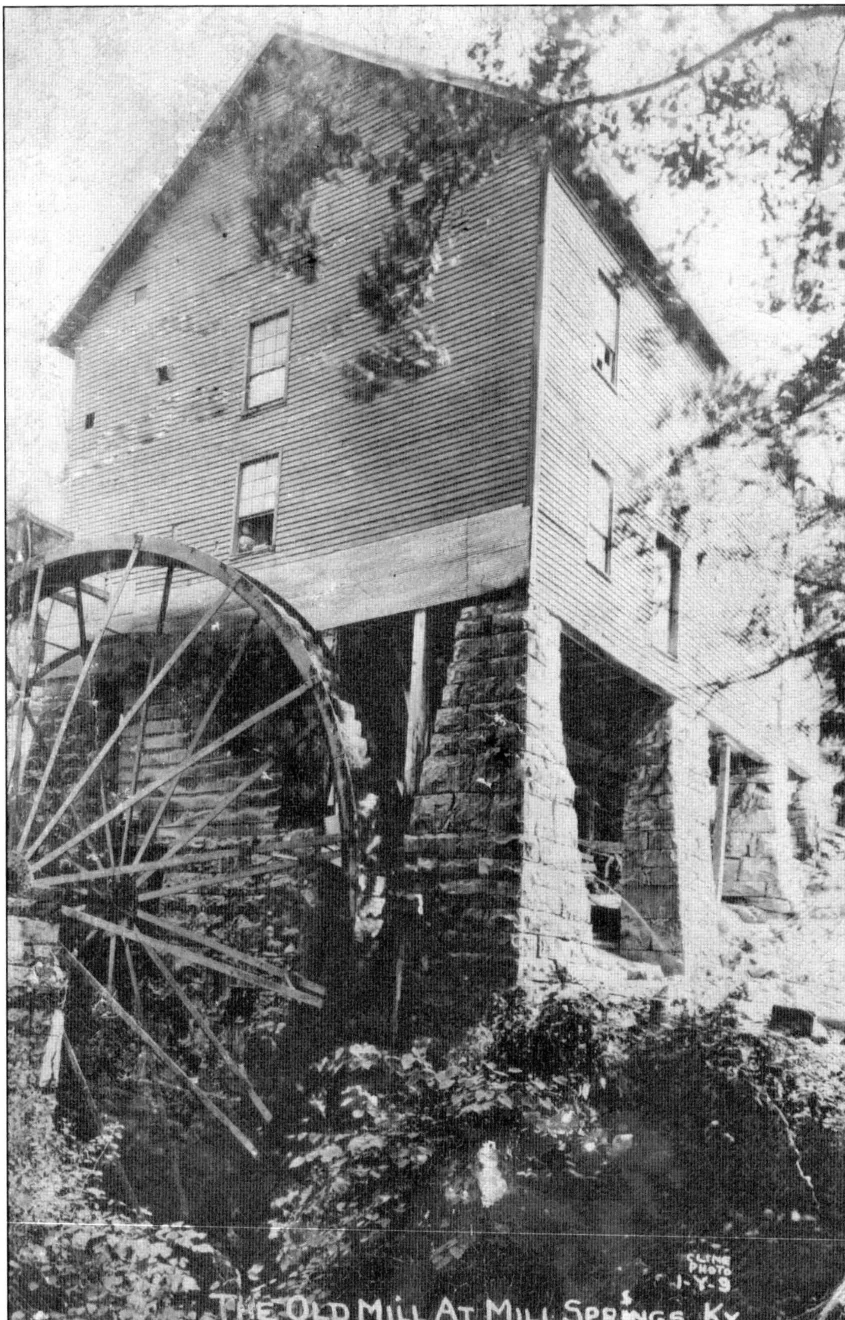

Mill Springs Mill is very much a Wayne County landmark. In 2010, it boasts the largest overshot water wheel in the United States and possibly the world. The mill was constructed in 1877, and the present wheel, which is 40 feet in diameter, was added in 1911–1912. The mill closed in 1948; its last operator was T. S. Roberts. Thanks to the efforts of the Monticello Woman's Club and the Kentucky Department of Highways, the mill was reactivated in 1963. Now, during summer weekends, the trap that releases the water from 13 springs is opened, the big wheel goes into motion, and corn is water-ground and packaged to sell as unbolted cornmeal. (Wayne County Museum.)

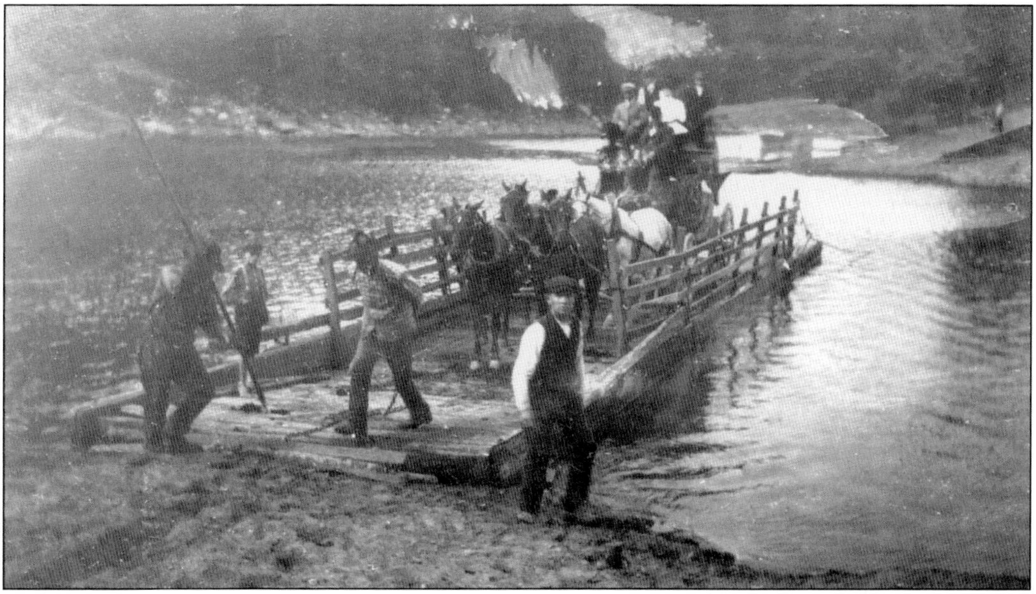

Carrying a full load, the Monticello-Burnside Stagecoach has crossed Cumberland River on the ferry at Burnside. Between 1897 and 1915, this stagecoach made a daily trip to Burnside to meet the train. This was the last operating stage line east of the Mississippi River. The stagecoach, No. 599 of the Albert Downing Company of Concord, New Hampshire, now sits in a Wells Fargo Bank lobby in Los Angeles, California. (Vera Garner.)

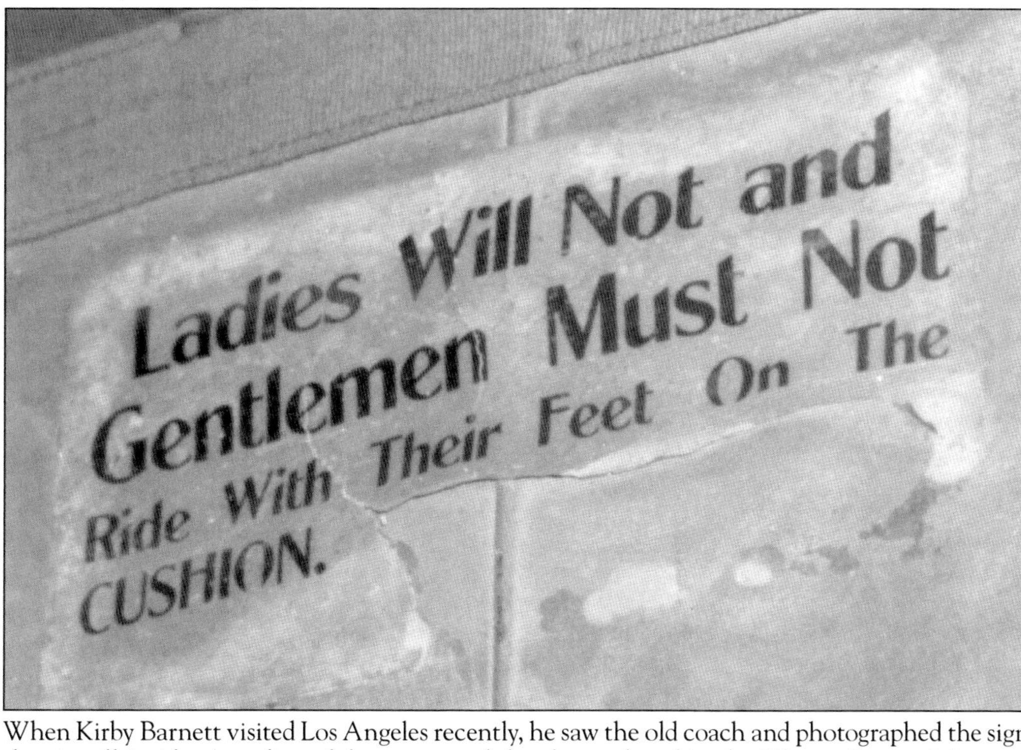

When Kirby Barnett visited Los Angeles recently, he saw the old coach and photographed the sign that is still inside. A replica of the stagecoach has been placed in the Wayne County Museum. (Kirby Barnett.)

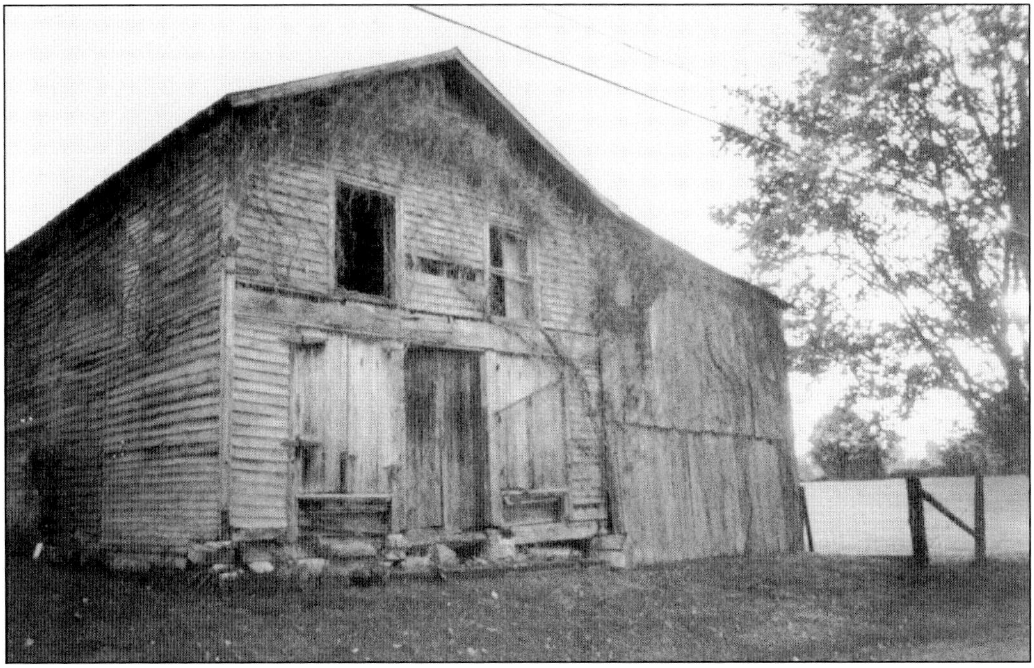

This old store once served as one of many stagecoach stops between Monticello and the train at Burnside. At the edge of Pulaski County, it was located across the road from the present site of Raintree Inn. (Joyce New.)

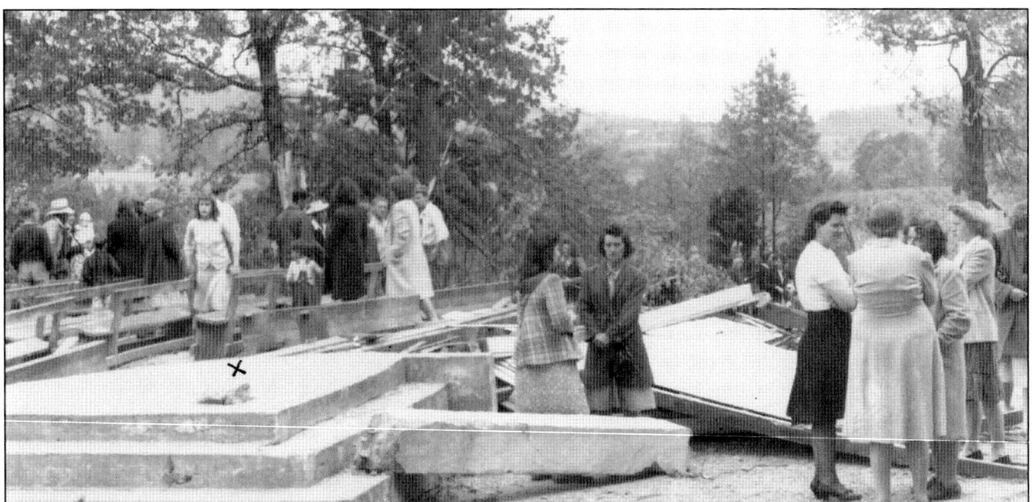

In 1948, on a Sunday evening in May, a tornado struck Clinton and Wayne Counties, killing five persons and injuring 20–30 others and destroying all kinds of livestock and other property. Fifty people were gathered for worship at Davis Chapel Church at Alpha (at the edge of Clinton County) that evening. When the storm came, the minister advised everyone to lie down on the floor. The building blew away, but none of those present were killed. After the storm passed, the Bible that had been on the pulpit was found on the floor. In this picture, the X marks the spot where Oscar Franklin was crouched when the storm destroyed the church building. (Oscar Franklin.)

Shelby Moore Cullom was born in Wayne County not far from Cullom Rock, the giant sandstone boulder that towers over Elk Ridge and the surrounding hills. This pinnacle is named for the man who became such a prominent figure on the national stage. While he was still an infant, Cullom moved with his family to Illinois. He grew up there and was admitted to the bar in 1855. Along the way he became the friend of another Kentuckian, Abraham Lincoln. He served several terms in the Illinois Legislature, then became governor of Illinois in 1877. During his second term in that office, he resigned to run for the U.S. Senate. He served five terms as a senator, and few men of his day achieved more in the way of public service. President Taft appointed him to supervise the building of the Lincoln Memorial at Springfield. He died in 1914 and is buried in the Springfield Cemetery near the tomb of his friend, Abraham Lincoln. Engraved on his tombstone is a mention of his birthplace—Wayne County, Kentucky. (Garnett Walker.)

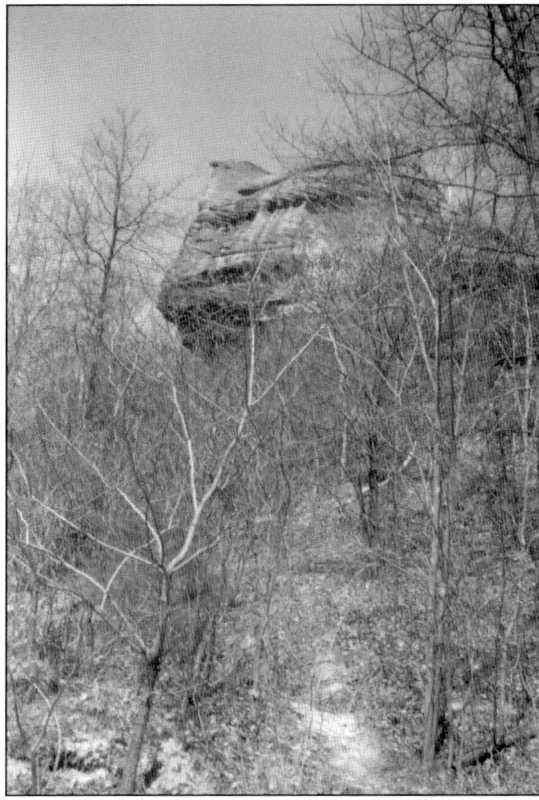

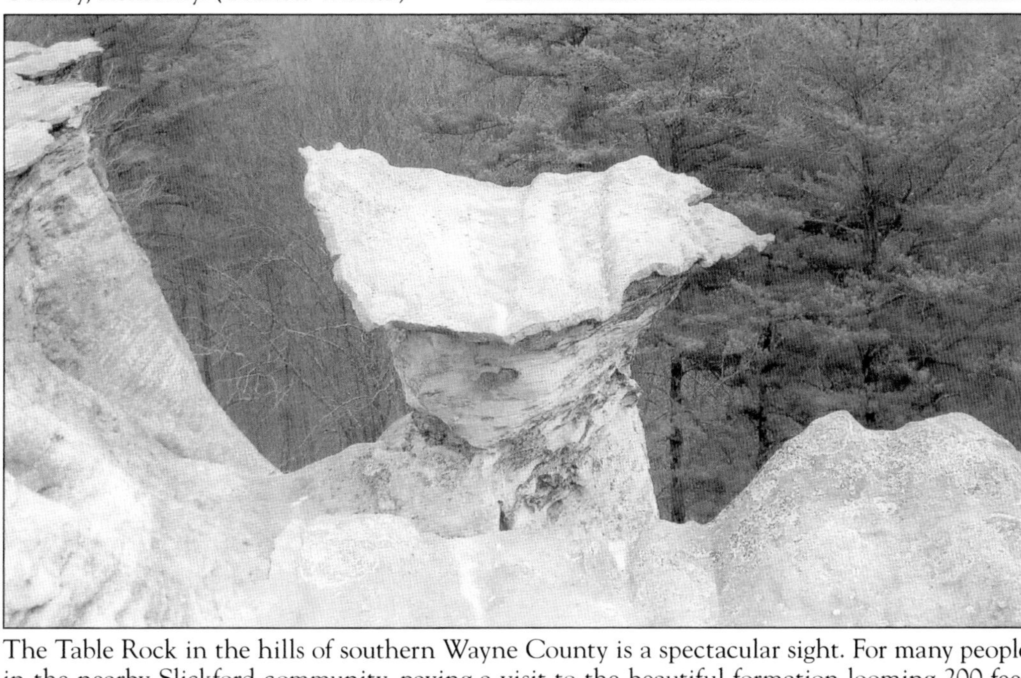

The Table Rock in the hills of southern Wayne County is a spectacular sight. For many people in the nearby Slickford community, paying a visit to the beautiful formation looming 200 feet above the valley floor is something they have done their entire lives. This photograph was taken from an old logging road. (Sue Wright.)

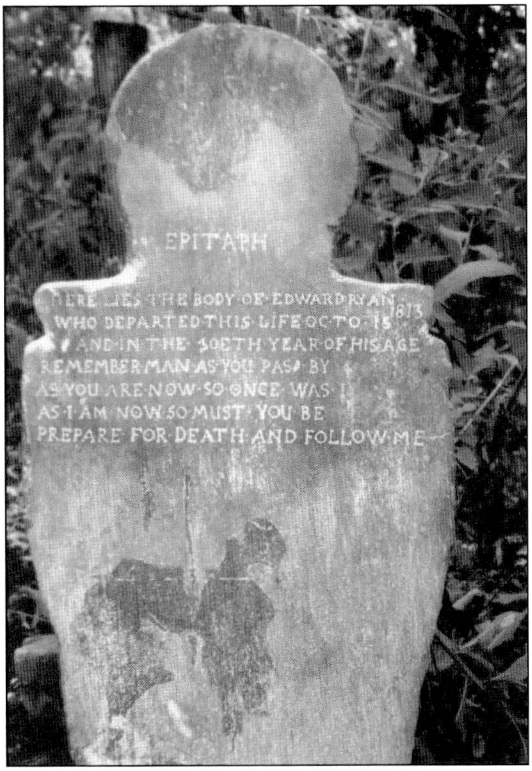

Beginning in 1976, historians Ben and Juanita Coffey spent five years searching, walking, driving, and deciphering in their quest to make the first comprehensive survey and record of Wayne County's cemeteries. As they worked, a startling fact became apparent: About half of Wayne County's deceased citizens are buried in unmarked graves. Another apparent fact was that many Wayne County people put much thought and effort into the creation of tombstones, such as the one shown here. (Ben and Juanita Coffey.)

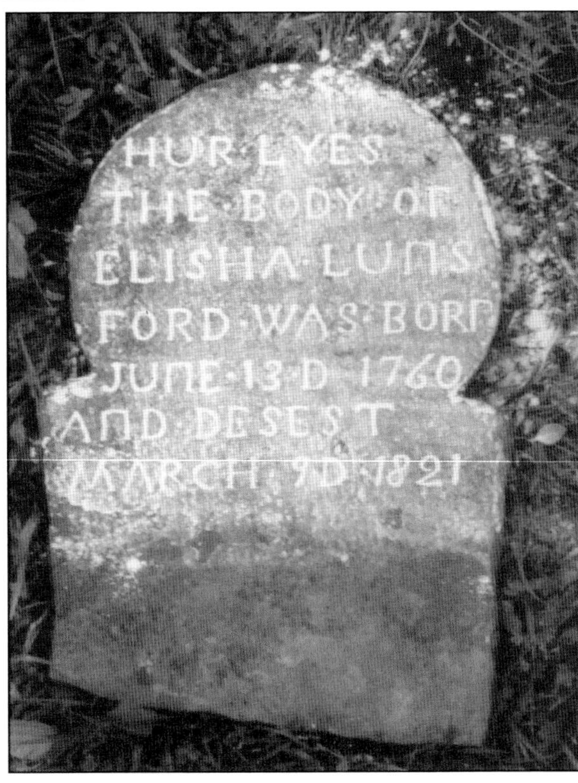

As Ben and Juanita Coffey worked so diligently to document thousands of Wayne County grave sites, they found many old hand-hewn tombstones with inscriptions chiseled by a friend or relative of the deceased. Mindful of the value of these markers, Ben photographed most of them. (Ben and Juanita Coffey.)

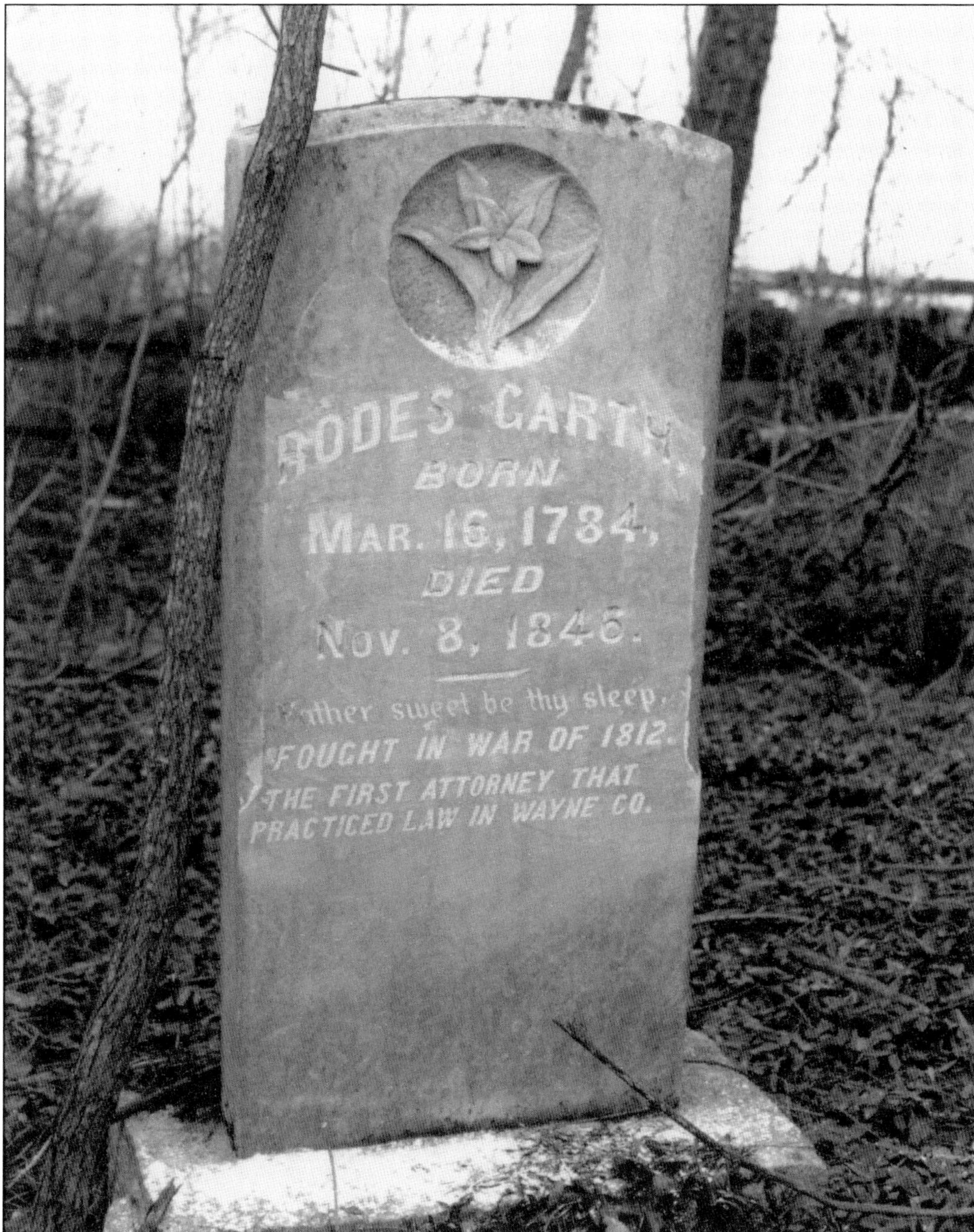

Rodes Garth was an outstanding Wayne County citizen. His grave, along with a number of others, lies inside a sturdy stone enclosure near the Frank Bell Lumber Company on White Way Inn Road. Garth came to Monticello and opened the county's earliest-known school in 1807. By all accounts, it offered an excellent education. In the War of 1812, Garth served with Micah Taul's company and kept a remarkable journal of the daily occurrences of that company. He was admitted to the bar and represented Wayne County in the Kentucky State Legislature on numerous occasions, in both the house and the senate. Although few people may remember his name, the impact of Rodes Garth's life is undoubtedly still felt in the community. (Ben and Juanita Coffey.)

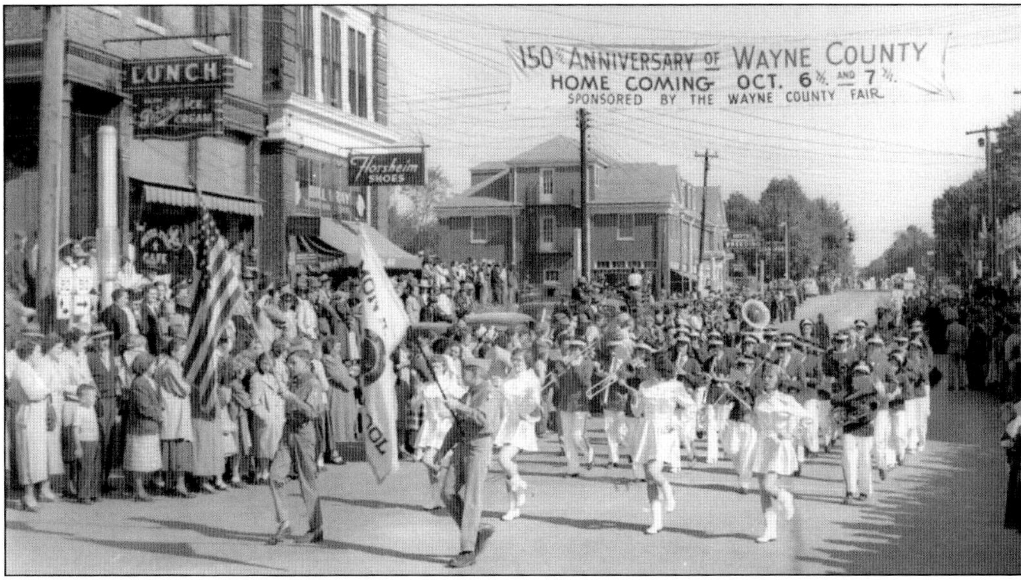

Citizens of Wayne County had a dual reason for celebrating on October 6 and 7 in 1950. Not only was it the county's sesquicentennial, it was time for the Wayne County Fair, and it seemed that just about every single one of the 17,000 persons in the county turned out to enjoy the events. Celebration highlights included a school parade, a parade of floats, and a pageant depicting the county from its early days until 1950. In addition to those events, almost every type of fair activity that one could name was successfully carried out. The fair was a suitable celebration to cap the first 150 years of county history. (Oscar Franklin.)

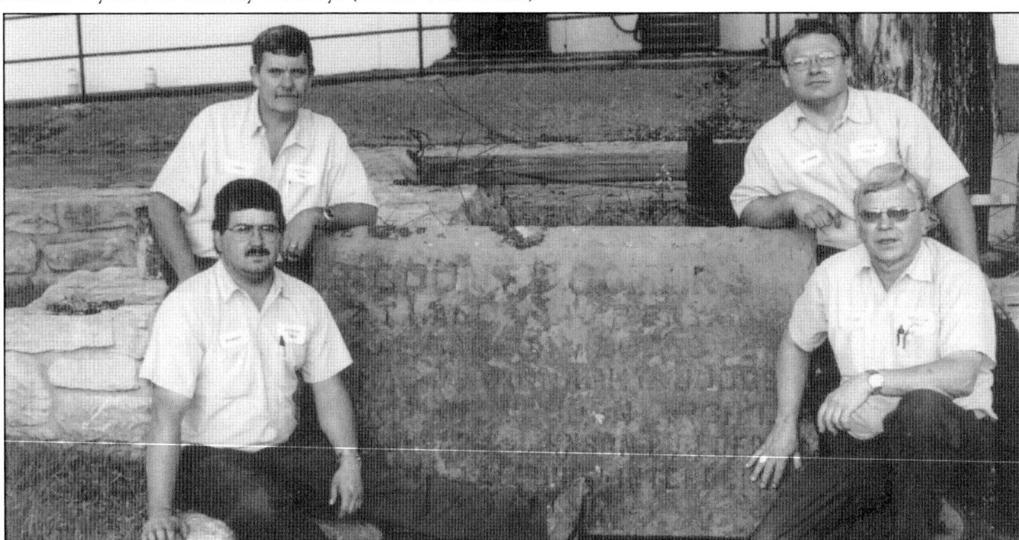

When Wayne County's fifth courthouse was torn down in 1949, its cornerstone somehow ended up in a field in the Susie community. In 2003, the men pictured here learned that the field was about to be bulldozed, so they rescued the stone and brought it to the Wayne County Museum. From left to right, they are (first row) Robert Bridgeman and Stuart Dolen; (second row) Larry Patton and Donnie Young. Engraved in the cornerstone are the names of the county commissioners and the judge at the time the courthouse was built in 1898, plus the names of the architect, the builders, and the superintendent. (Wayne County Historical Society.)

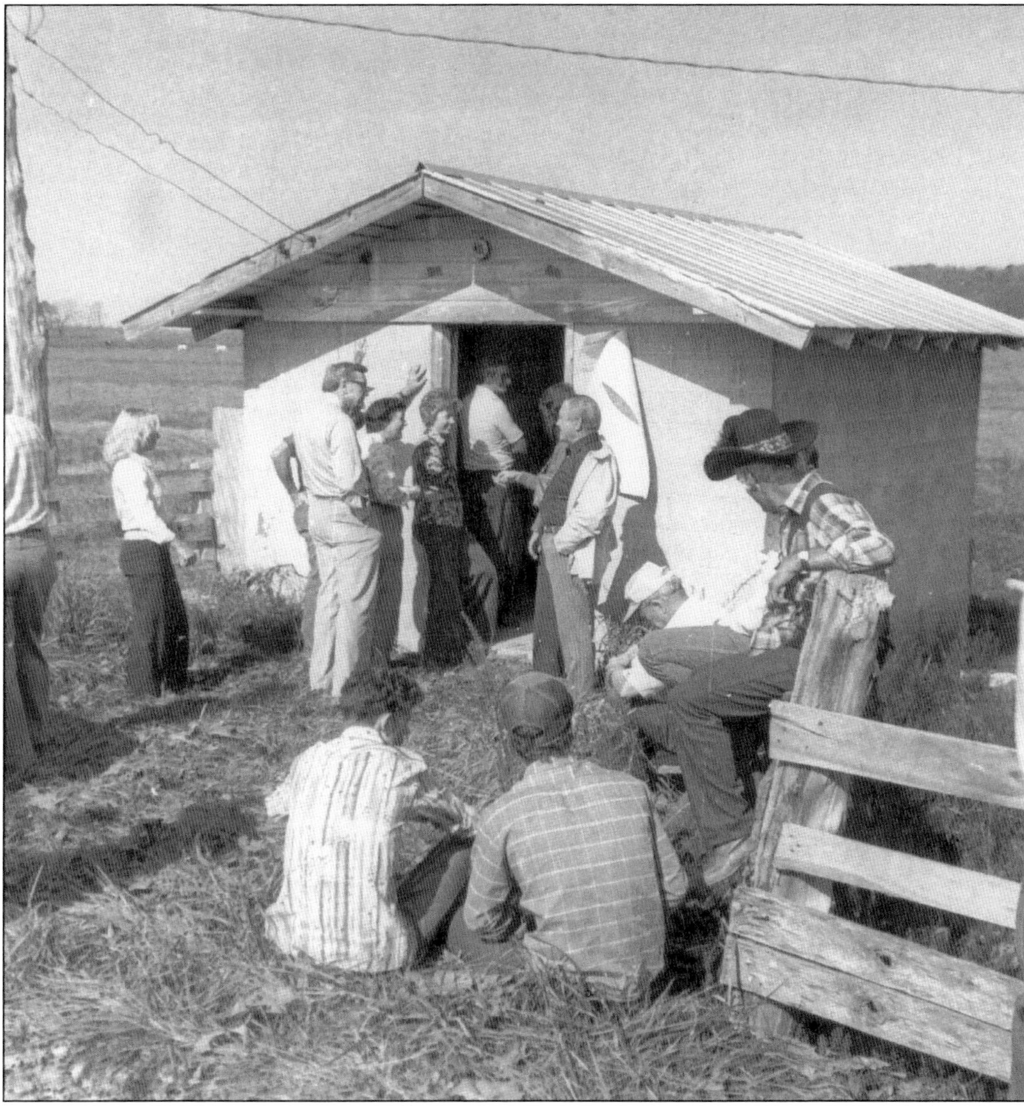

In Wayne County, going to vote has always been a social occasion as well as a political activity. In 1981, these Collett's Hill residents enjoyed the company of their neighbors at the voting house of Precinct No. 6. (Wayne County Historical Society.)

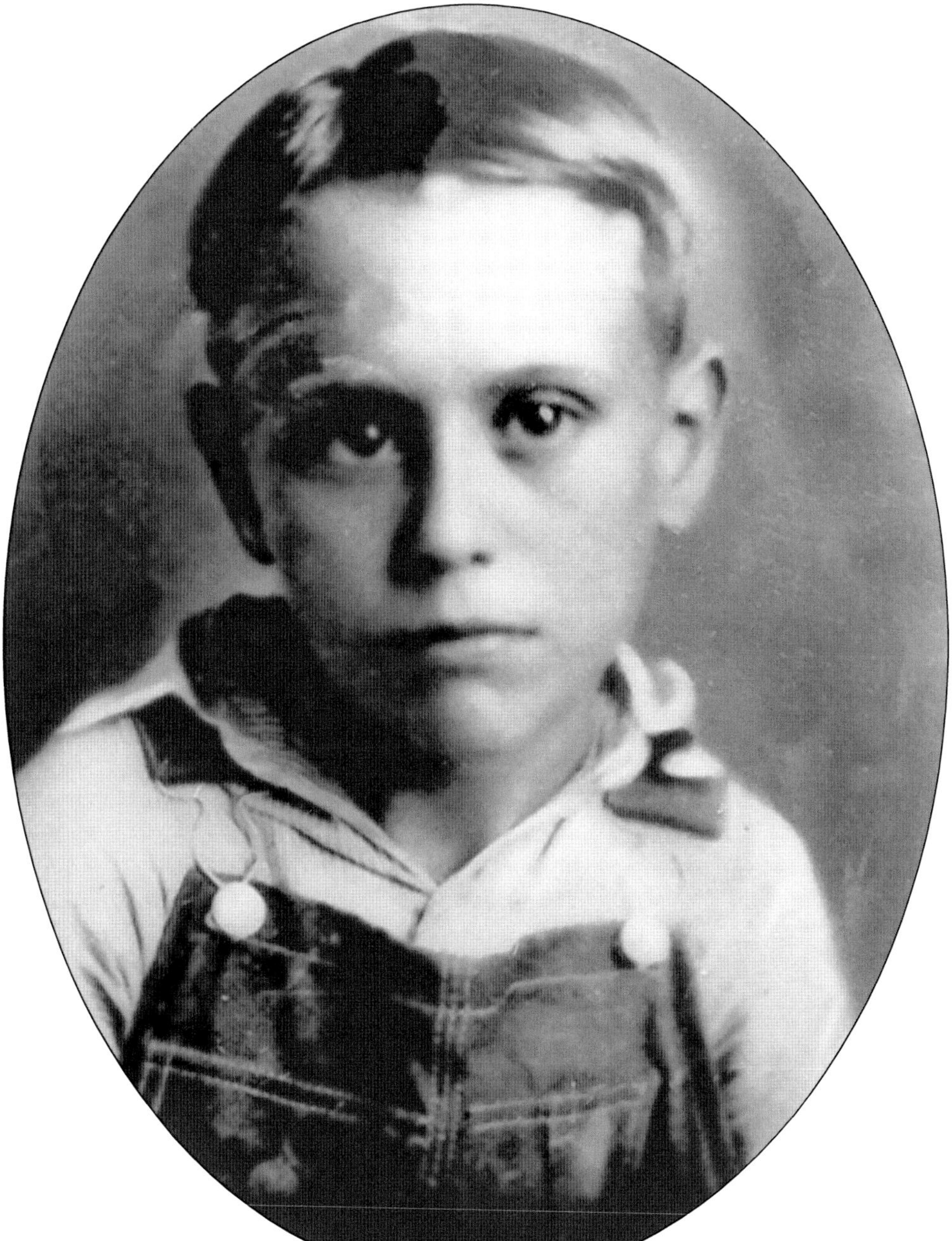

Each life is a precious gift and, no matter how brief, should be remembered as such. Born in 1928, James C. Perdue and Maggie Davis Perdue's son, Otto, only lived until 1940, when he died of appendicitis. This photograph is mounted above Otto's name on his tombstone in Davis Chapel Cemetery. Otto liked baseball, and though it was the midst of the Great Depression, his parents had managed to buy him a baseball glove. His mother also made him a professional-looking baseball uniform, lovingly sewn together from feed sacks. These two treasures, the uniform and the baseball glove, have been placed at the Wayne County Museum—reminders of a small boy who had a place of his own in the tapestry of Wayne County life. (Wayne County Museum.)

Four

Work And Recreation

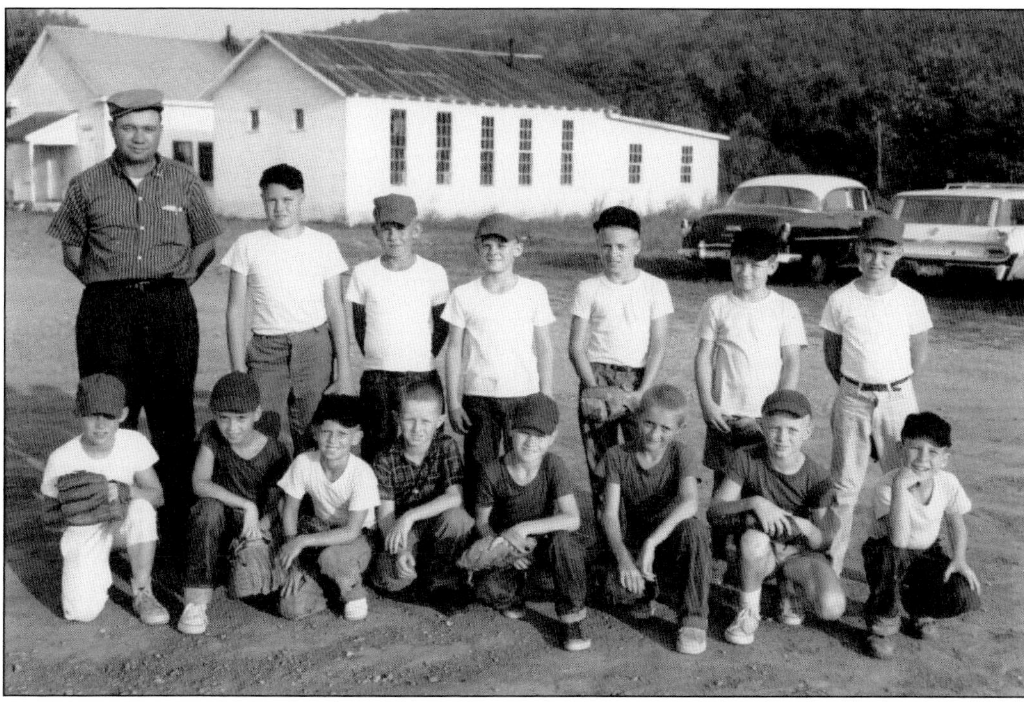

A Little League baseball team from around 1960 is pictured on the sports field of the old Wayne County High School on South Main Street. From left to right are (first row) Joe Phillips, an unidentified player, Buddy Troxell, David Catron, Gary Dishman, Gary Patton, and two unidentified players; (second row) coach Jim Forshee, Darrell Dunagan, Paul Upchurch, Henry West, Bobby Breeding, Monte Wayne Lair, and Sam Rankin. Visible in the background are old one-room schoolhouses, which have been transported to the grounds of the high school from their original locations to serve various purposes. (Dr. Robert B. Breeding.)

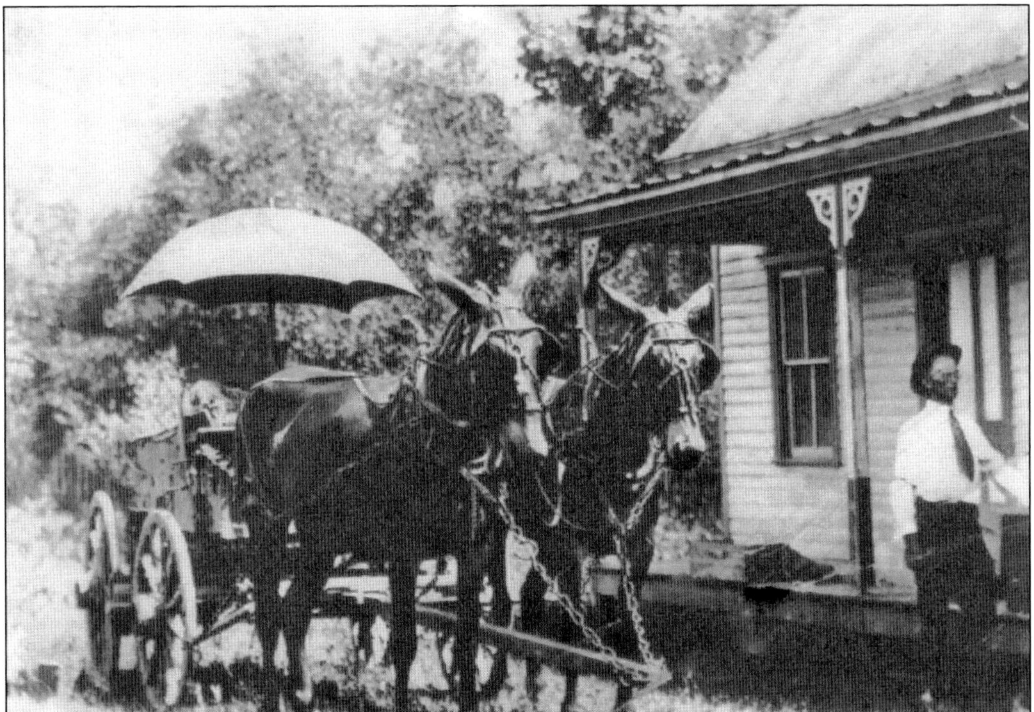

Charles Omer "Ped" Kelsay was a peddler who lived in the Gap Creek community. He sold Raleigh and Watkins products by hauling them over rough roads in a wagon pulled by two mules. He later upgraded to a covered wagon with four horses. Because it was impossible to make a trip in a day, Kelsay would stay with people along the way. He did this for many years until he bought a farm in the Shearer Valley community, which he farmed for the rest of his life. (Roxie Dalton.)

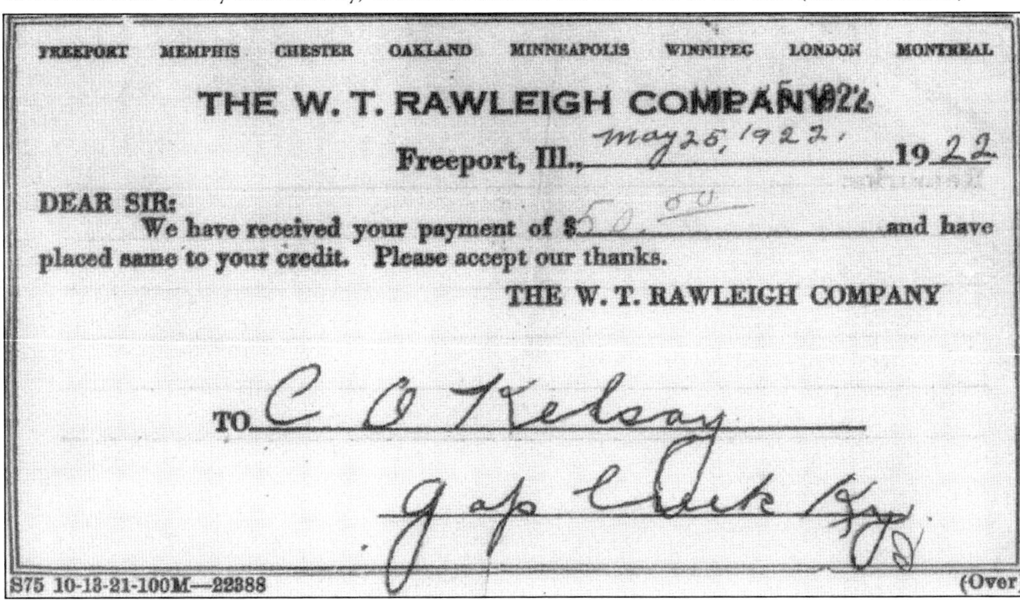

FREEPORT MEMPHIS CHESTER OAKLAND MINNEAPOLIS WINNIPEG LONDON MONTREAL

THE W. T. RAWLEIGH COMPANY

Freeport, Ill., May 25, 1922. 1922

DEAR SIR:
We have received your payment of $50.00 and have placed same to your credit. Please accept our thanks.

THE W. T. RAWLEIGH COMPANY

TO C O Kelsay
Gap Creek Ky

875 10-13-21-100M—22388 (Over)

The W. T. Rawleigh Company issued this acknowledgment of payment from Charles Omer Kelsay for products he would offer for sale to his customers. (Roxie Dalton.)

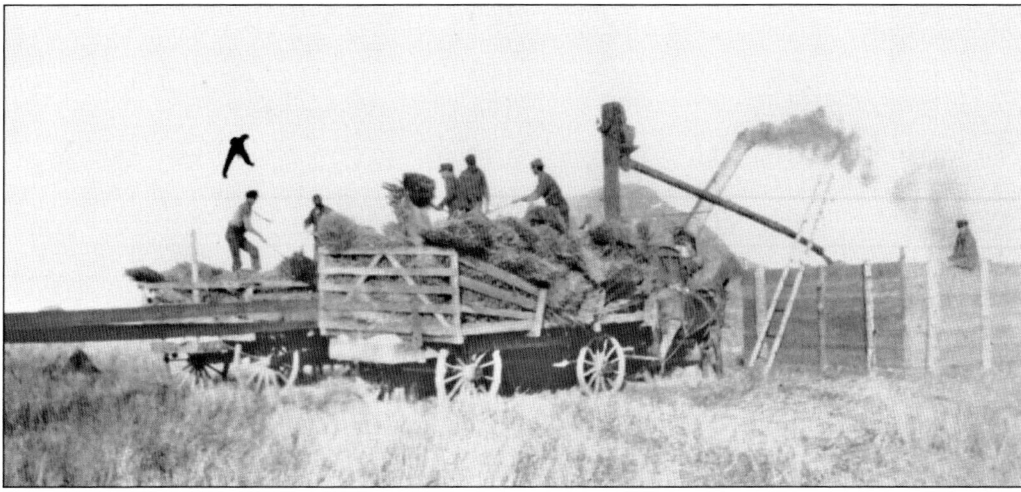

To say that farming in Wayne County has dramatically changed over the years is an understatement. Some Wayne County farmers today can still remember a time when motorized farm machinery was unknown to the average farmer. Almost everything had to be done by hand and brute force. Nowhere was this truer than in the harvesting of wheat. The stalks of golden grain had to be cut by hand, trimmed, and stacked into sheaves. Those sheaves would then have to be threshed by hand to separate the grain from the stalk. In time the steam-powered threshing machine made its appearance. A farmer in the Murl community obtained one of these machines, and a new way of life opened up to the farmers. Newel Hicks is identified with a mark on this photograph. (Vera Garner.)

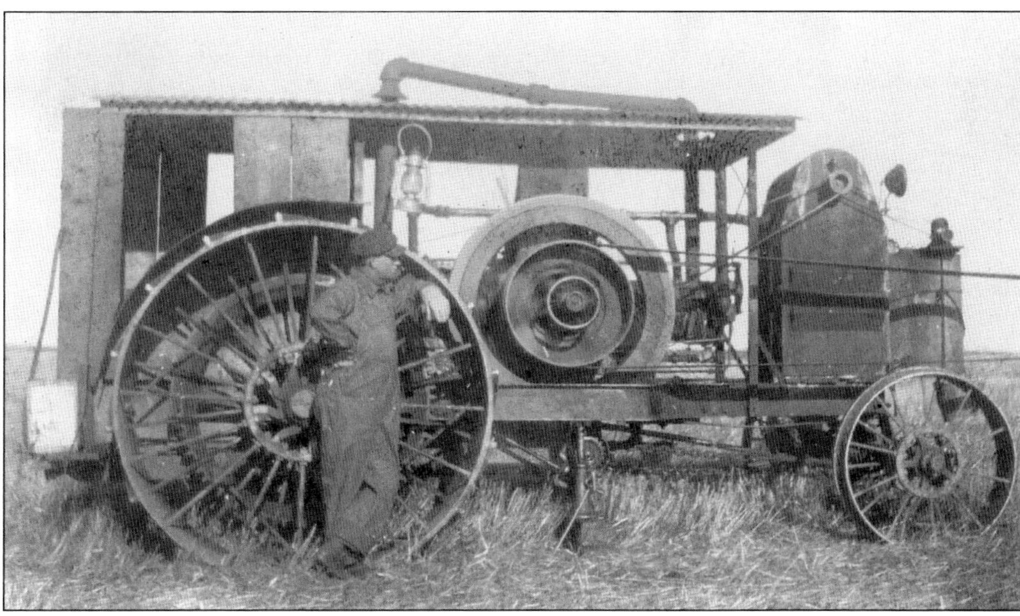

In this photograph of an early model of a threshing machine from the Murl community, a man identified only as "Willis" stands beside his iron horse while another man identified as "Delmer" runs the engine. (Vera Garner.)

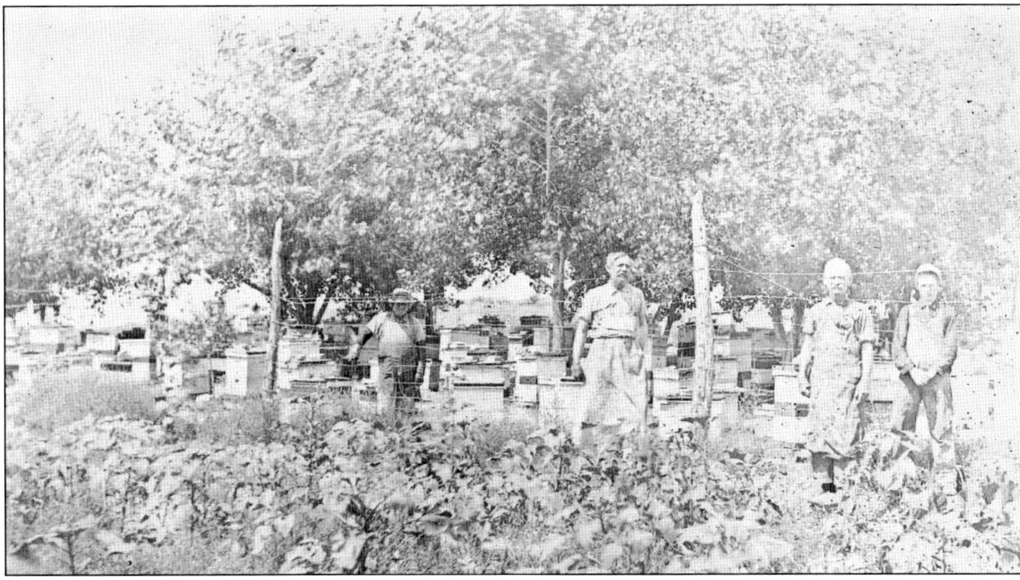

Beekeeping was more than a backyard hobby for the W. H. Bartleston family. In 1917, when this photograph was taken, they owned and tended 168 beehives. It seems safe to assume that the Bartlesons had a wealth of knowledge about bees. It is also certain that they had some labor-intensive days throughout the year, especially when it was time to extract and market the honey. (Vera Garner.)

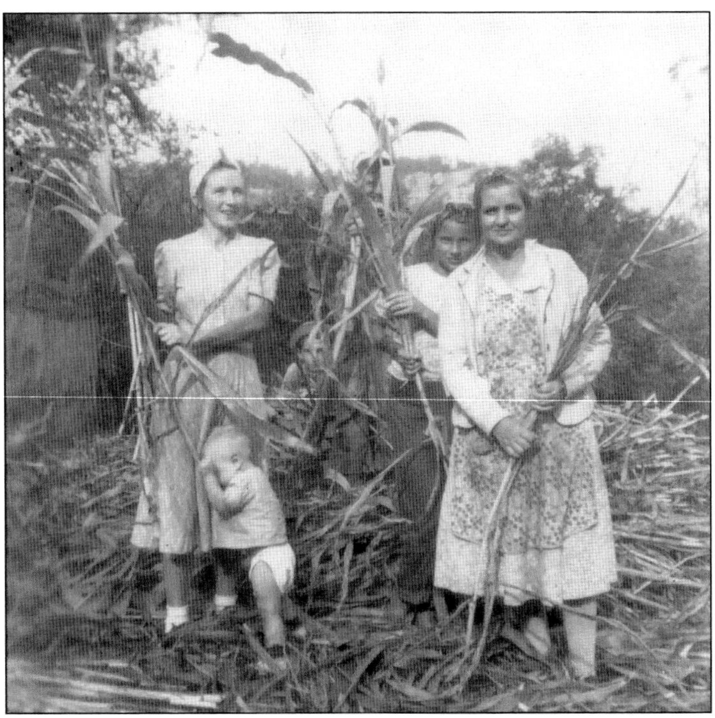

It was a beautiful autumn day in 1950 on Bridgeman Mountain at the Frazier Morgan place. Relatives and friends from the nearby Harmon Hollow community gathered, and the process of making sorghum molasses from sugarcane began. Lena Morgan (left) and Mauda Morgan (right), assisted by the four youngsters seen between them, stripped the leaves from the cane. A knowledgeable person oversaw the working of the cane mill and the series of tasks that followed. At the end of the day, the reward was a batch of delicious molasses. (Lena Morgan.)

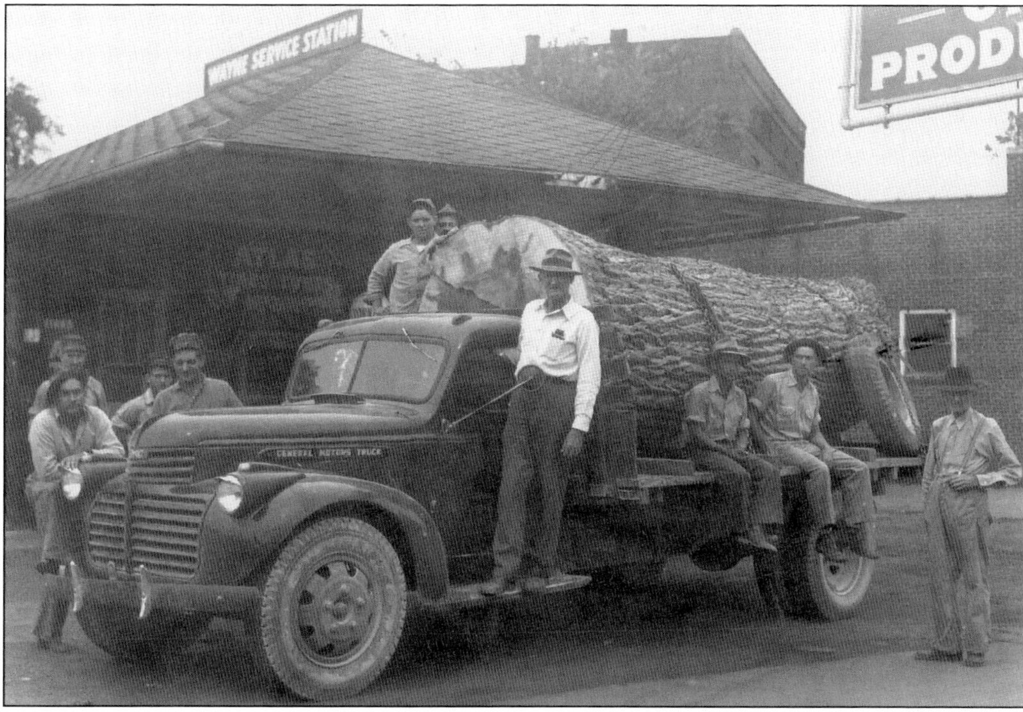

Wayne County has been blessed by an abundance of timber. Since the mid-1800s, when the first sawmill began operating in the Mount Pisgah community, the timber business has played a major role in the economy. Pictured here around 1947 with a heavy load is Hulen Baker's truck parked in front of Fred Crouch's service station. (William Roberts.)

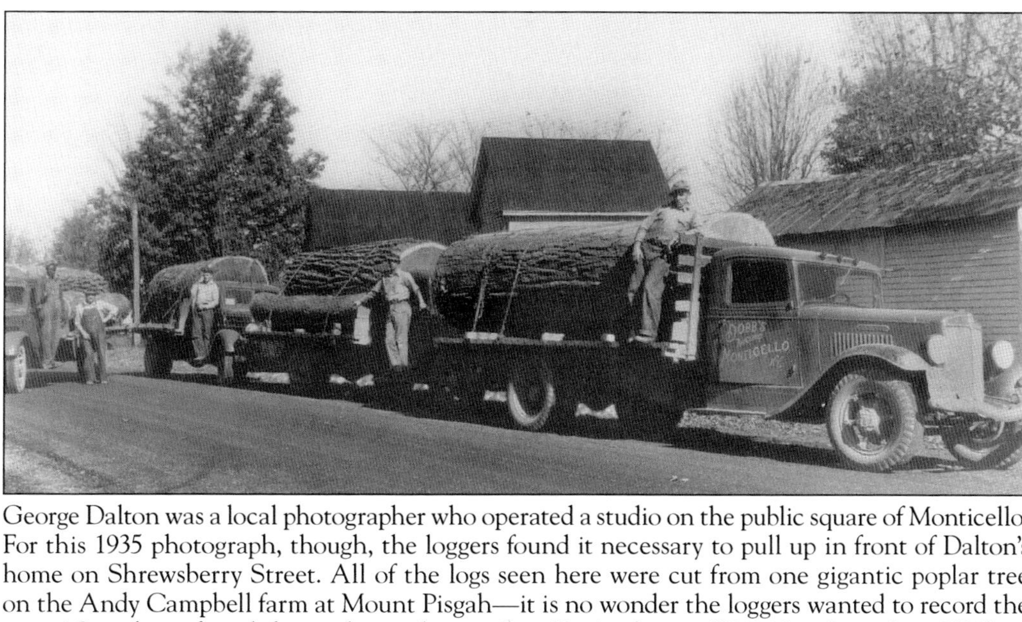

George Dalton was a local photographer who operated a studio on the public square of Monticello. For this 1935 photograph, though, the loggers found it necessary to pull up in front of Dalton's home on Shrewsberry Street. All of the logs seen here were cut from one gigantic poplar tree on the Andy Campbell farm at Mount Pisgah—it is no wonder the loggers wanted to record the event! Seen here, from left to right, are loggers Sam Bo Anderson, W. E. Noe, Irvin Lair, Wallace Bryant, and Hal Holbrook. (Paul and Katherine Dunnington.)

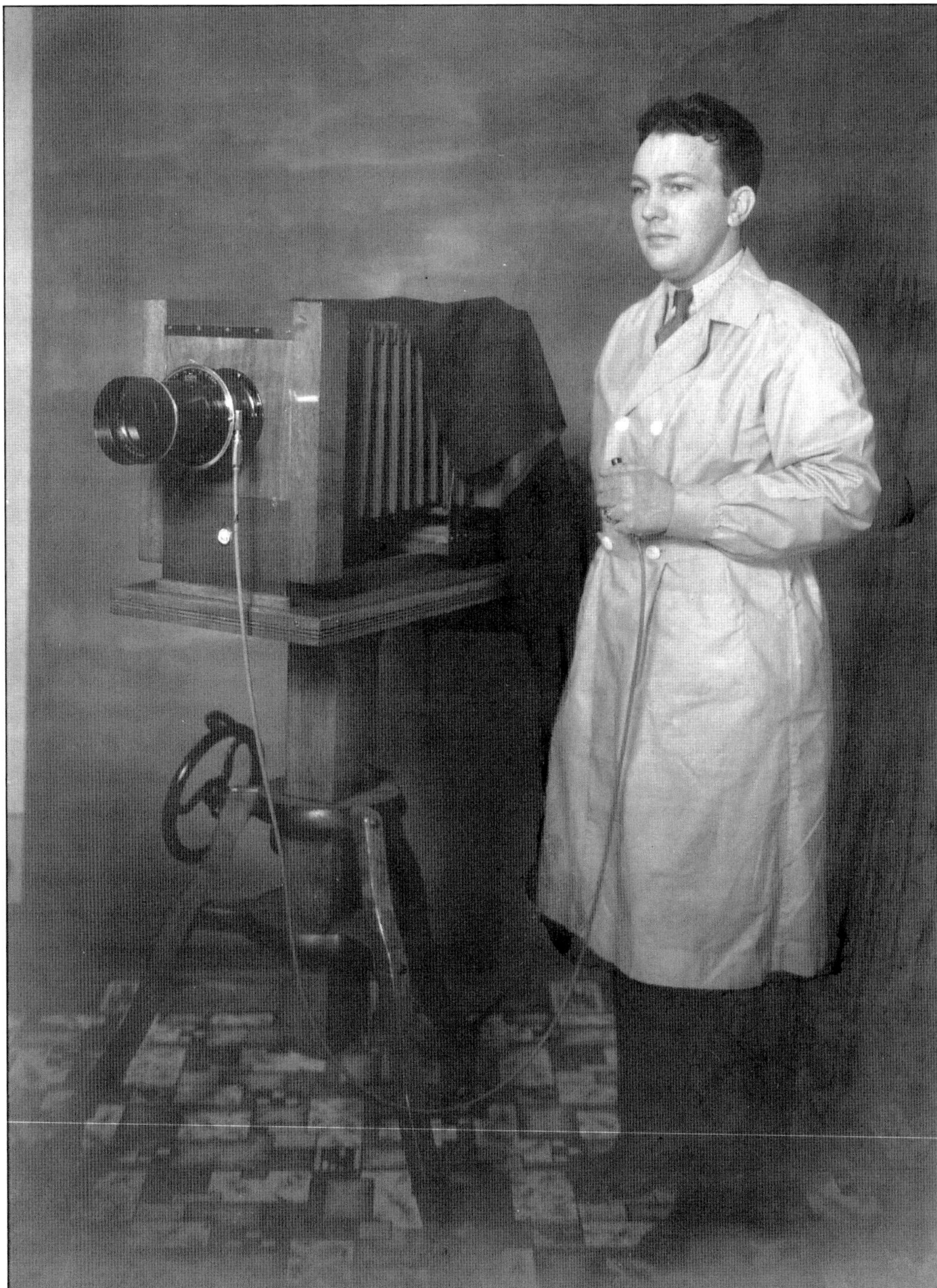

The Dalton Photography Studio occupied a unit in what is now known as the Van Phillips building on the public square. George Dalton, the photographer, was often assisted by his brother, Wendell Dalton. In this 1935 photograph, Wendell wears one of the smocks that his wife, Mildred, made for the brothers to wear when they worked in the dark room. (Mildred Dalton.)

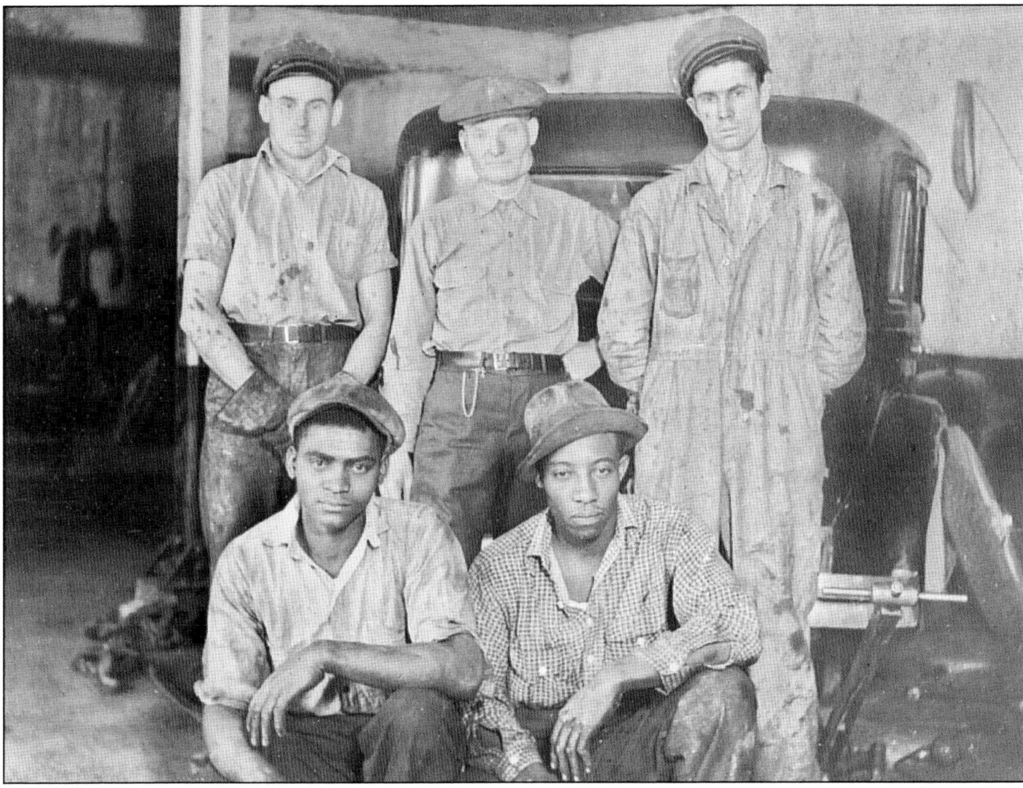

This late-1930s photograph shows the staff at the Ford Garage on Short Street. Seen here, from left to right, are (first row) Oliver Duncan and Johnny Brown; (second row) Ras Ferrell, Pierce McClain, and Leland Eads. (Wayne County Historical Society.)

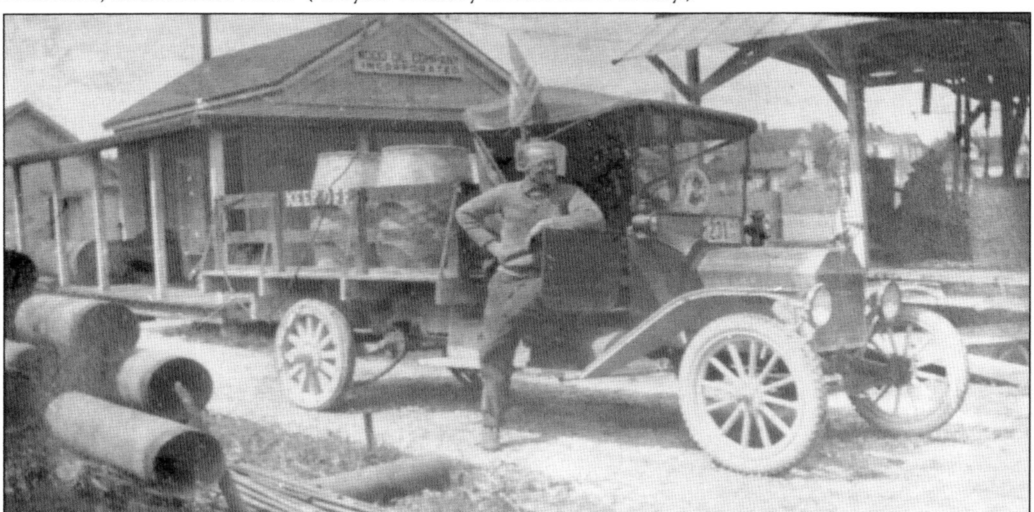

In 2010, a Wood Oil Company building still stands on North Main Street in Monticello. The late 1800s and early 1900s saw an oil boom in Wayne County, and the Wood Oil Company drilled and produced more oil than any other company. Wood Oil built and operated a gasoline distillation plant in Oil Valley and had a compressor station on the Miller lease. (Wayne County Historical Society.)

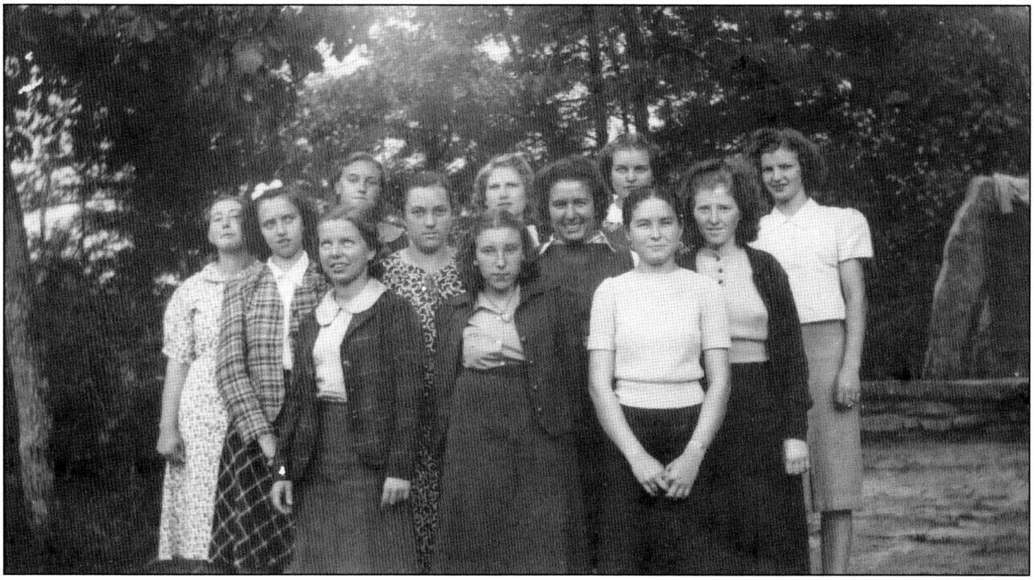

During the Great Depression, the National Youth Administration (NYA) program gave employment to young people, ages 18–24. Female NYA members made children's clothing and did clerical tasks and janitorial work within the Wayne County School System. For one year, they provided food service for Wayne County High School. The group pictured here in 1937 is on a trip to Cumberland Falls. (Dolores Morris.)

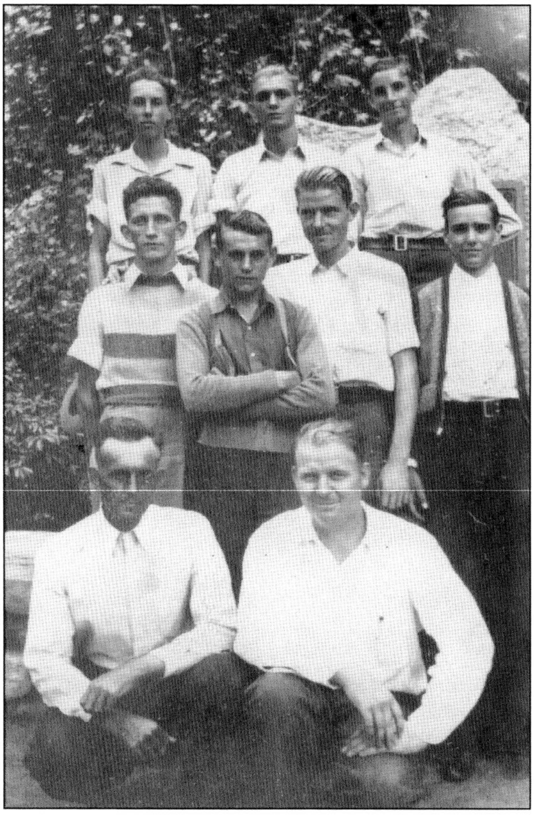

These young men of the NYA worked on carpentry items from an old school building on Sandusky Street. Charles Crabtree (left), supervisor, and Gilmer Morris, teacher, are pictured at the front of this group. Ben Hancock, Thomas Terrill, and Romer Coffey also provided leadership for this program. In 1941, they made furniture for the new Wayne County High School. They produced 1,000 folding chairs, 250 chair desks, numerous desks for teachers, and several filing cabinets. Most of the young men were paid $14 per month. Some who were skilled were paid $16 or $17 per month. (Dolores Morris.)

Tasks necessary to the wash day of yesteryear included the following: pumping and heating lots of water, scrubbing every item of clothing (including bedclothes) on the washboard, boiling the white clothes in a big black kettle in the back yard, rinsing clothes, starching clothes, cleaning the clothesline, and hanging the clothes in a neat manner so that they looked nice on the clothesline. Bonnie Denney is pictured here pumping water. (Abbott family.)

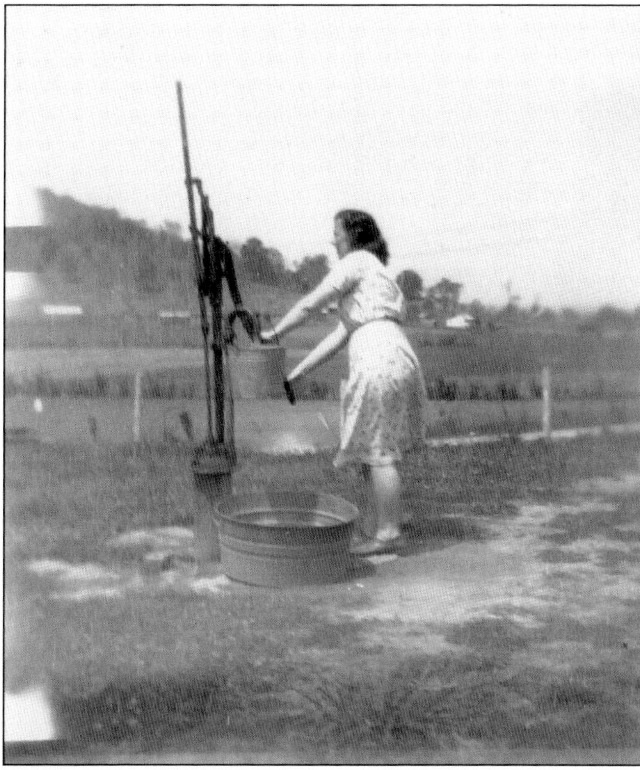

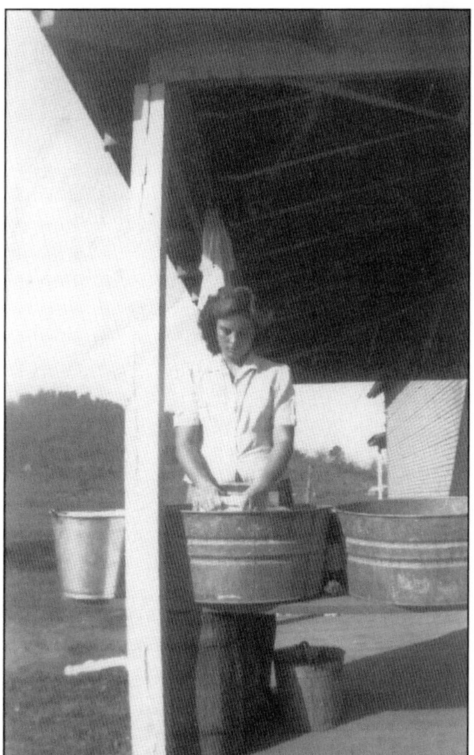

After all the preparations were made to wash the clothes, the old washboard was brought out, and the real work began. Though many homes were furnished with some electrical appliances, like a refrigerator or cookstove, it was considered a luxury to have an electric washing machine. Juanita Abbott is seen here scrubbing clothes on the washboard. (Abbott family.)

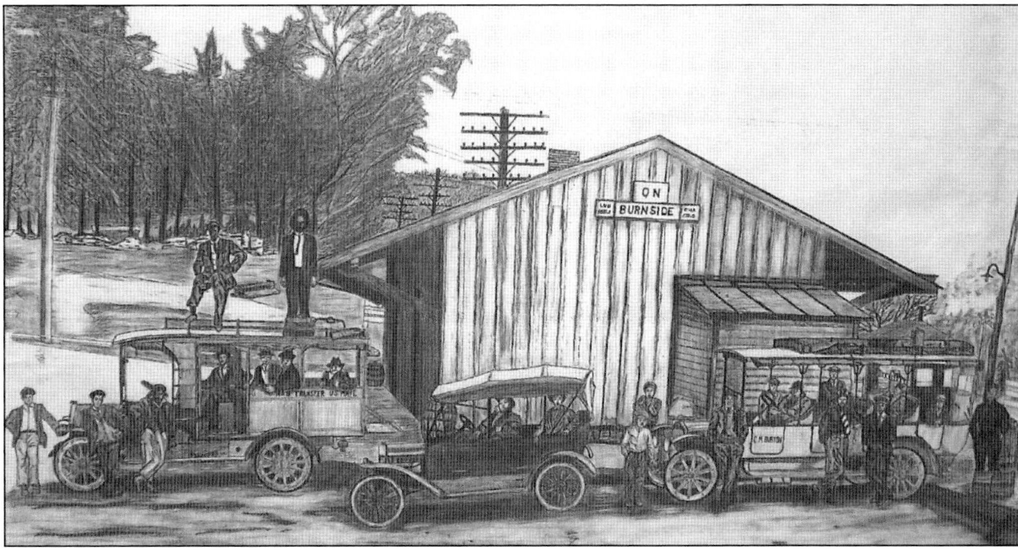

After a railroad was built through Pulaski County in 1877, the train station at Burnside became an important place for Wayne County people. How best to transport mail, passengers, and freight to and from the train station was a major concern for many years. The motorized vehicles shown here appear to belong to C. H. Burton and to the M and B Transportation Company. According to a 1913 *Wayne County Outlook* article, C. H. Burton owned four vehicles. For $1.50, a passenger could travel on one of these "machines" from Monticello to the train station in Burnside. The M and B Transportation Company, owned by T. M. Ragan, Martin Back, and T. J. Alexander, put a variety of vehicles on the Monticello-to-Burnside route, including a 3-ton Garfield truck. (Cliff Appleby.)

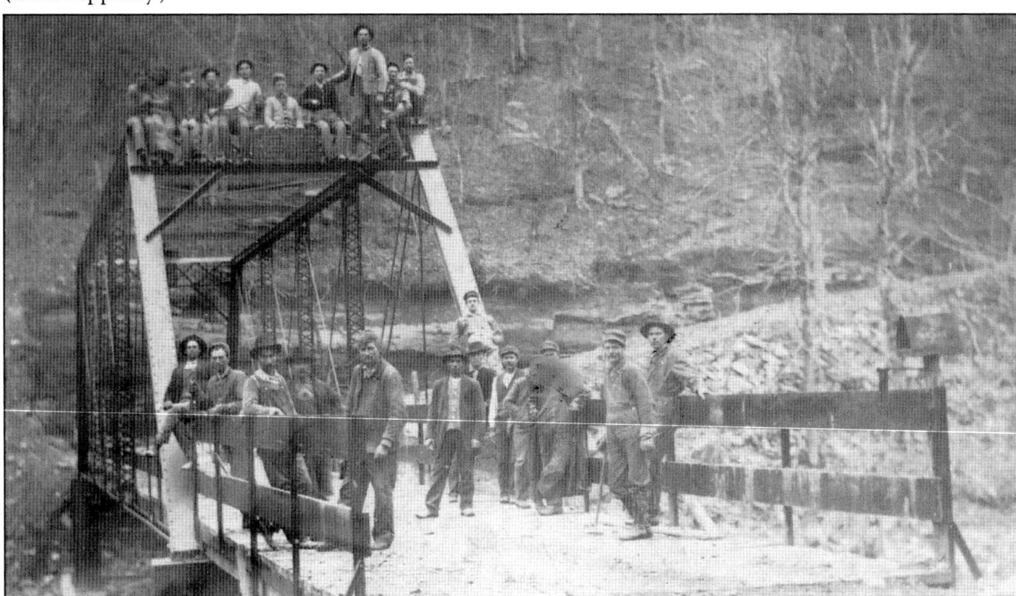

The men who built the first bridge over Beaver Creek posed for this picture when their task was finished. At that time, the Albany Road (now Highway 90) crossing the bridge was rough and winding. The bridge was built south of Monticello at the foot of what is still called Pump Station Hill, a name that harkens back to oil boom days. (Katy Lou Rector.)

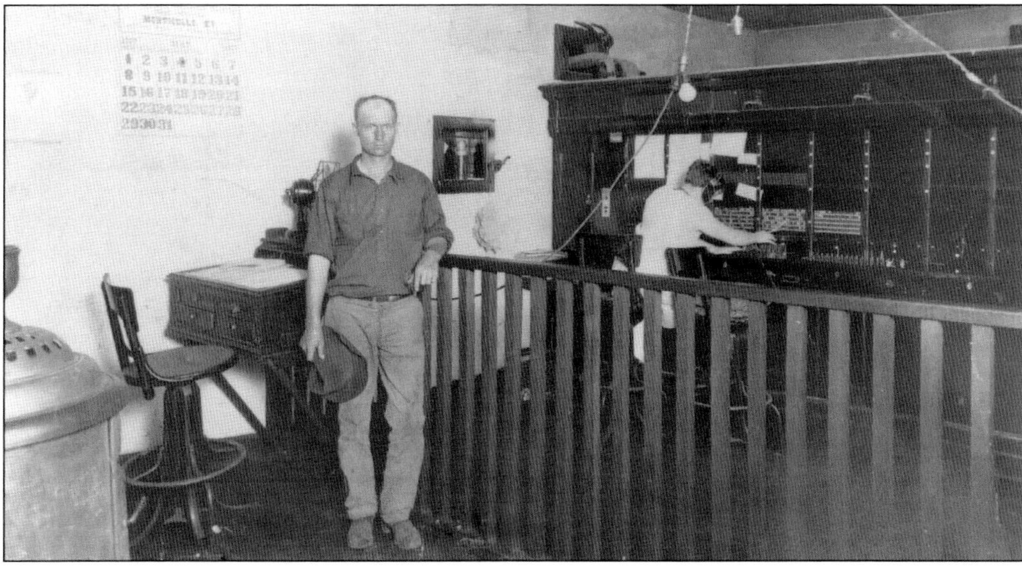

Ben Davis (standing) and Irene Lee (seated at the switchboard) are pictured in 1927 inside the old telephone office on Michigan Avenue. Erected in 1923, the building was located behind the present site of F and H Drugstore and served as the telephone office until 1958, when the new dial telephone system came to Wayne County. It was demolished in 2000. (Wayne County Historical Society.)

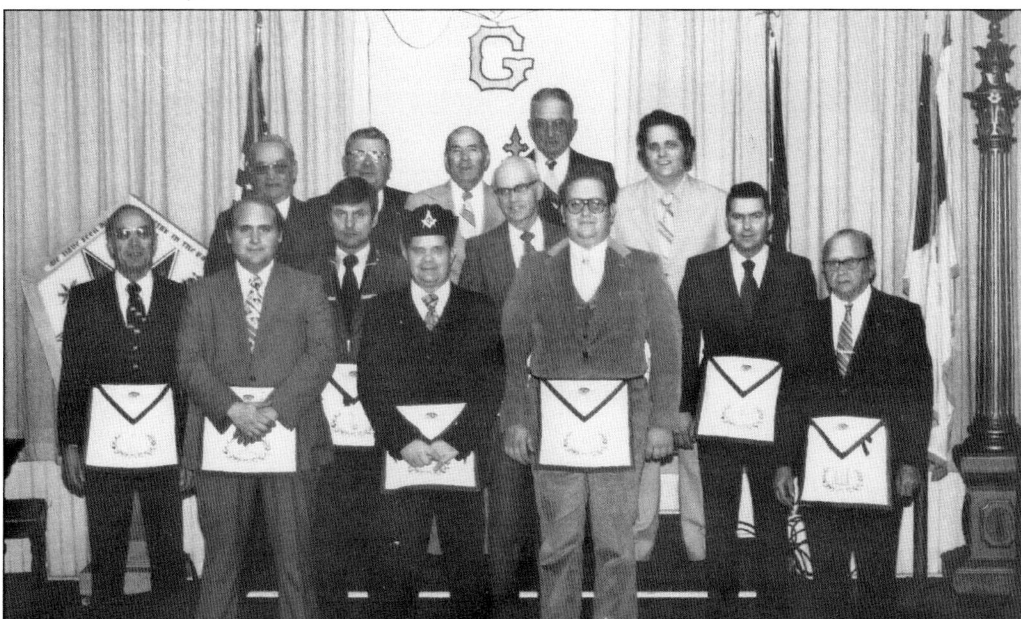

The Monticello Masonic Lodge No. 431 elected this group of men as officers for 1980. From left to right are (first row) James E. Barnes, Glen Hickey, Richard Morrow, Larry Humble, Phillip York, and Cletis Nelson; (second row) Dillard Duvall and Shelby Keeton; (third row) Obie Corder, Barnett Abbott, Henry Blevins, Ozro Marsh, and Harold Norfleet. Additional lodges in Wayne County are at Gap Creek (the Otter Creek Lodge) and at Pleasant Hill (the Freedom Lodge). (Wayne County Historical Society.)

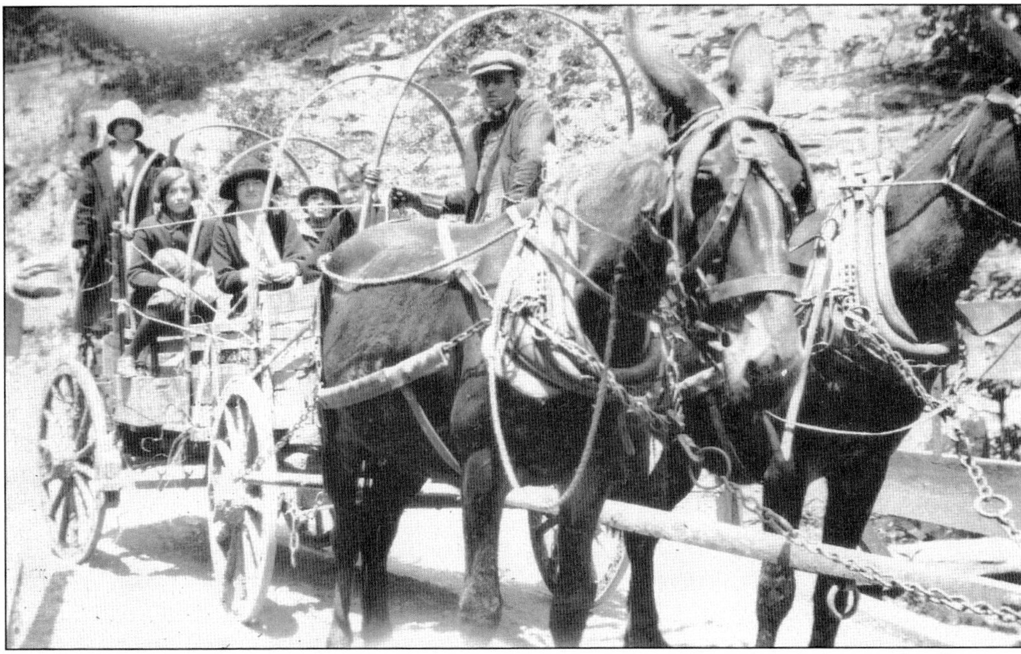

These Wayne County campers pictured in this 1920s photograph are headed toward Zula. Level areas of land near Otter Creek drew generations of campers to that community. (Vera Garner.)

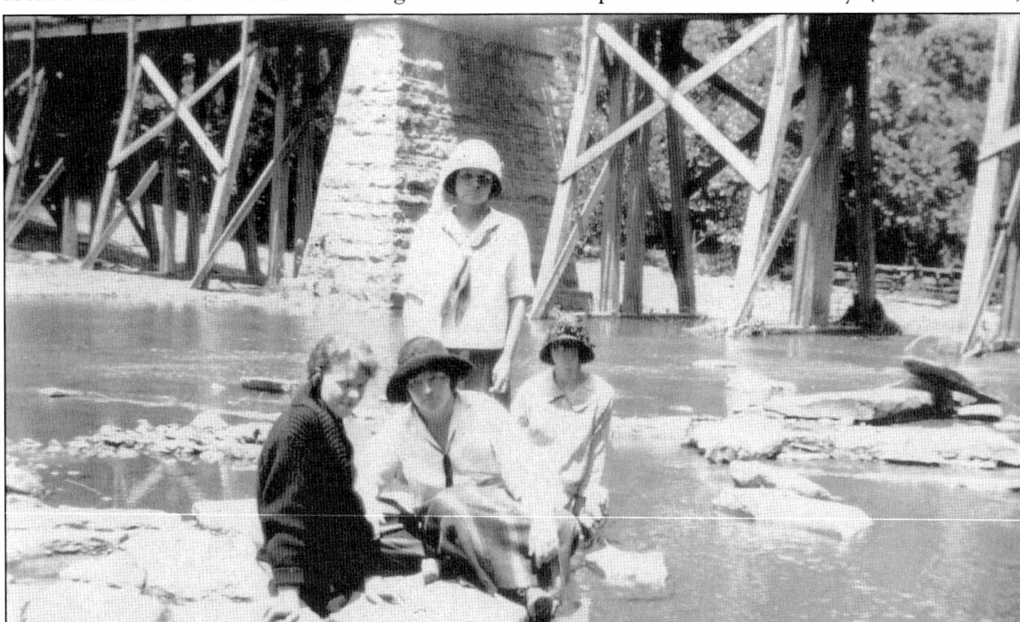

It seems that four bridges have been built across Otter Creek (on what is now Highway 90) in the Zula vicinity. The bridge seen behind these campers was, as far as is known, the first. In 2010, because of the low water level in Lake Cumberland, a person could stand on the third bridge and see an abutment of the first bridge as well as the entire second bridge. Nearby and high above the other bridges is today's bridge, so nicely constructed that a traveler can drive across it scarcely realizing it is a bridge. (Vera Garner.)

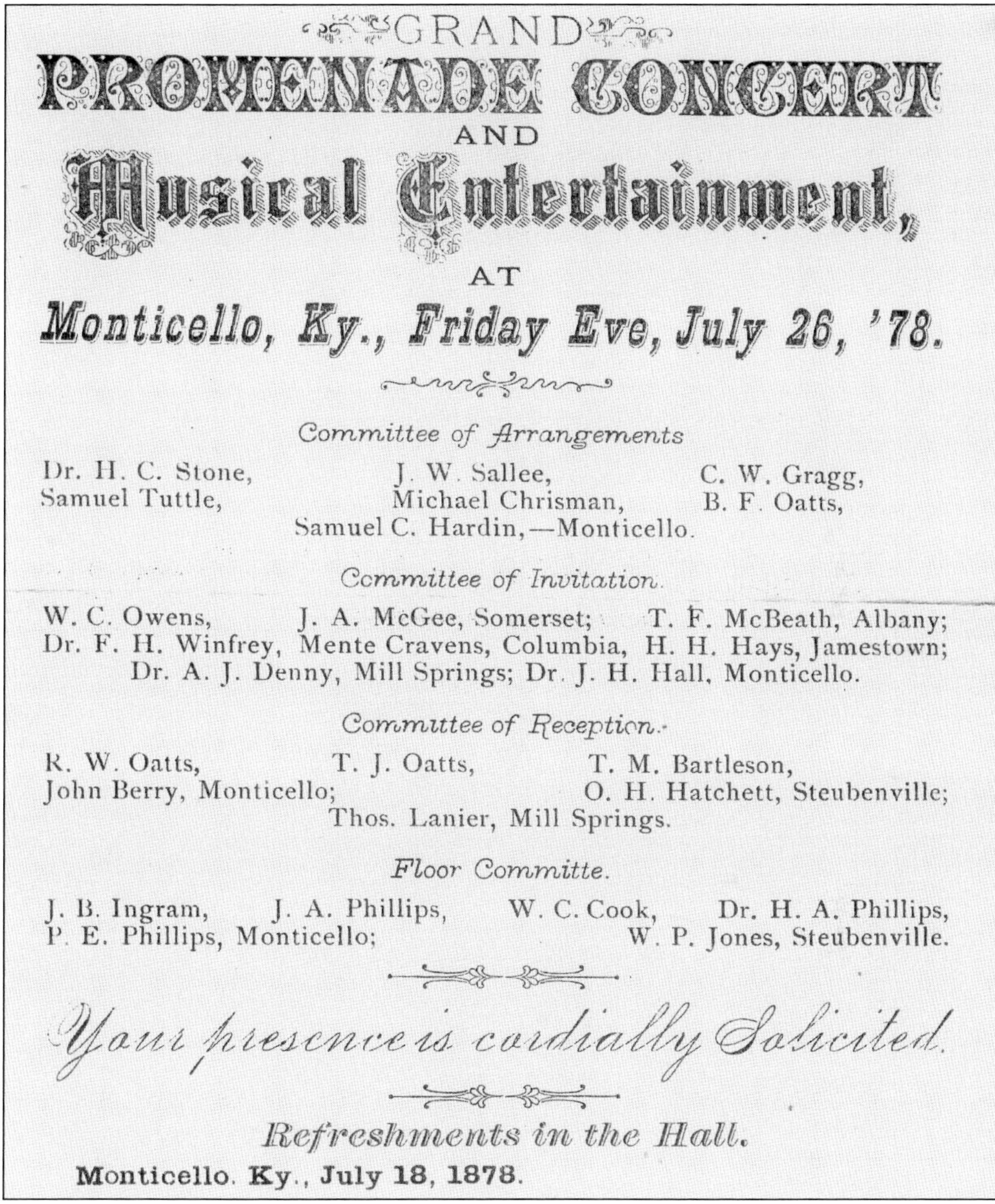

GRAND

PROMENADE CONCERT

AND

Musical Entertainment,

AT

Monticello, Ky., Friday Eve, July 26, '78.

Committee of Arrangements

Dr. H. C. Stone, J. W. Sallee, C. W. Gragg,
Samuel Tuttle, Michael Chrisman, B. F. Oatts,
Samuel C. Hardin,—Monticello.

Committee of Invitation.

W. C. Owens, J. A. McGee, Somerset; T. F. McBeath, Albany;
Dr. F. H. Winfrey, Mente Cravens, Columbia, H. H. Hays, Jamestown;
Dr. A. J. Denny, Mill Springs; Dr. J. H. Hall, Monticello.

Committee of Reception.

R. W. Oatts, T. J. Oatts, T. M. Bartleson,
John Berry, Monticello; O. H. Hatchett, Steubenville;
Thos. Lanier, Mill Springs.

Floor Committe.

J. B. Ingram, J. A. Phillips, W. C. Cook, Dr. H. A. Phillips,
P. E. Phillips, Monticello; W. P. Jones, Steubenville.

Your presence is cordially Solicited.

Refreshments in the Hall.

Monticello, Ky., July 18, 1878.

A promenade concert is a performance, usually featuring classical music, during which at least part of the audience stands and is free to move about. The 1878 invitation shown here gives a tiny glimpse into what must have been a rather sophisticated social event in Monticello. The men listed as committee members were leading citizens of Wayne and surrounding counties. (Wayne County Museum.)

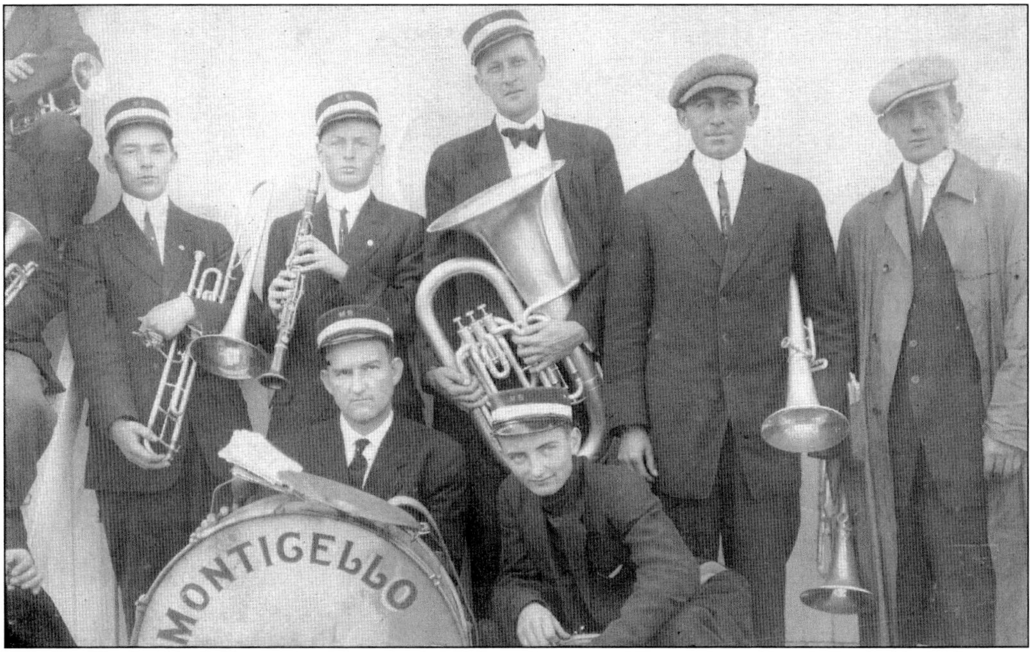

In the early 1900s, the Monticello Melodius Band was an important part of many social activities in Monticello. For some occasions the band members wore elaborately trimmed jackets. (Wayne County Museum.)

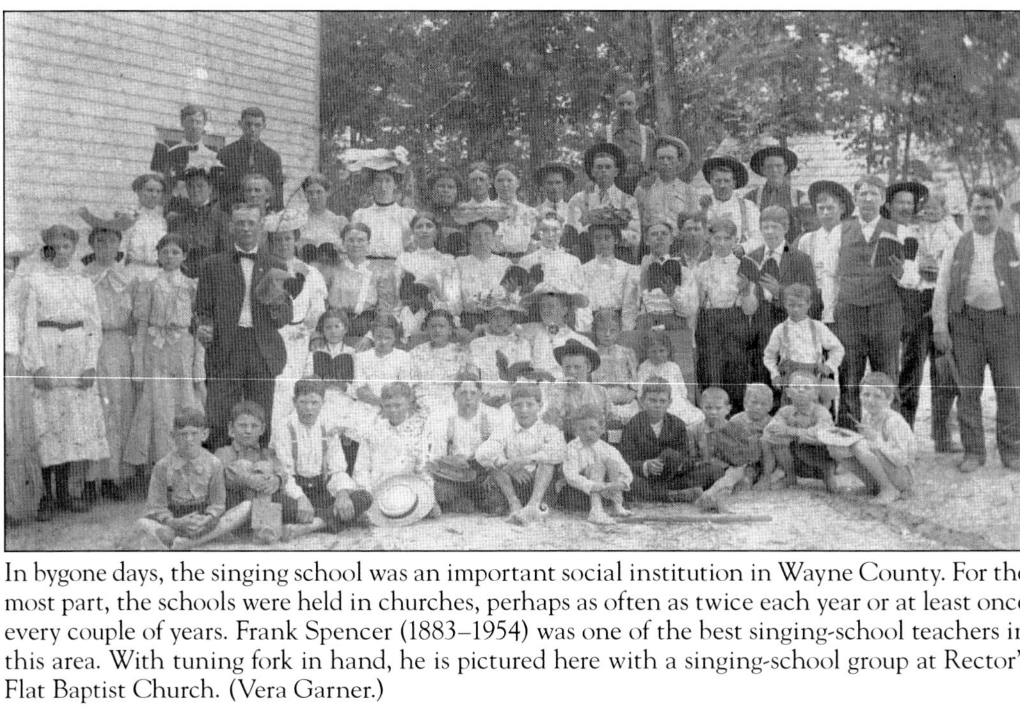

In bygone days, the singing school was an important social institution in Wayne County. For the most part, the schools were held in churches, perhaps as often as twice each year or at least once every couple of years. Frank Spencer (1883–1954) was one of the best singing-school teachers in this area. With tuning fork in hand, he is pictured here with a singing-school group at Rector's Flat Baptist Church. (Vera Garner.)

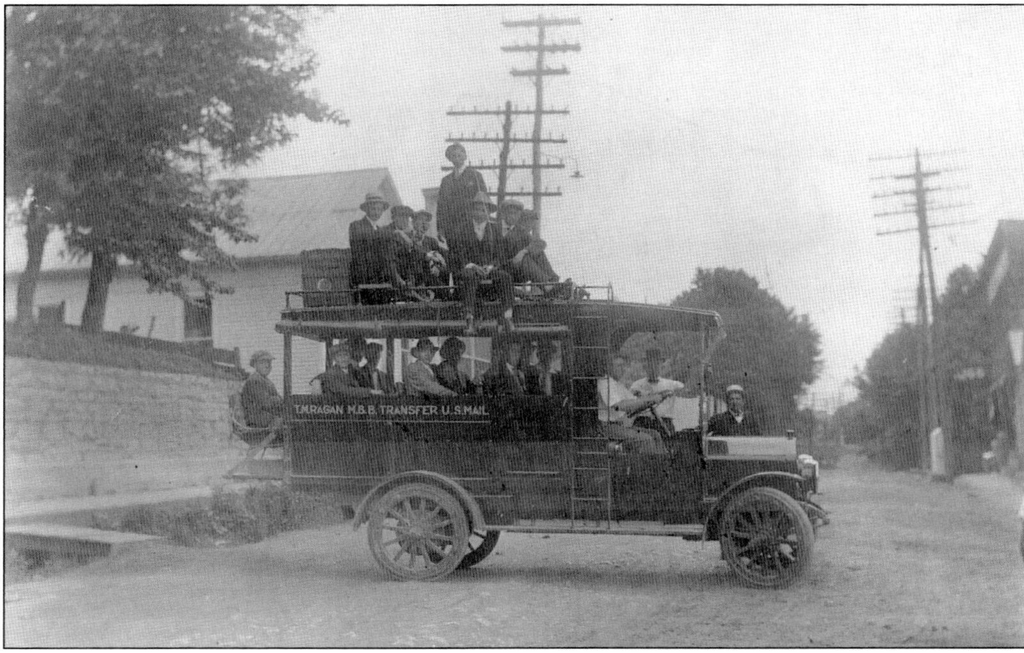

Tom Ragan drove this bus to carry the mail between Burnside and Monticello. He is seen here in the front seat with Ellis Ragan beside him. Belfry Brown occupies the tailgate seat. The crowd shown here has been to Burnside for a Sunday afternoon ball game. (Wayne County Museum.)

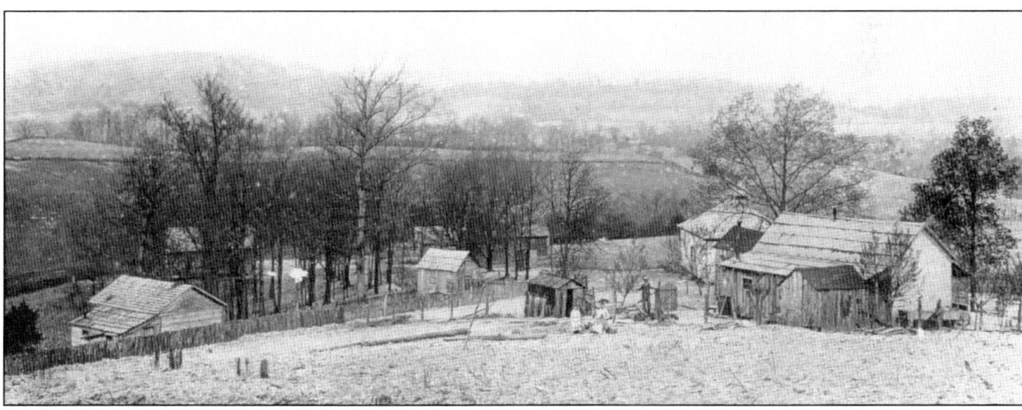

This idyllic scene shows the Hidalgo community in 1919. A church and school are visible in this picture. A country store is there as well, but it is hidden from view by the cluster of buildings on the right, where the home of Mary Dishman also stands in this image. The shed on the largest building shown here contained a gristmill that operated each Saturday afternoon. The house on the left underwent extensive remodeling in the 1940s. The church congregation pitched in and did the work so that Nell Buck Blevins would have a good place to live while her husband was in military service. Most of these buildings still stand in 2010, but the road has been changed—WPA road workers were responsible for that. (Hattie Edwards.)

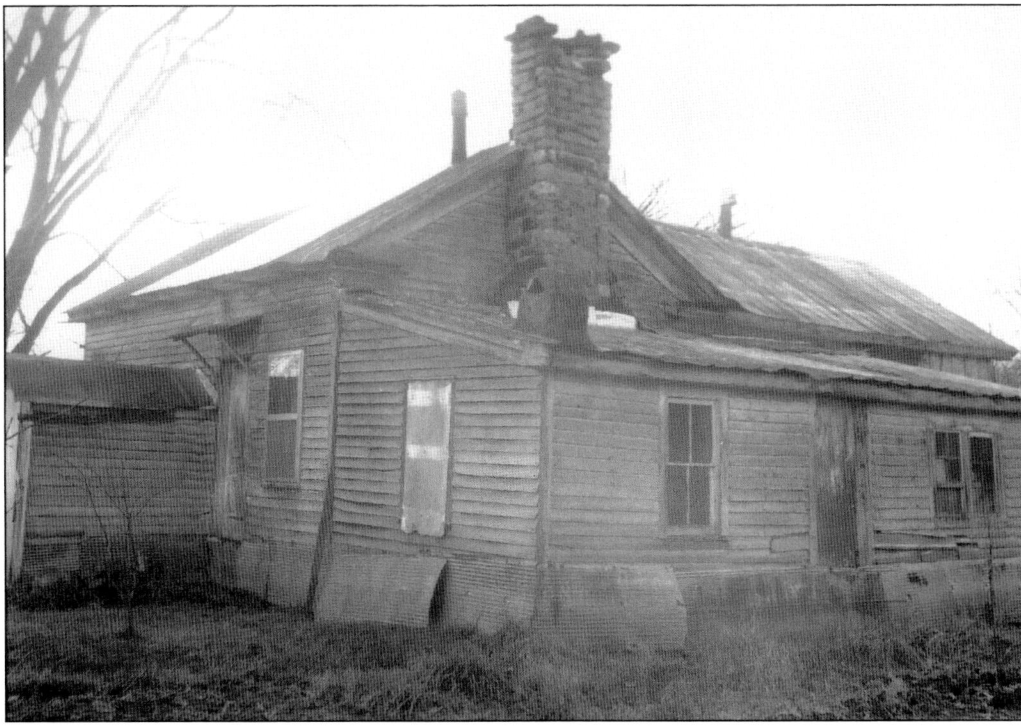

Rankin was once a bustling community at the end of Fall Creek Road. The Rankin family came from Paisley, Scotland, and it was largely their business acumen that developed this community. They built one of the big mills that the Rankins became noted for in this area. A carding factory, a blacksmith shop, and a country store were added, and of course, the community had a church and a school. The Arthur Rankin family lived in this house. (Wayne County Historical Society.)

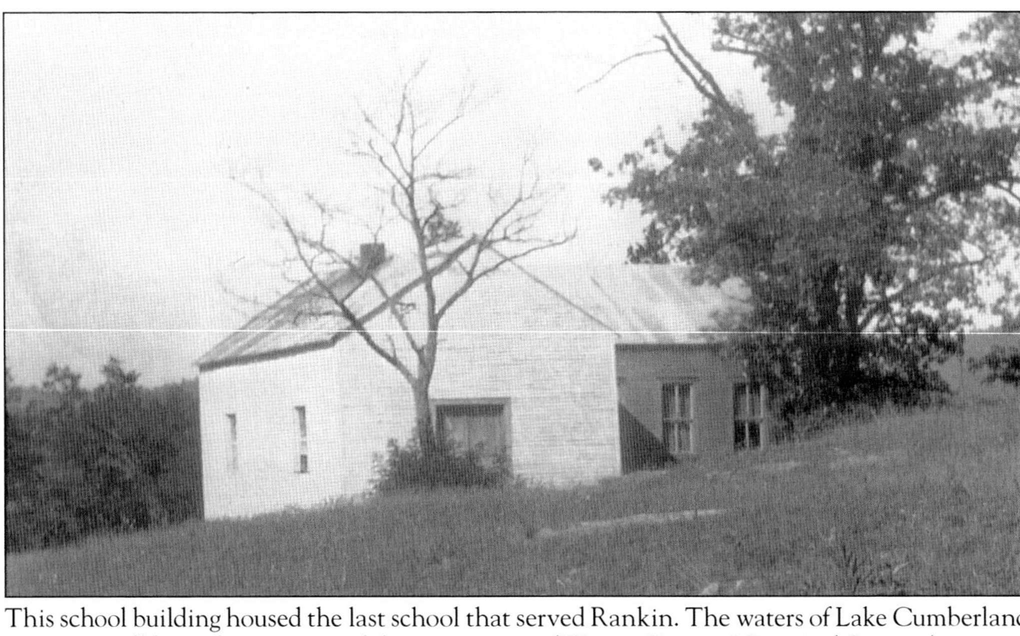

This school building housed the last school that served Rankin. The waters of Lake Cumberland now cover all but a few vestiges of the community. (Wayne County Historical Society.)

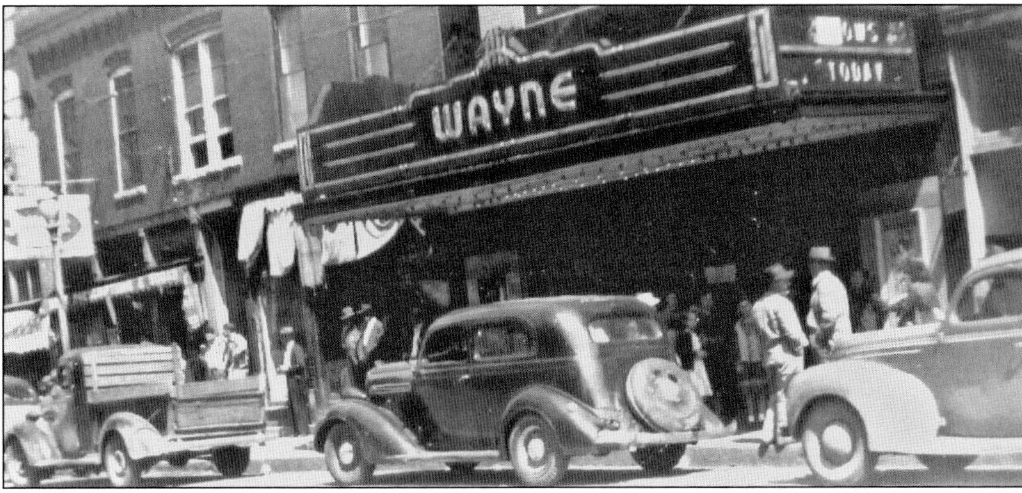

Nothing but the side walls of the old Gem Theater building remained when A. E. Christian remodeled it and opened it in 1931 as the new Wayne Theatre. Modern equipment was installed throughout, including RCA sound, cushioned seats, and an air-conditioning plant. When the photograph above was taken, moviegoing was a major means of entertainment. Crowds showed up at the beautiful theater for both matinees and evening movies. Wayne Theatre operated until 1965, when the last movie was shown on the big screen. Happily for Monticello, in October 2009, decades after it closed, Wayne Theatre again opened its doors. Its restoration, thanks to Monticello Bank, gives Monticello's downtown area a big boost and brings the past and the present a little closer together. Once again, movies and other quality entertainment are being presented at the historical Wayne Theatre. (Wayne County Museum.)

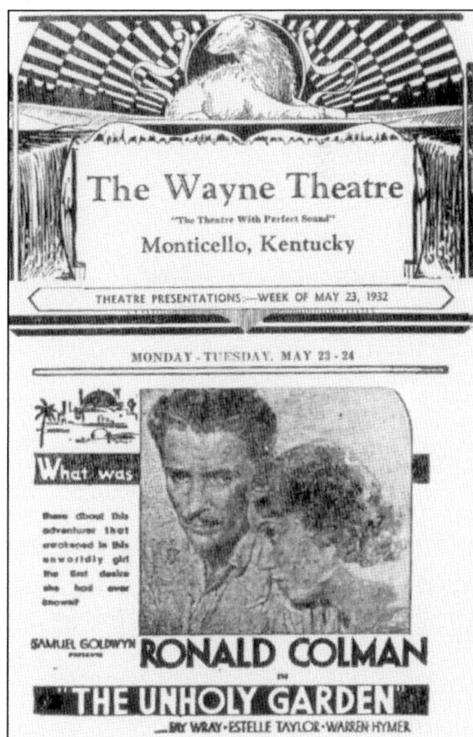

The Wayne Theatre in downtown Monticello provided entertainment by showing all the current movies. Weekly movie advertisements appeared in the *Wayne County Outlook* in an attempt to lure theatergoers to come enjoy a movie. This particular advertisement appeared in 1932. (*Wayne County Outlook*).

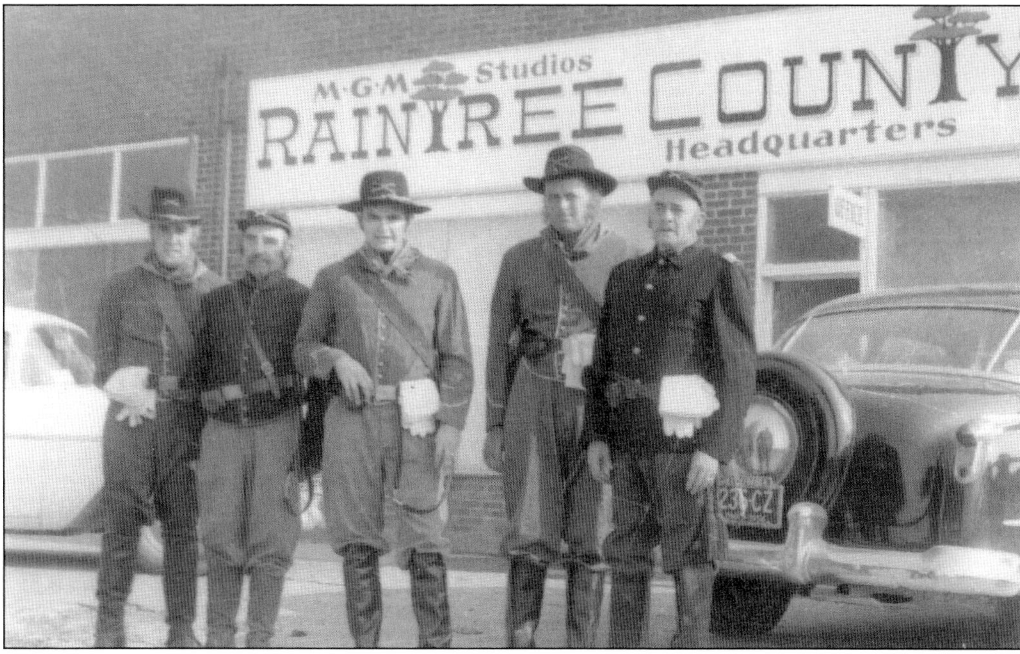

During the summer of 1956, a number of Wayne County people worked as extras with Elizabeth Taylor, Montgomery Clift, and Eva Marie Saint in MGM Studios' Civil War epic, *Raintree County*. Part of the movie was filmed in Danville. When the script called for a six-horse team pulling a caisson at full speed, three Wayne County men—Tolbert Guffey and twins Hugh and Herbert Bell—took the reins because no one else could control the horses like they could. The Wayne County men pictured here are standing in front of the MGM Studios in Danville. From left to right, they are Roe Bertie Hicks, Herbert Bell, Jack McIntyre, unidentified, and Capt. Lewis Stokes. (Katy Lou Rector.)

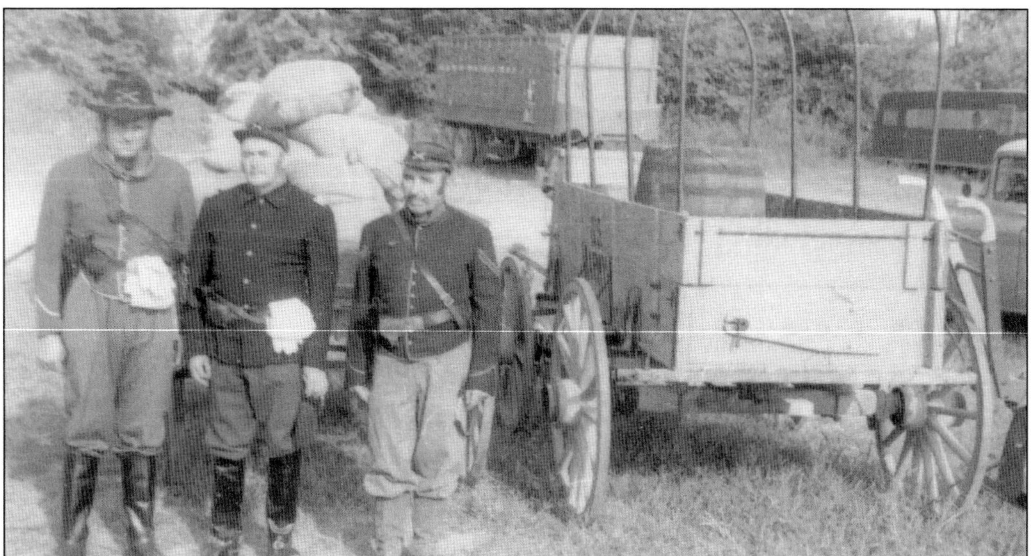

These Wayne County men are ready for action as they pose with some of the props used in the production of *Raintree County*. (Katy Lou Rector.)

Five

Church and School

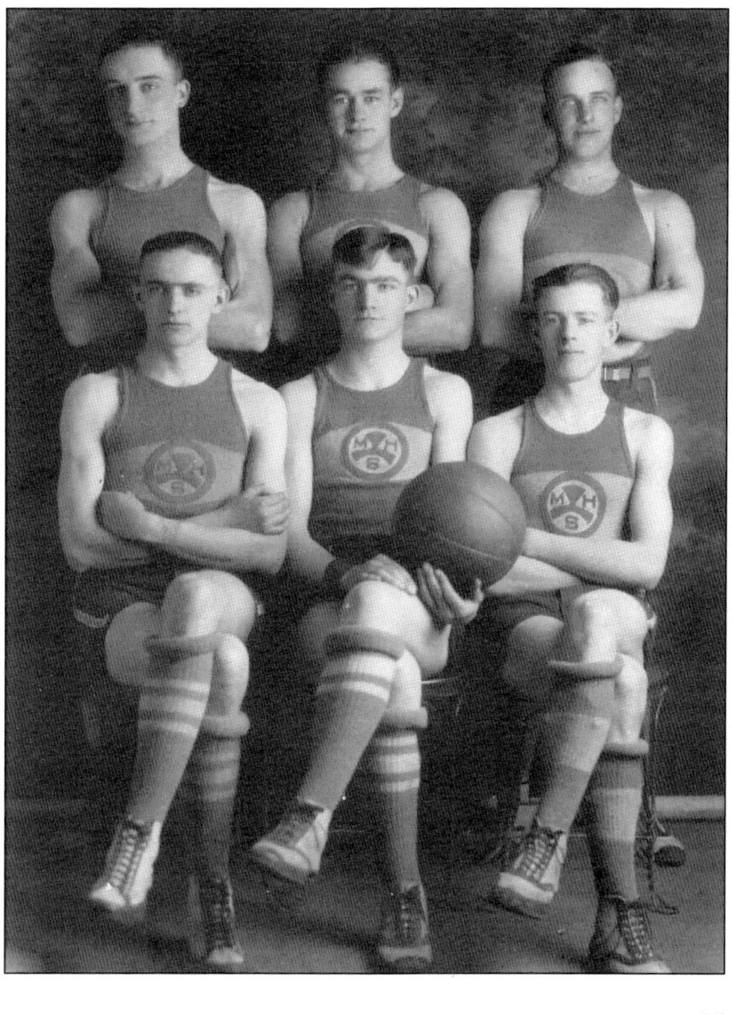

In 1922, when this Monticello High School basketball team went to the Kentucky State Tournament, Monticello was a little town of about 1,400. In the tournament, they defeated Owensboro and Carrollton before being defeated by Frankfort. From left to right are (first row) Roy Bartleson, Will Rankin, and R. O. "Casey" Cook; (second row) John Back, Grider Anderson, and Allen Bertram. (Mollie Shearer.)

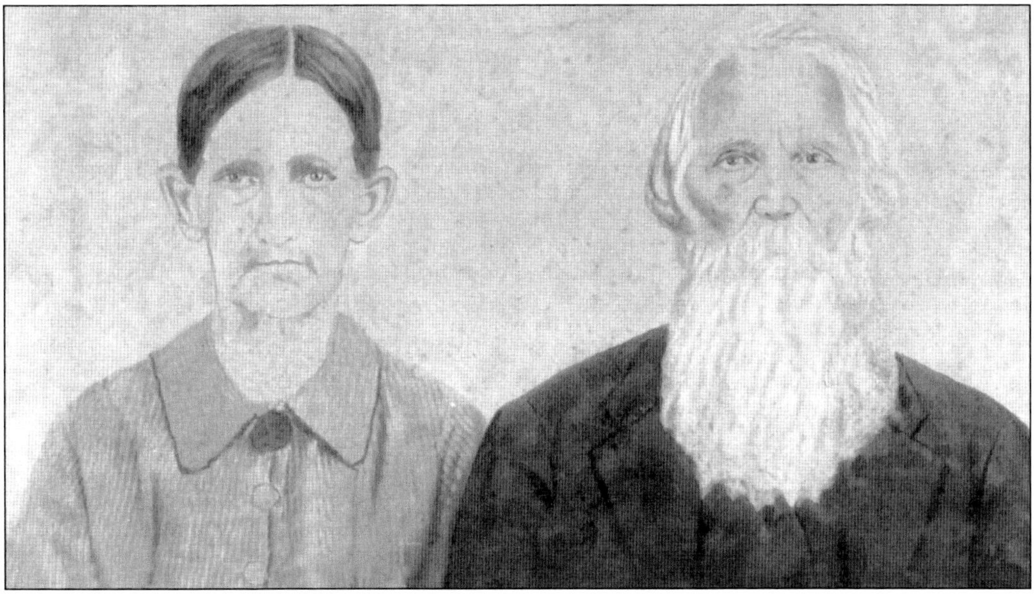

Prof. Josephus Newton Davis and his wife, Virginia, were born in Virginia. After many moves, they settled in the Mill Springs community, where they owned a farm and built a large house, which was later purchased by Clarence and Edna Mae Bates. For many years, Professor Davis taught a school called Davis Seminary in a building across from the farmhouse, and on Sundays, he preached in the same building. In 2010, this building, now covered with brick siding, still stands. Davis and his wife are buried on a knoll on the back side of the farm. (Wayne County Museum.)

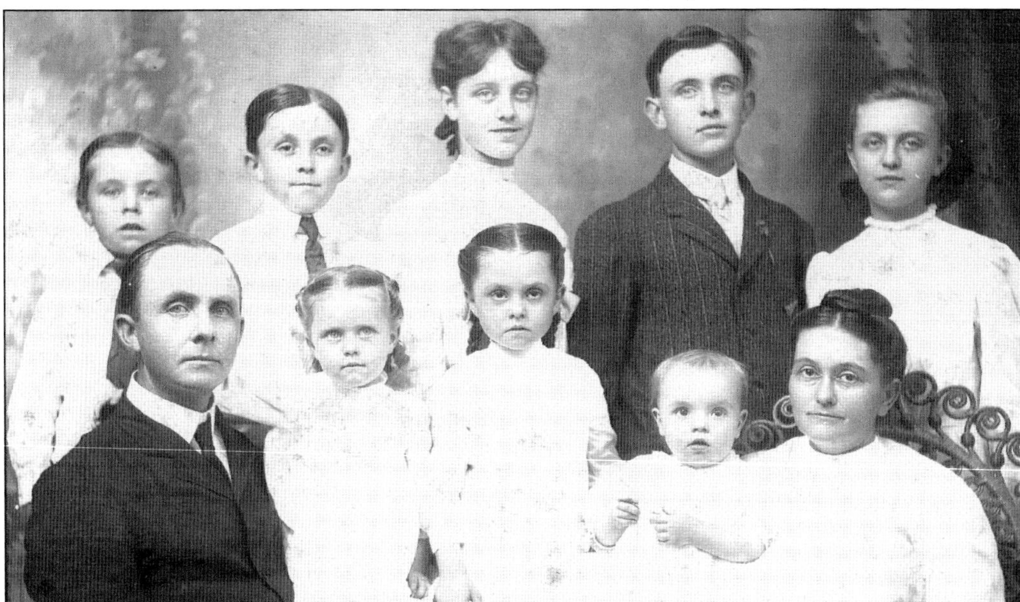

In the early 1900s, Rev. T. L. Hulse was pastor of both the Lockett's Chapel Methodist Church and the Monticello Methodist Church. He also preached at a small Methodist church, which at that time stood in Oak Grove. While in Monticello, he and his family lived in a parsonage owned by the Lockett's Chapel Church on Kendrick Avenue. After leaving Monticello, Reverend Hulse often returned for special occasions. (Clyde and Opal Bridgeman.)

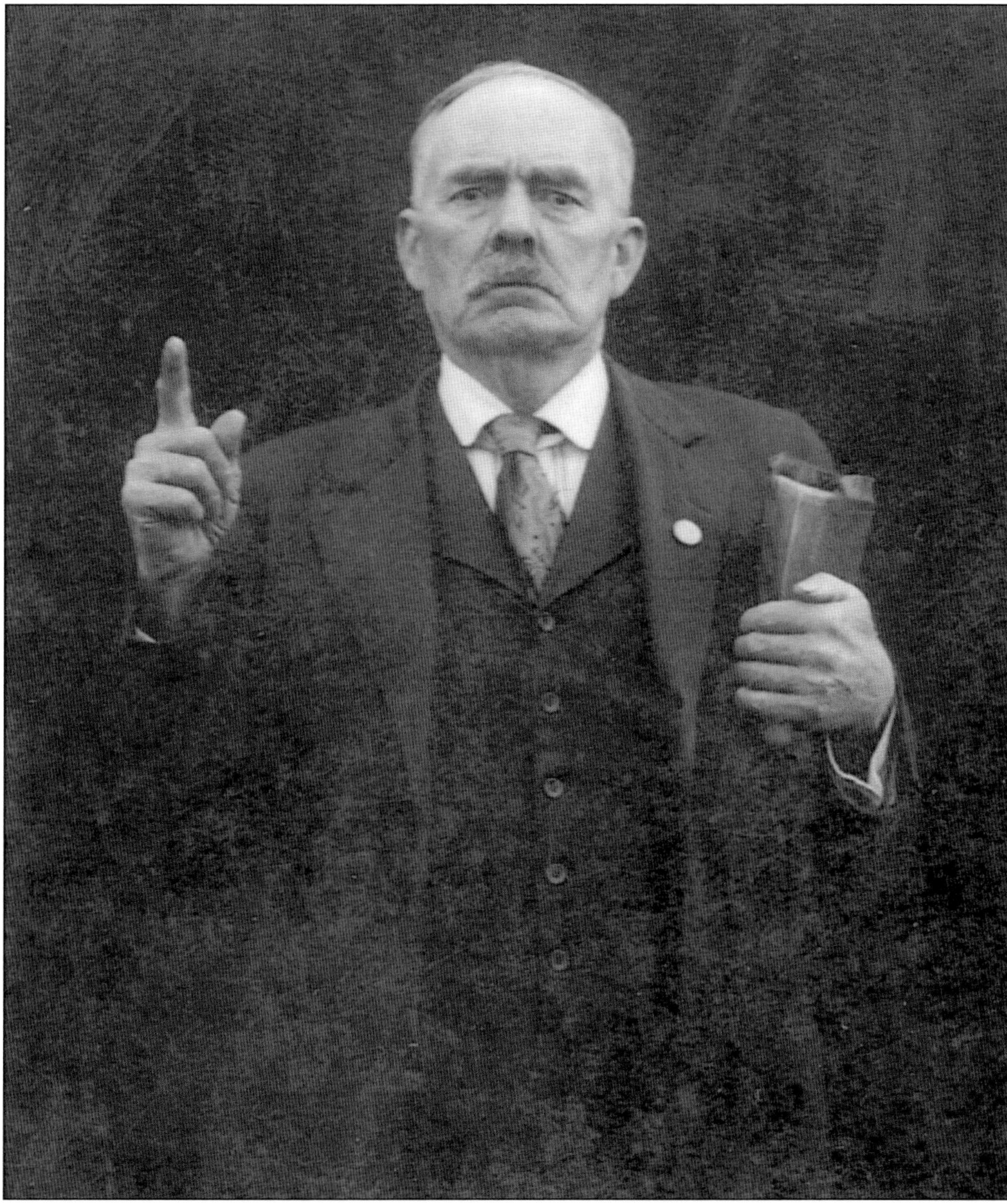

Bro. John Wesley Denney of the Powersburg community strikes a pose that gives no hint of the delight he took in playing practical jokes on his fellow Baptist preachers. For nearly 50 years, Brother Denney preached in the churches of Wayne County, Clinton County, and various other counties in Kentucky and Tennessee. A 1931 *Wayne County Outlook* article tells of how Denney was scalped when the horse he was riding became frightened and ran under the barn shed of P. R. Edwards. Denney's forehead struck the barn's low ceiling, completely severing his scalp from his skull. The wound required 19 stitches. "He showed unusual nerve and willpower," wrote the *Outlook*'s reporter, "considering his advanced age of 78 years, by permitting the physician to sew up the wound without the aid of an anesthetic, and he laughed and joked while it was being done." Brother Denney recovered from this accident and preached for a few more years. He also farmed and ran a small store. (Wayne County Museum.)

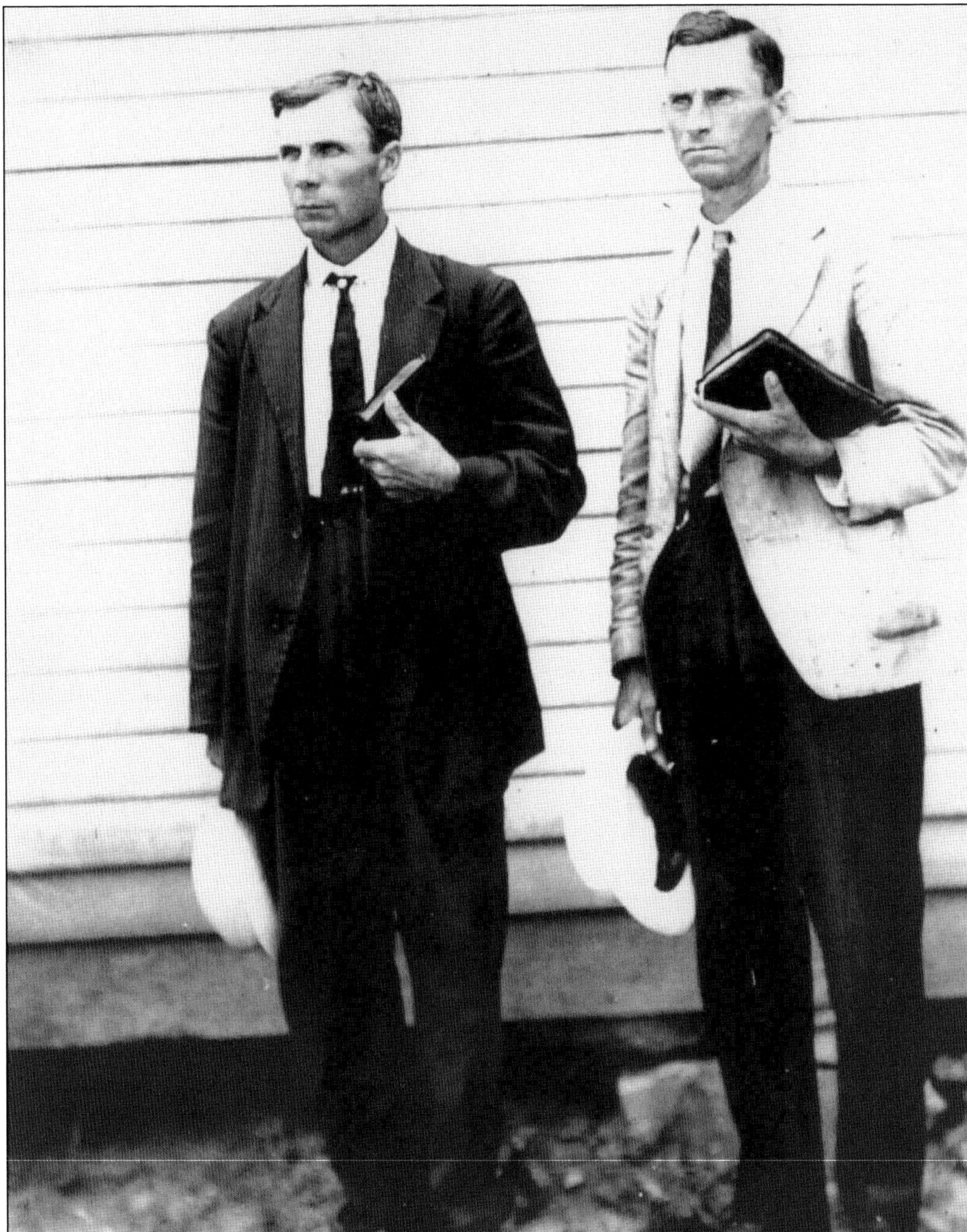

In 1920, Bro. J. D. Selvidge (right) posed with a friend of his, Bro. Marcus Denney, for this photograph at Gap Creek in Wayne County. Brother Selvidge was born on May 22, 1876, in Clinton County, Kentucky, and was ordained as a Baptist minister in 1912. He served as pastor in Spann Hill, New Hope, New Charity, New Salem, Cedar Hill, Bethel, Shiloh, Gap Creek, Elk Spring Valley, Mount Hermon, Rector's Flat, Big Sinking, and possibly others. He served his longest term of ministry at Stony Point Baptist Church in Clinton County. For several decades, Brother Selvidge was a great influence for good in the area. (Wayne County Museum.)

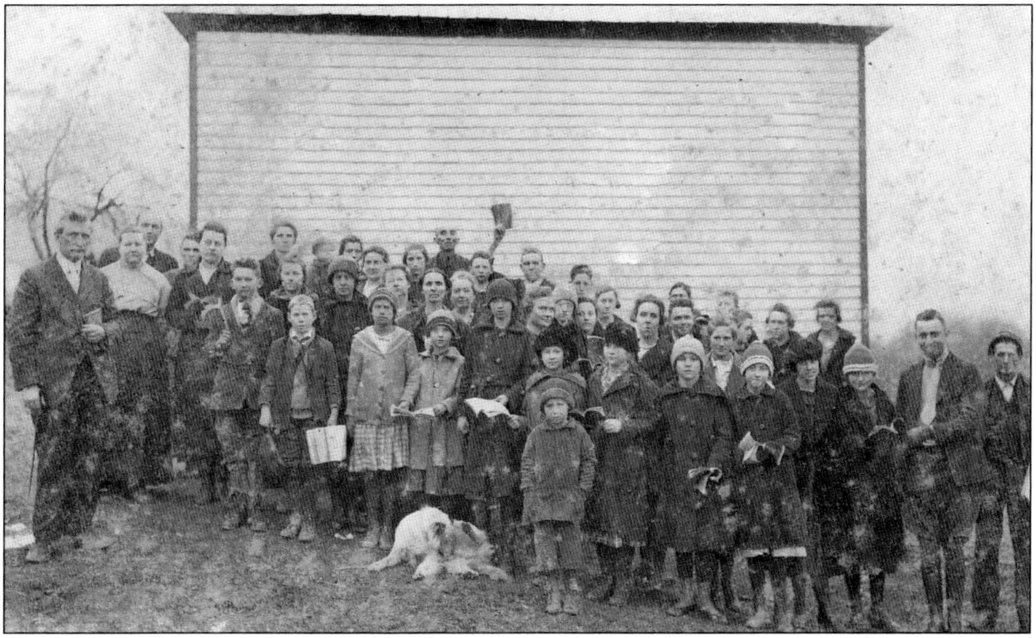

When this photograph was taken, it was a common practice for both school and church to be held in the same building. The group seen here has met to worship at the Duncan Valley Schoolhouse. Among those present are Pernie Edwards, Hattie Morgan, Bessie Wilson, Maggie Hurt, Bert Edwards, Irene Shearer, Sissie Wayne Hughes, and Jabe Edwards. The preacher is Brother Smith (far left). (Dolores Morris.)

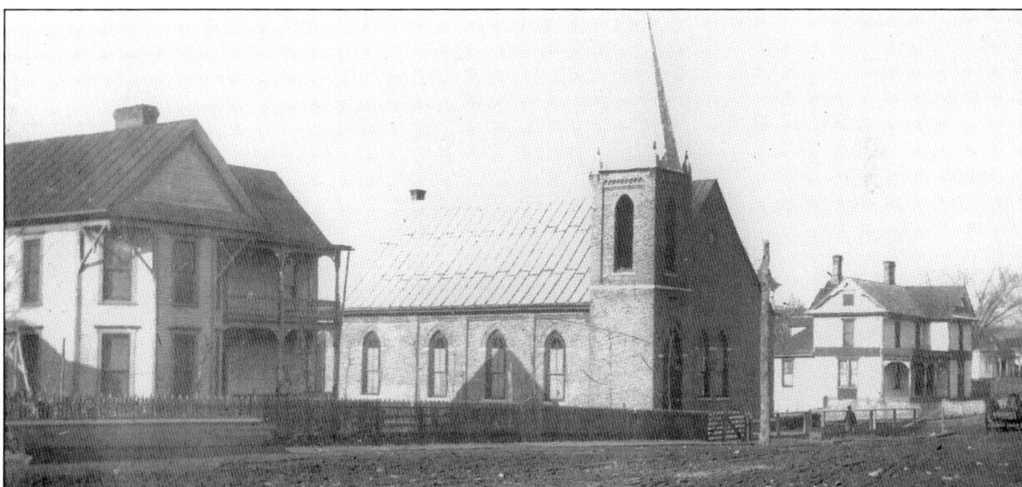

In 1904, the First Presbyterian Church was built at the intersection of North Main Street and Walnut Street. Because there was a cave underneath it, the structure started sinking and breaking apart about 1913. At that time, local Baptists worshiped in a frame building down the street. Always crowded on its tiny lot, the frame building burned in 1918. By that time, the Presbyterian Church had disbanded, and the Baptists had purchased the Presbyterian building and lot. They razed the collapsing structure, filled in the cave, and started building the large, gray stone building that stood there until 1986. In 2010, the law office of Jeffrey Hoehler stands on that site. (Wayne County Museum.)

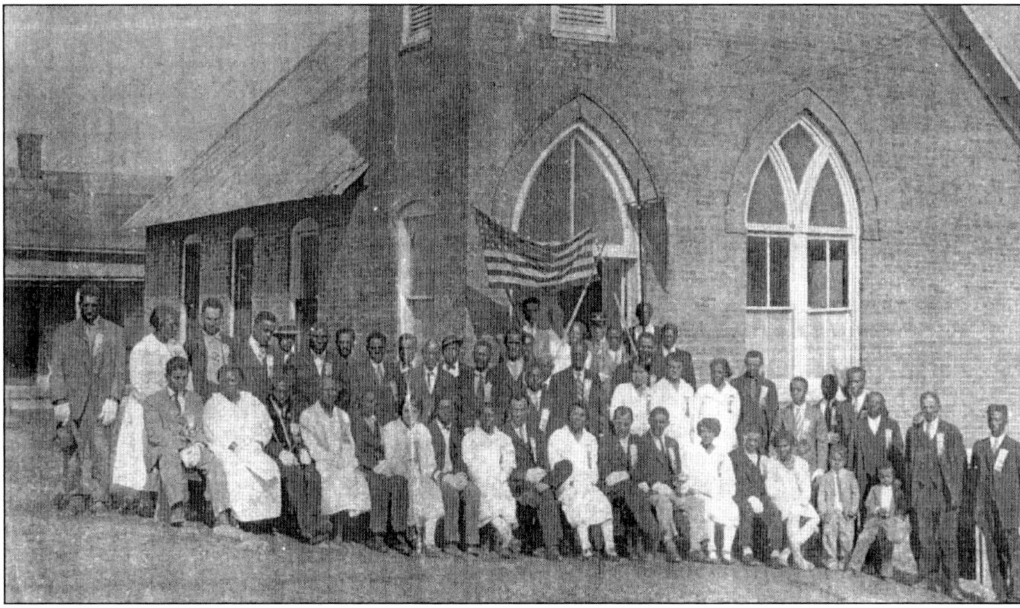

St. John's AME Church began on Morris Hill. The congregation erected its next building on Short Street. In 1904, a fire swept down Short Street, and the church was one of the buildings destroyed. In 1913, the present building was constructed at the end of High Street. (Wayne County Museum.)

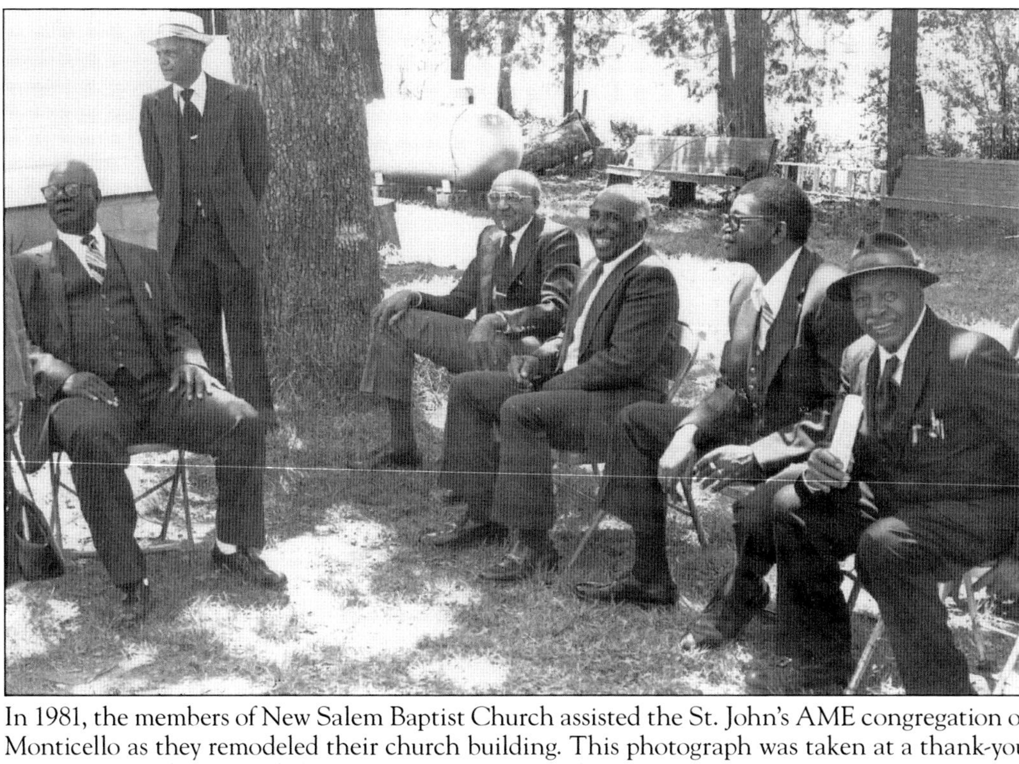

In 1981, the members of New Salem Baptist Church assisted the St. John's AME congregation of Monticello as they remodeled their church building. This photograph was taken at a thank-you celebration held afterward. (Wayne County Historical Society.)

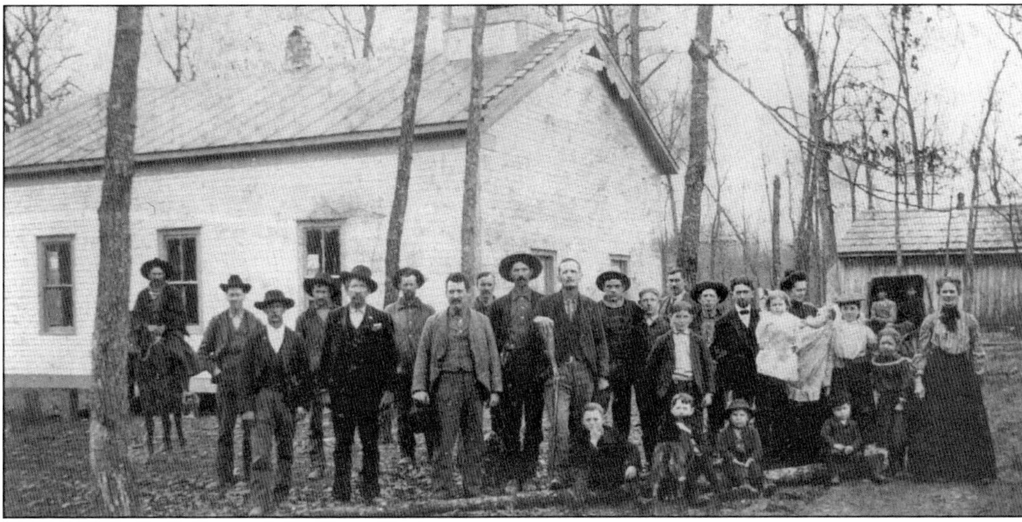

After their work was completed in 1906, the group that built Rector's Flat Baptist Church posed for this picture. Seen here from left to right, they are (first row) George Shearer, Joe Shearer and his dog, Hubert Denney, and Everette Rector; (second row) John Upchurch, Jesse Rector, James Denny, Marshall Poe, D. W. C. Rector, John Ramsey, Lewis Shearer, Hencie Hughes, Thomas Upchurch, J. Lewis Beck (with gun), Harrison Ramsey, Wes Baker, Sampson Baker, pastor H. Clay Bell, Willie Thurston, Wayne Rector, Emma Rector (holding Lythia Rector), Elsie Rector (baby), Ida Shearer, Gertie Denney, and Ellen Shearer. Mr. and Mrs. J. F. Chrisman are in the buggy. Rector's Flat Baptist Church was constituted in 1905. (Vera Garner.)

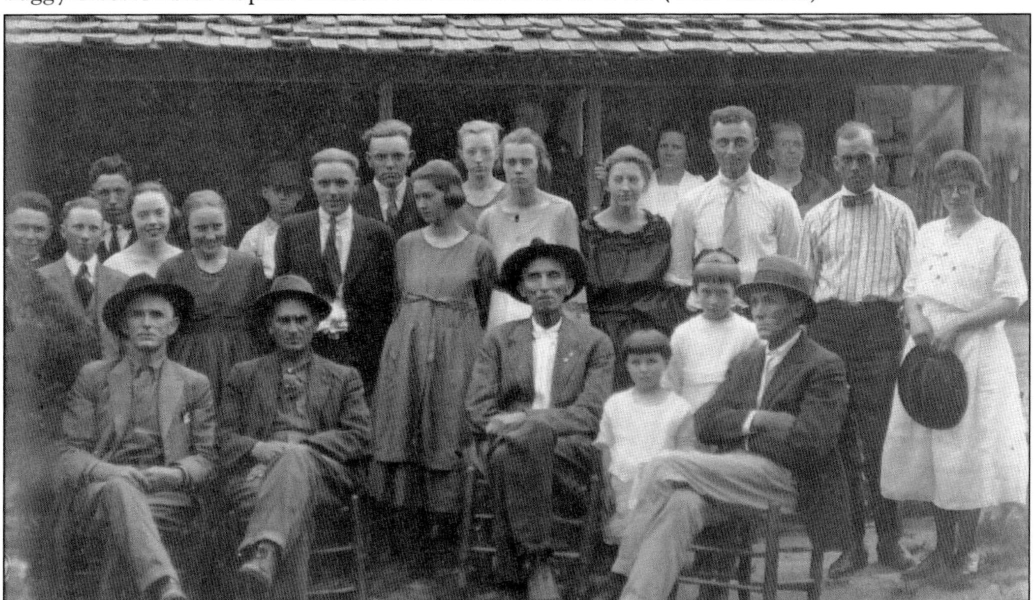

The group in this photograph is simply identified as a Sunday school class meeting in the Hidalgo community. It is interesting because the building in the background does not seem to be a typical church building or schoolhouse. It could be that the group does not have a church building available to them, or as some have suggested, the class may be meeting at the home of one of its members. This photograph is an example of how the effort to identify old images is an ongoing process. (Dolores Morris.)

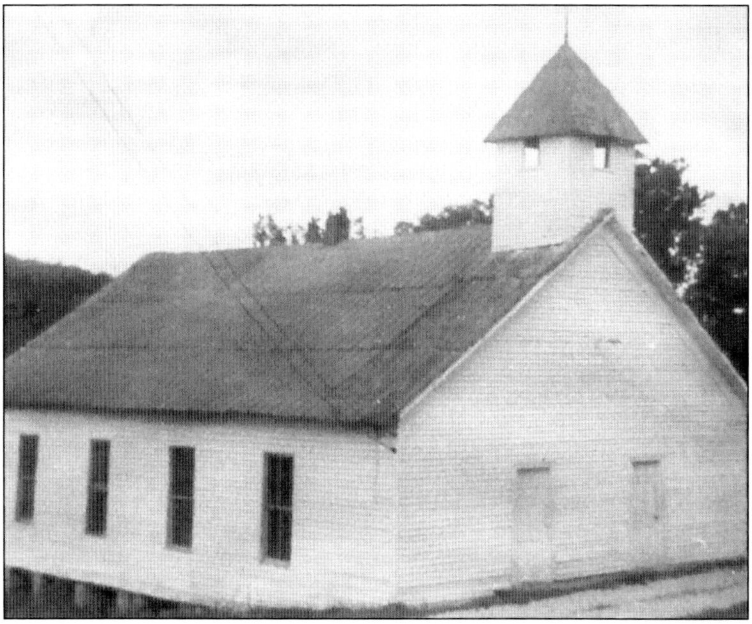

The church that began at Kidder 190 years ago has been called by different names: Kidder Church, Cedar Sinking Church, Liberty Baptist Meetinghouse, and finally, Liberty Baptist Church. The building pictured here was constructed in 1903. Two log structures, both lost to fire, preceded this building. The beautiful brick building that now stands just off Highway 790 was built in 1971. (Wayne County Museum.)

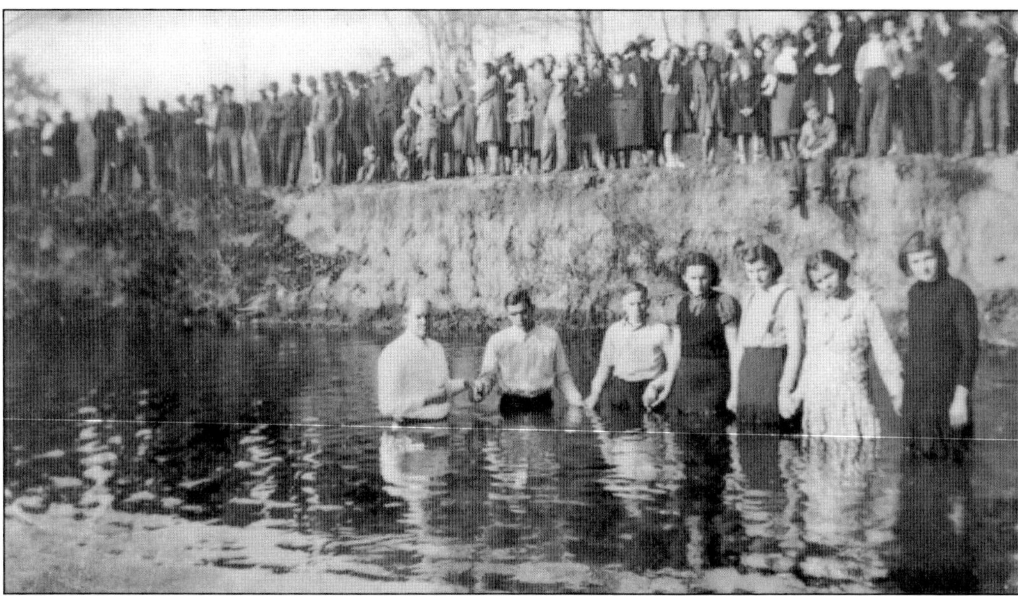

Bro. Isaac Hucaby began preaching at age 18 and baptized more than 500 people during the years of his ministry. Seen here on November 5, 1939, is a group of people awaiting baptism. From left to right, they are Hucaby, Johnny West, Ray Smith, Laura Bertram, Alta Baker (West), Velma Baker (Foster), and Polly Marcum. Two of these young people, Johnny West and Alta Baker, eventually became husband and wife. (John and Alta West.)

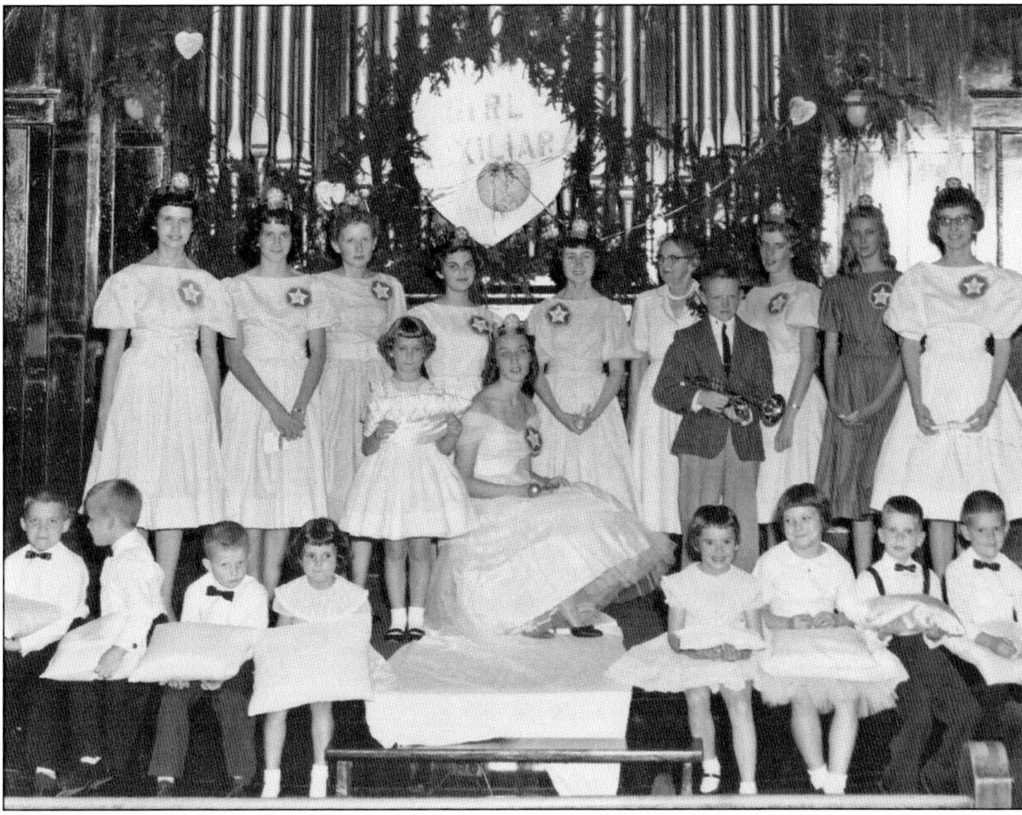

This Girl's Auxiliary Coronation took place at First Baptist Church in 1962 or 1963. The coronation services, which were intended to promote both spiritual values and social skills, also encouraged the young people to consider themselves as valued members of the church family. Pictured with the group, Bess Cook Ryan (fourth woman from right, standing), wife of Charles O. Ryan, served as leader of this auxiliary. Year after year, Bess organized wonderful programs for the church. The Christmas pageants that she directed were not to be missed. (Sue Johnson Woolums.)

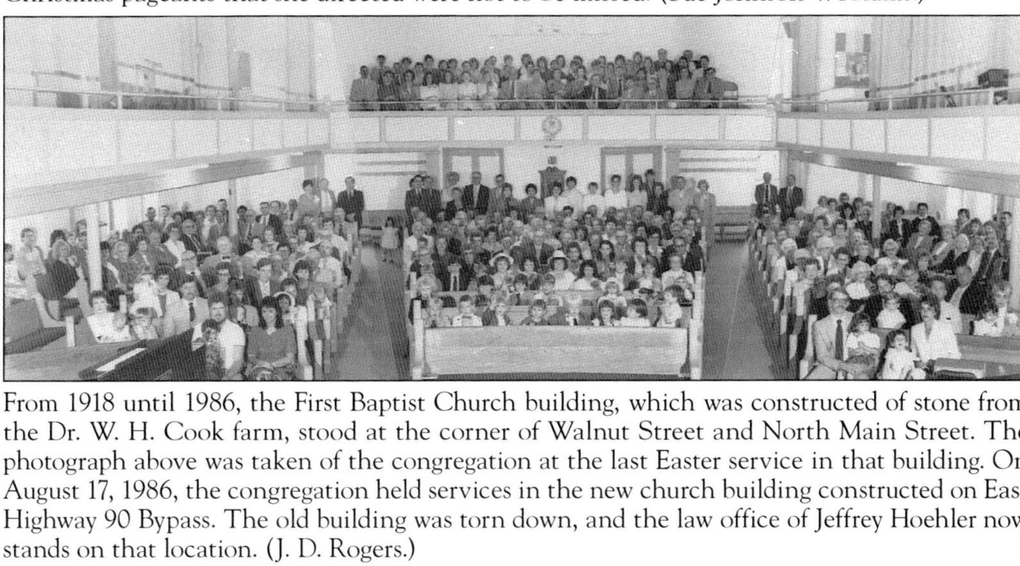

From 1918 until 1986, the First Baptist Church building, which was constructed of stone from the Dr. W. H. Cook farm, stood at the corner of Walnut Street and North Main Street. The photograph above was taken of the congregation at the last Easter service in that building. On August 17, 1986, the congregation held services in the new church building constructed on East Highway 90 Bypass. The old building was torn down, and the law office of Jeffrey Hoehler now stands on that location. (J. D. Rogers.)

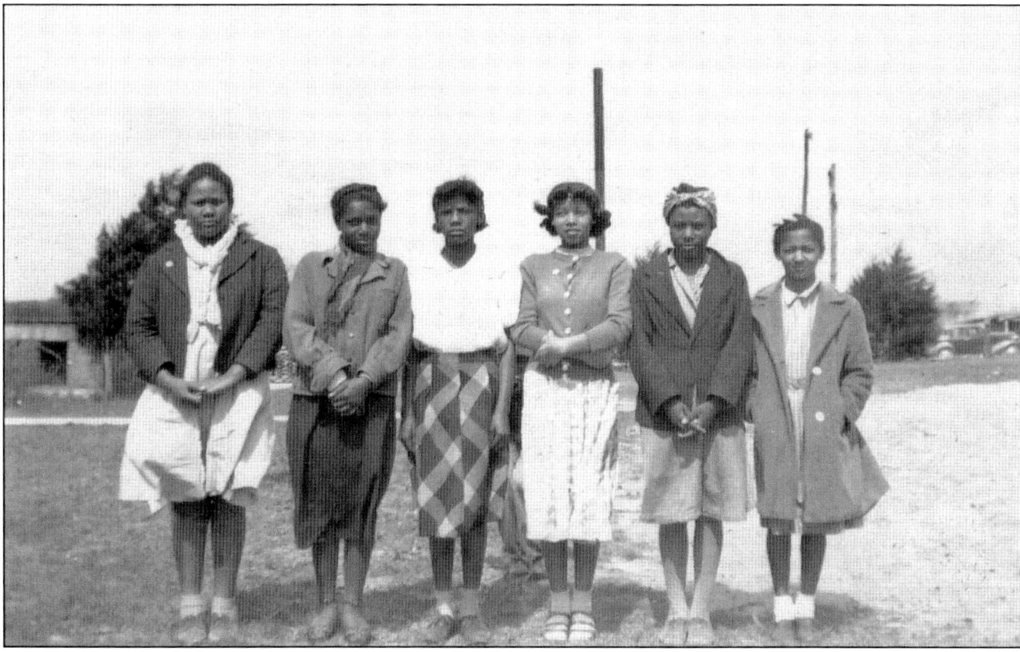

For many students, 4-H programs and activities became a major part of their education, leading to lifelong interests. Officers of the Travis School club are pictured above. From left to right, they are Margaret Barnes, Juanita (Coffey) Allen, Gertrude Duncan, Betty Brown, Katie Garrett, and Gardinia Hawkins. (Wayne County Historical Society.)

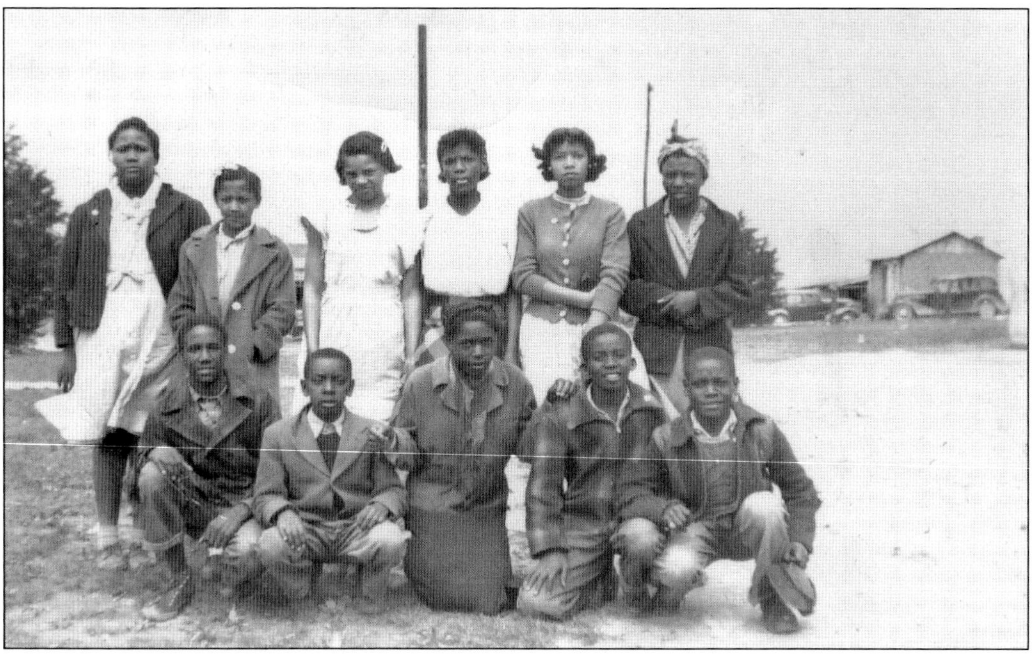

Most adults have great memories of the years they spent in school. In an earlier time, school and church were the two main places to develop relationships with peers. Many of these relationships continued throughout the students' lives. This photograph is of young people at the Travis School. (Melvin Jones.)

This nursery school on Michigan Avenue operated under the umbrella of a Depression-era federal program. In this late-1930s image, the children bow for prayer before a meal or snack. The adults are, from left to right, Mrs. Grider, Martha Pedigo, and Flonnie Edwards. (Dolores Morris.)

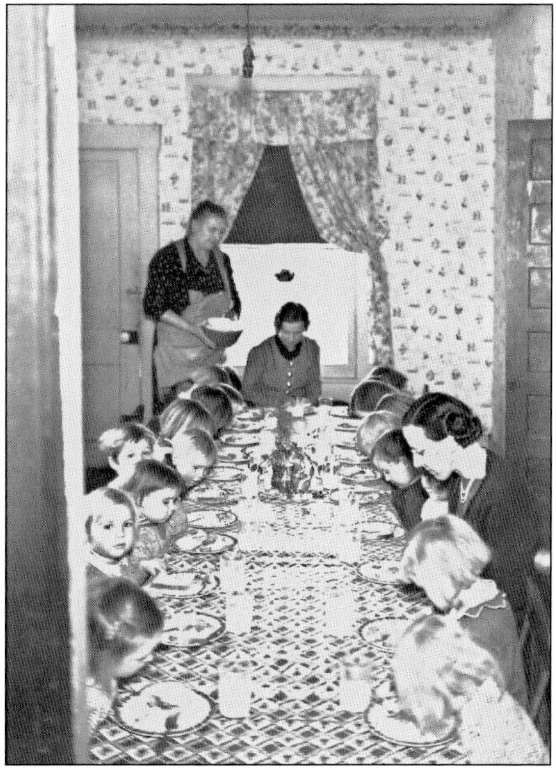

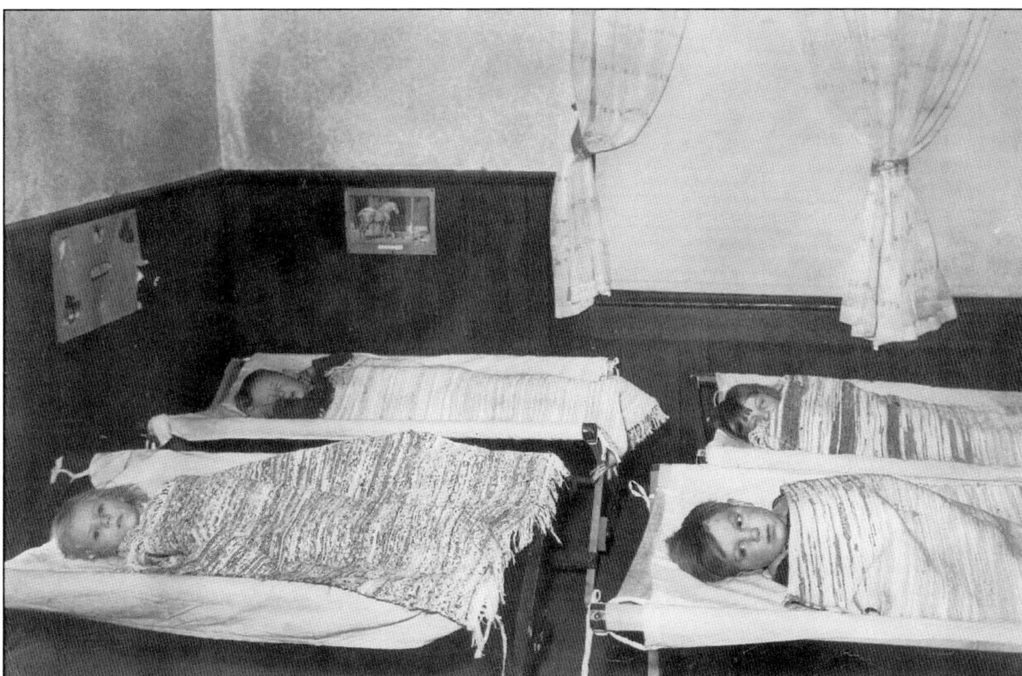

The nursery school children were given time for a nap, whether or not they considered a nap necessary, as seen by some of their wide-eyed faces. (Dolores Morris.)

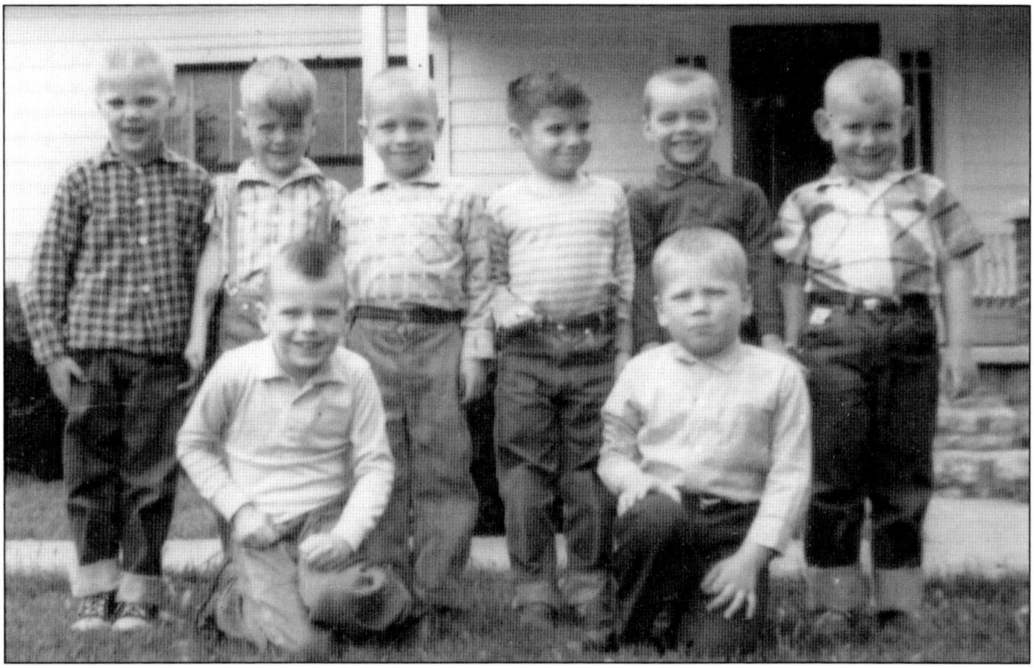

For some years, Sara Huff operated a kindergarten class in her home on North Main Street. The 1959–1960 class is pictured here. From left to right are (first row) Ernest Johnson and Ches Brandon; (second row) Robbie Underwood, Joey Gray, Lyle Breeding, Van Back, Del Goodwin, and Glen Hickey. (Dr. Robert B. Breeding.)

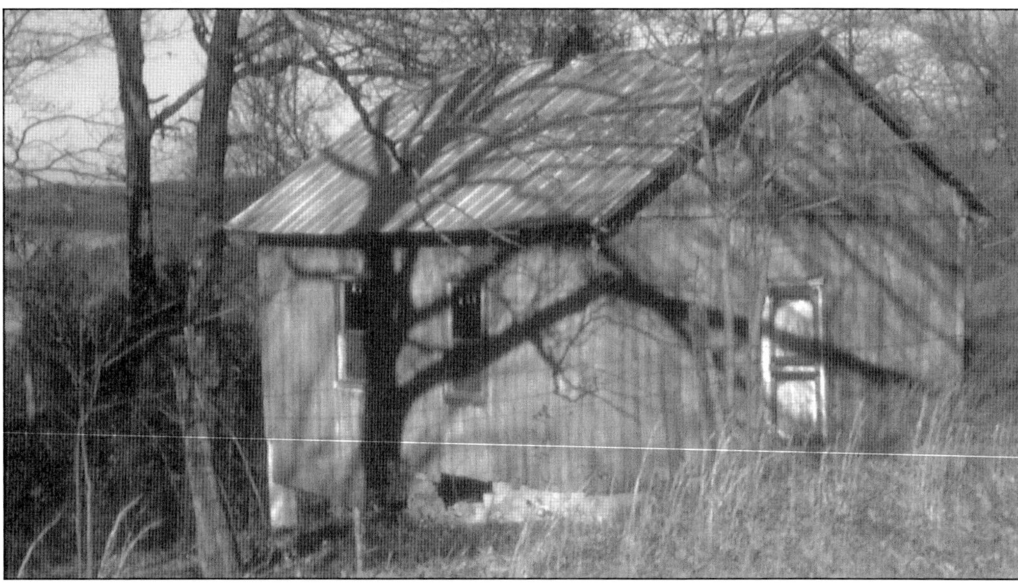

African American children attended this school in the Mill Springs community until 1931. Travis School opened that year, and eight African American schools were consolidated. In addition to Mill Springs, this involved children from the following schools: Weaver (Mount Zion community), Gap of the Ridge, Pleasant View (Lockett's Chapel community), Sheep Lot (in southern Monticello), Dogwood (Stokes Road community), Wray Hill, and St. Paul's (Meadow Creek community). (Garnett Walker.)

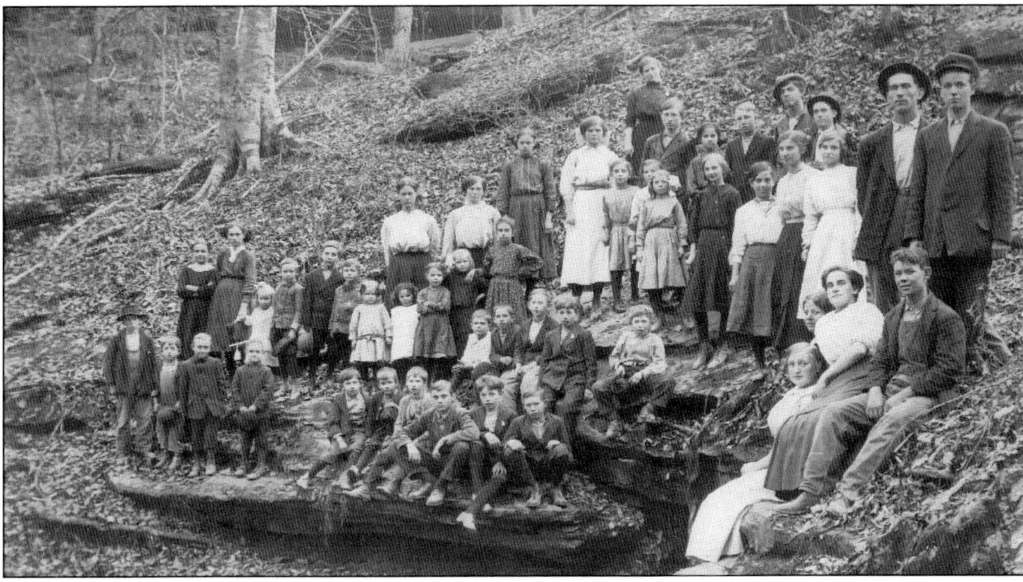

Wild Kitchen School was so named because it was built on the site where a "kitchen in the wild" stood in pioneer times. Shortly after the War of 1812, a group of settlers came to Wayne County from Virginia and set up camp in the Cabell area. Their horses escaped one night and simply went back to their homes in Virginia. The men followed the horses to round them up, leaving the women and children alone in the camp for three months. Years later, a school was built on the spot that had been used for the camp kitchen. The picture above shows the school around 1917. The teacher, Clara Brown (seated second from right) is pictured with her students grouped around a spring in the community—perhaps the same spring that furnished water for those early campers. (Katy Lou Rector.)

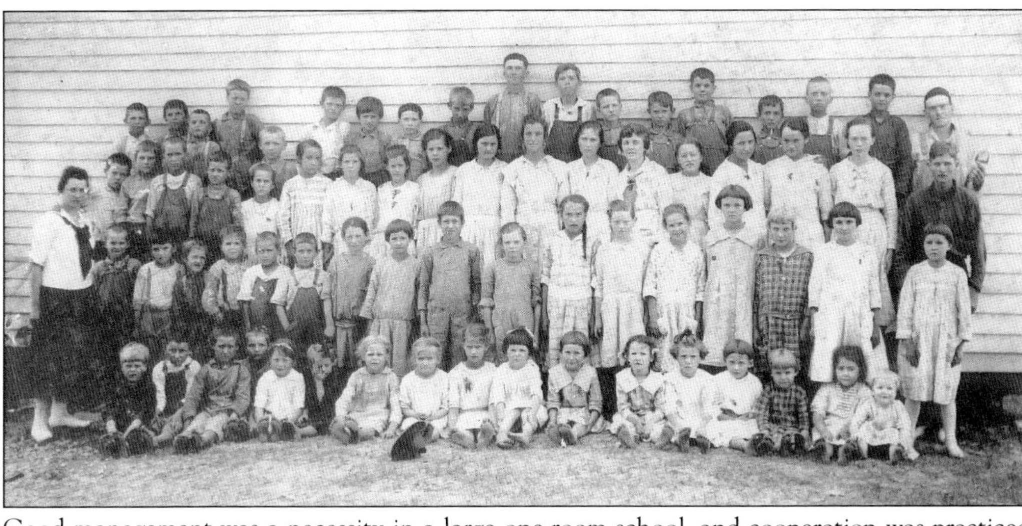

Good management was a necessity in a large one-room school, and cooperation was practiced daily as older children helped younger ones. Much learning took place as students heard children of all ages recite their lessons throughout the school day. Ala Shearer Vickery, pictured at left, taught this school at Hidalgo in 1918. (Bob and Gladys Vickery.)

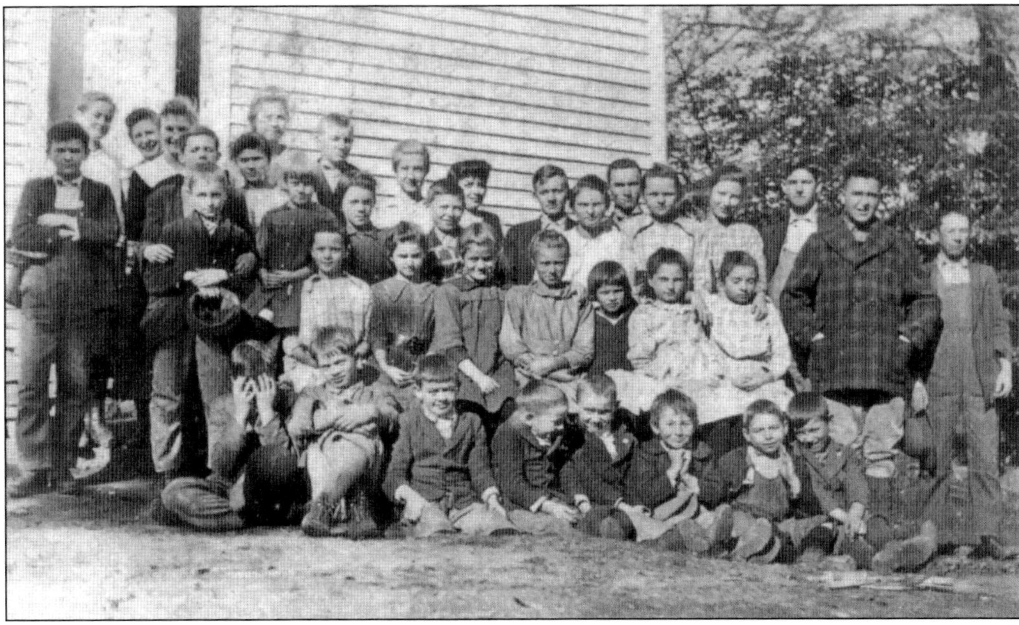

Lacking access to a high school, the older students in this 1918 Sunnybrook School photograph simply repeated the eighth grade. The woman at left with the large white collar on her dress is Lola Bertram, who was in her third or fourth year of eighth grade. Her teachers brought in several advanced books for her to study, and she, in turn, helped with classes for the younger students. (Wayne County Museum.)

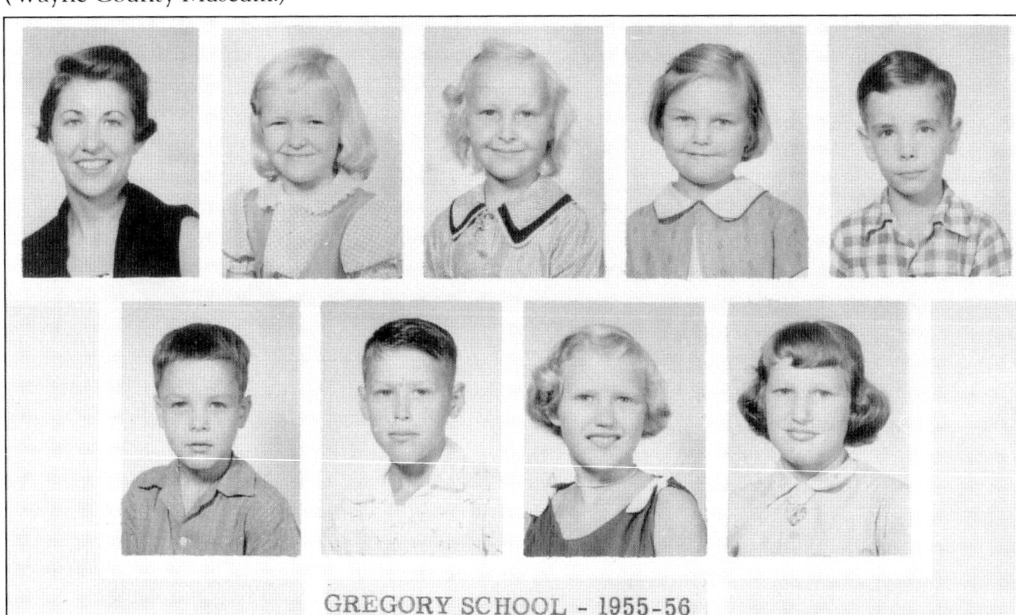

The number of students attending a one-room school varied with the local population. In 1955–1956, when Eloise Morrow taught Gregory School, the student body consisted of eight students. From left to right are (first row) Gene Jones, Richard Dunagan, Margie New, and Wilma Dunagan; (second row) Morrow, Carol New, Betty Abbott, Mary Sue Dick, and Carmel Vaughn. (Margie Williams.)

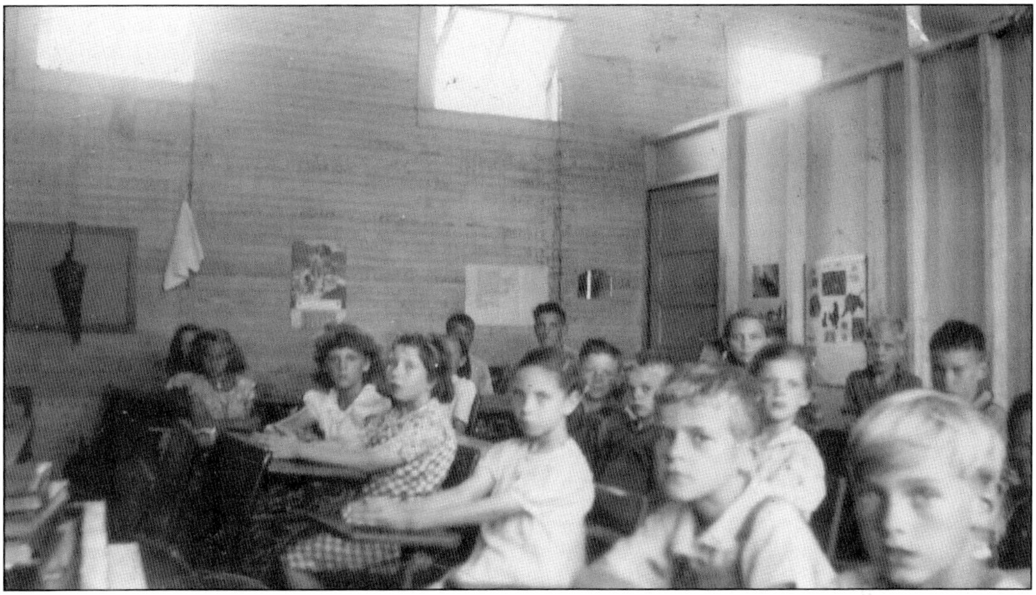

When this photograph was taken of Spann Hill School in 1947, there were more than a hundred small community schools such as this one in Wayne County. Among the younger students pictured above are Gladys Hicks, Hazel Koontz, Iva Roberts, Esther Lou Prichett, Lois Roberts, Earl Troxell, Herbert Troxell, Leonard Jones, Glen Hicks, Marlene Brunner, Daniel Richardson, Beecher Daws, Frank Troxell, and Harold Roberts. (Beecher Daws.)

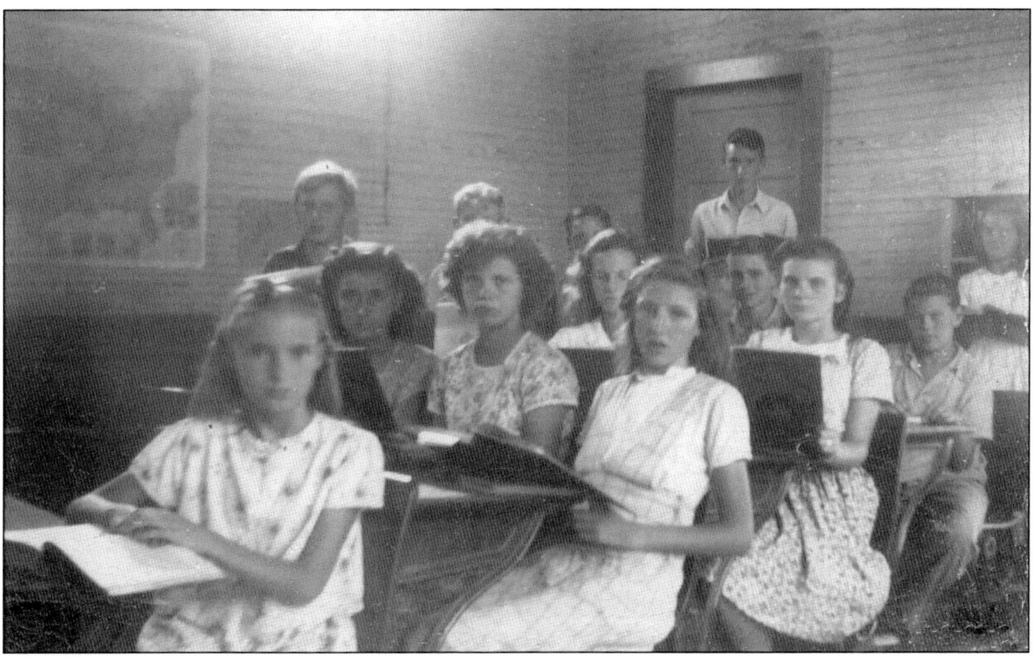

The older students pictured in this 1947 photograph of Spann Hill School are, in no particular order, Mary Carolyn Richardson, Fannie Criswell, Flossie Abbott, Betty Marcum, Ina Troxell, Junior Walker, Betty Jo Richardson, Farrell Nevels, David Koontz, Beryl Daws, Floyd Jones, Lorene Koontz, and Robert Pritchett. (Beecher Daws.)

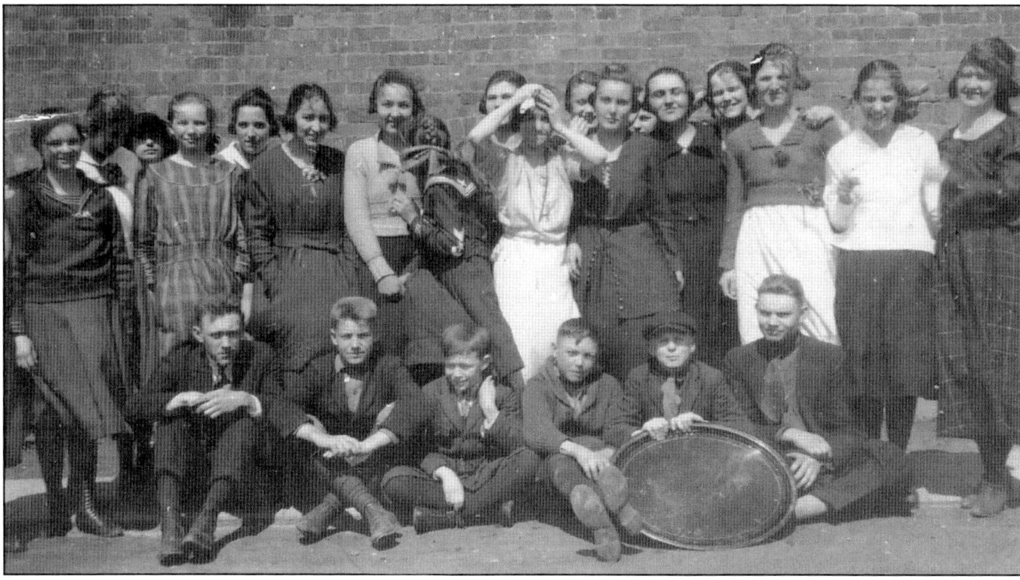

Monticello School's eighth grade class of 1920 is pictured here. In the first row, from left to right, are Homer Campbell, unidentified, Milton Fairchild, Lawrence Rankin, Loren Tate, and Chester Cook. The other students are unidentified. (Vera Garner.)

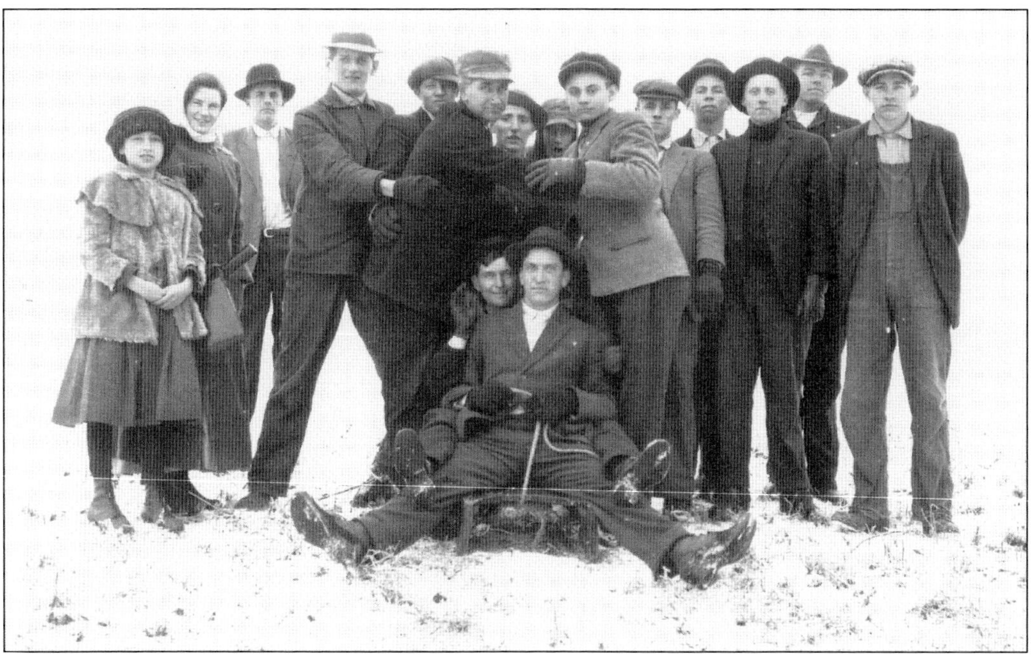

The work of a normal school was teacher training. Someone with a camera caught these students of the Murl Normal School at a time when they were not even pretending to study. The fellow seated in front on the sled is Herb Guffey. The small girl at left is Clara Barnes (Smart), and behind her is teacher Artemus Barnes. This school operated in the Murl community during the winter months from 1915 until 1919. (Vera Garner.)

Six

Cumberland River and Lake Cumberland

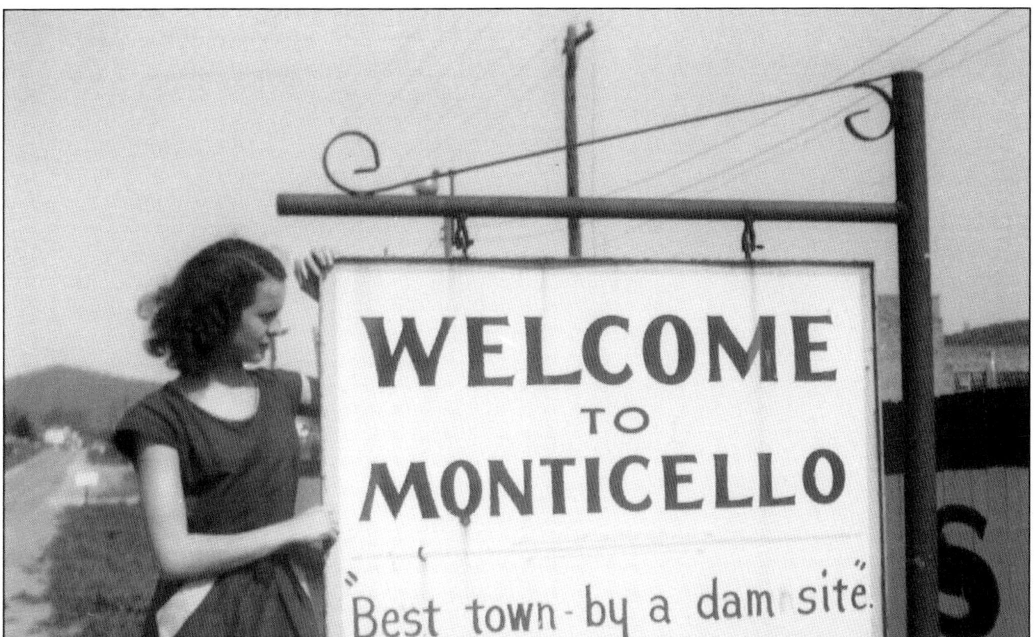

The building of Wolf Creek Dam and the formation of Lake Cumberland brought immense and lasting changes to Wayne County. Little wonder that for many years these topics were at the forefront of local thinking. "Best town by a dam site" was a much-used slogan across the country for towns located near dams, and it was adopted here. In 1965, Monticello replaced that slogan with another: "The Right City for a Bright Future." (Wayne County Museum.)

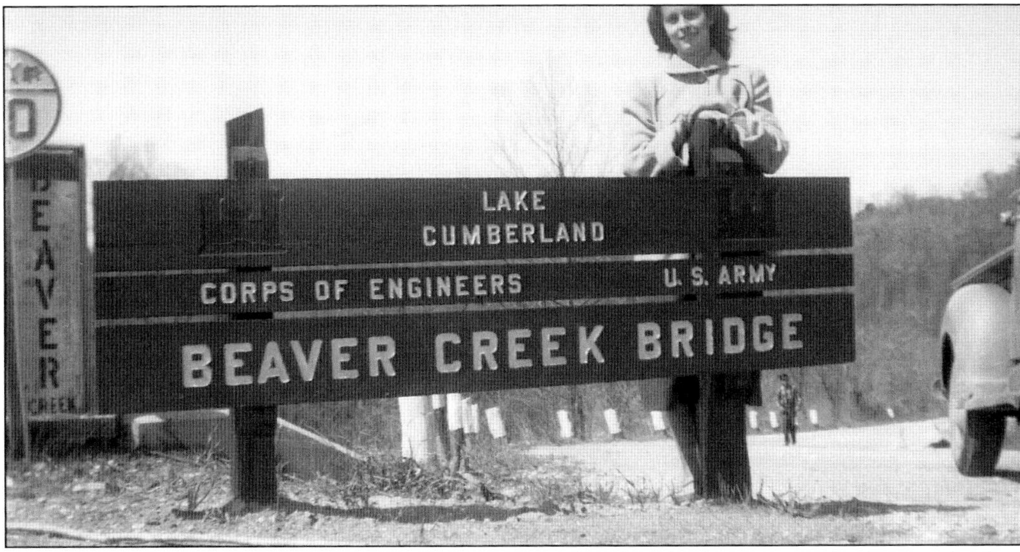

Many projects of the U.S. Army Corps of Engineers related to the formation of Lake Cumberland were blessings for the community. In this picture, taken just south of Monticello, the sign announces the building of a much-needed new bridge across Beaver Creek. (Wayne County Museum.)

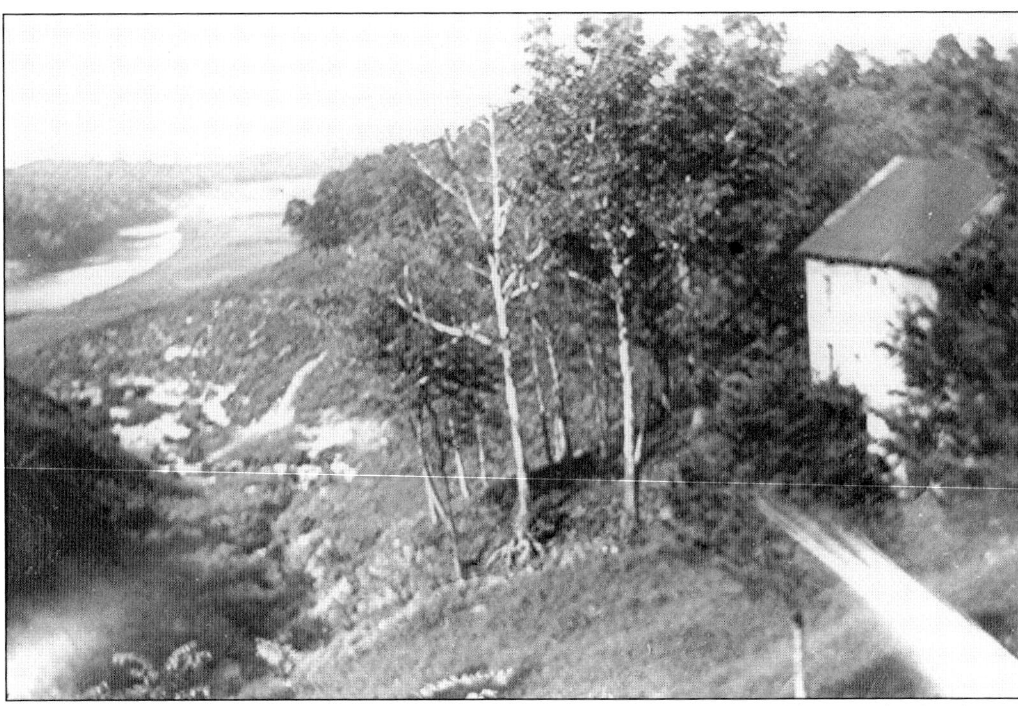
This scene is a poignant one for many people because it gives a glimpse of the Cumberland River near Mill Springs Mill. Since the Lake Cumberland Basin was filled in 1950, most of the landscape seen here has been underwater. (Samantha Suggett.)

Before Wolf Creek Dam was completed and a section of Cumberland River became Lake Cumberland, many Wayne County families had to move from their rich valley farms to higher ground. Pictured on the porch of the house they left behind are Bryan and Gladys Twyford, and their son, Bill Fred. Melvin McFarland stands at left. (Bill Fred Twyford.)

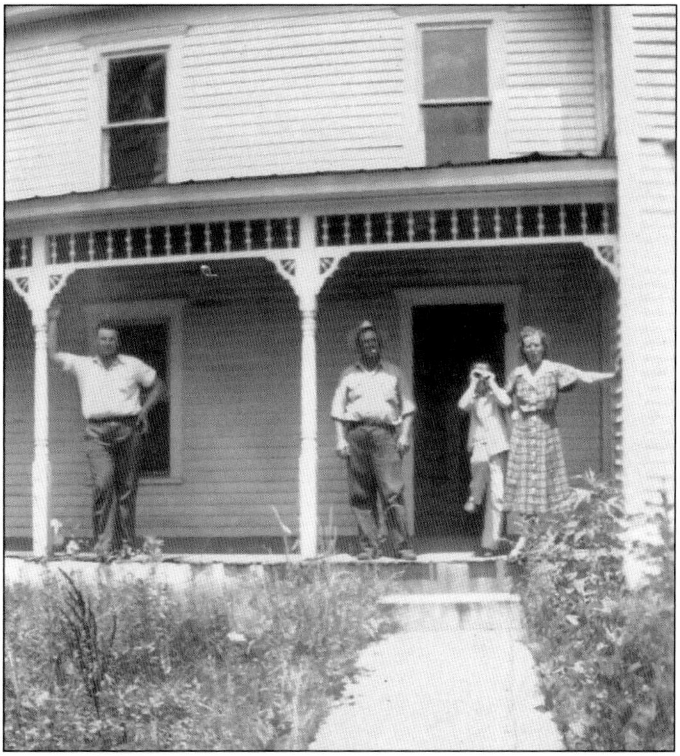

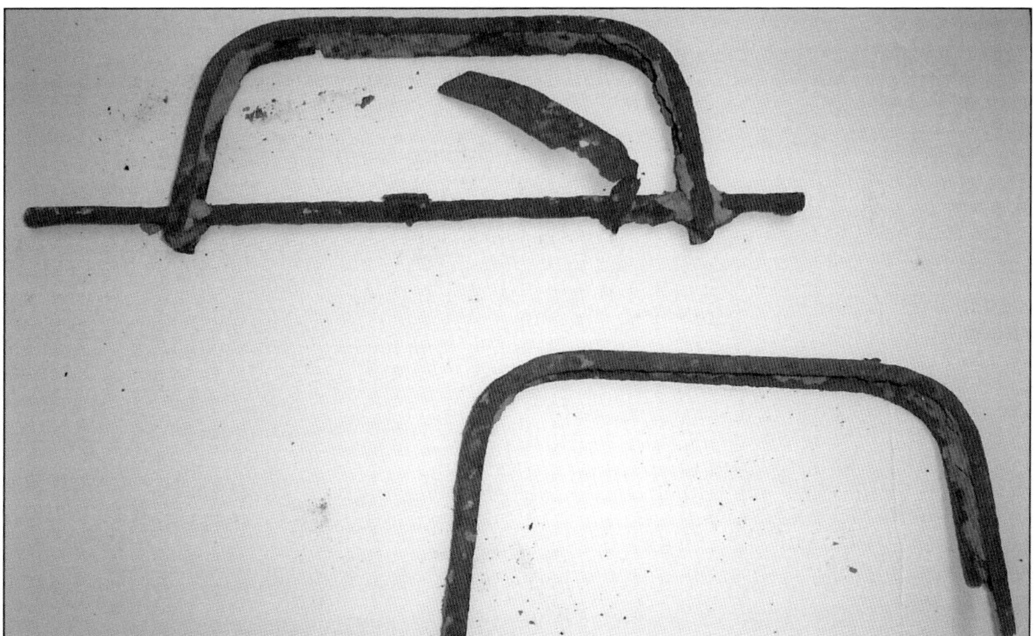

In 1981, when the water level of Lake Cumberland was low, Bill Fred Twyford was able to drive down to his old home place. Much to his surprise, he found the sidewalk and doorstep of their house still intact as well as the remains of what was once his little red wagon in the yard. (Bill Fred Twyford.)

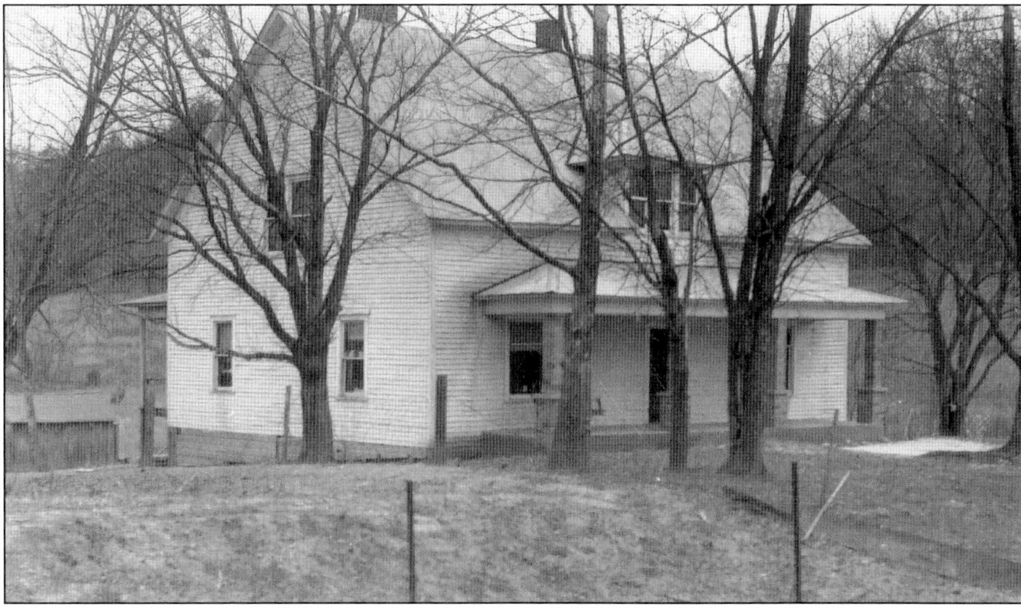

At one time, Horseshoe Bottom was a thriving rural community with two stores, a church, and a one-room school. The pictures of these buildings were taken shortly before the waters of Lake Cumberland covered the area. Located below Parnell, Horseshoe Bottom was about 16 miles from Monticello. The nearest town, though, was Jamestown, in Russell County. To get to Jamestown, Horseshoe Bottom residents had to cross Cumberland River by canoe or ferry. Most of the men of the community kept a car on the other side of the river so they could drive to Jamestown after crossing the river. Pictured here is the home of Edgar Johnson. (Sula Margaret Gregory.)

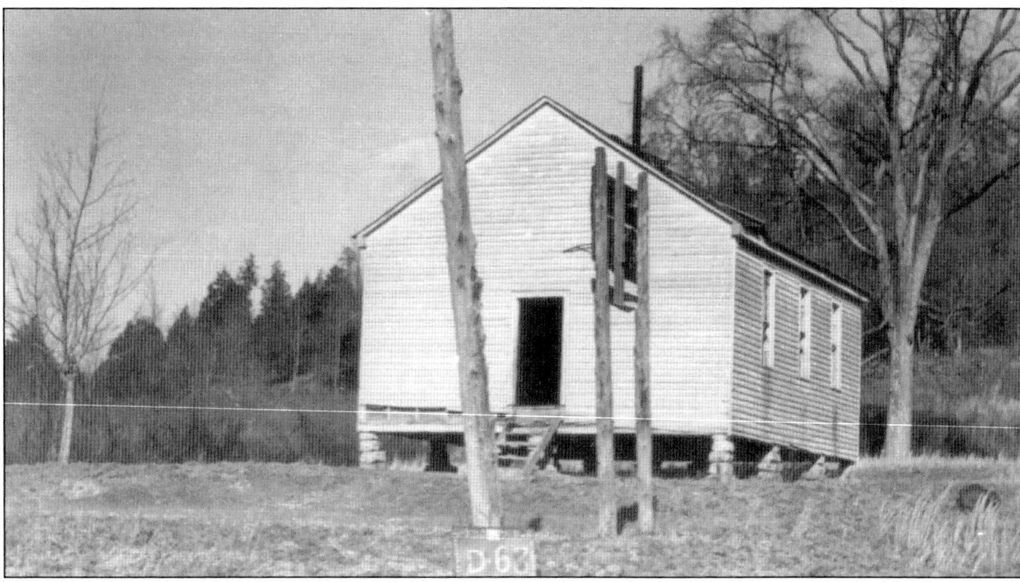

The construction of the Wolf Creek Dam and the creation of Lake Cumberland caused tremendous changes in the lives of Wayne County residents. Some important local landmarks were destroyed, including church buildings and schoolhouses. Horseshoe Bottom School was one of the schools that closed during this period. Now it exists only in the memories of those who gained much of their education within its walls. (Sula Margaret Gregory.)

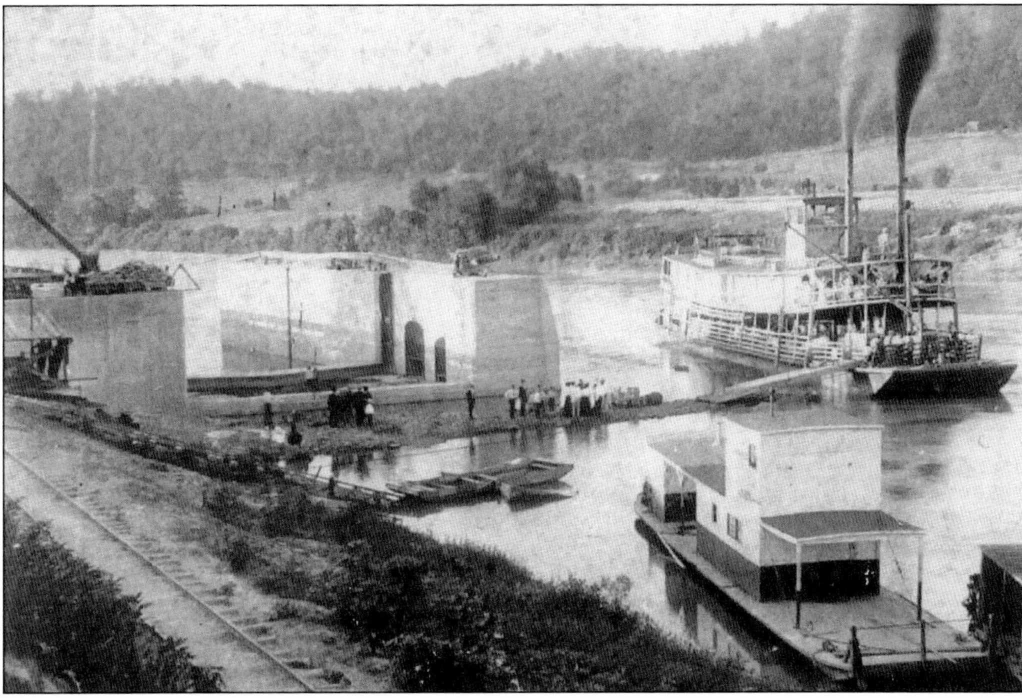

Lock No. 21 was constructed because the Upper Cumberland River was narrow and shallow. After the lock was put into operation in 1911, steamboats could travel up the river to Burnside in all seasons rather than in irregular and unpredictable periods of high water. The steamboat in the picture is the *Rowena*. (Wayne County Museum.)

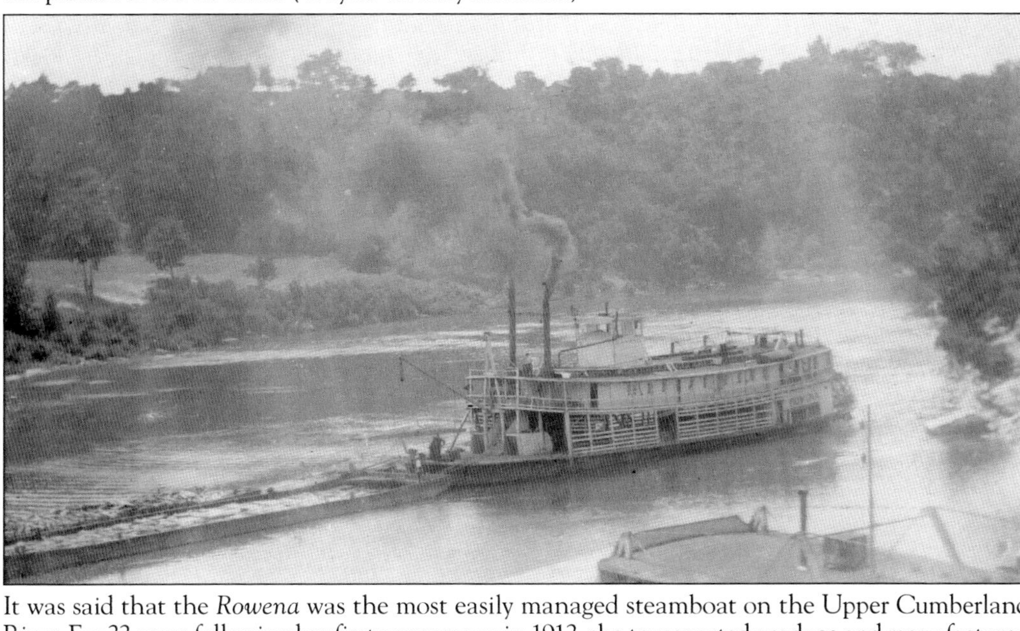

It was said that the *Rowena* was the most easily managed steamboat on the Upper Cumberland River. For 22 years following her first appearance in 1912, she transported produce and manufactured goods back and forth between this area and Tennessee. She could also carry up to 60 passengers and was often chartered for excursions. In this photograph, the *Rowena*'s glory days are over, and she has been reduced to the chore of pushing barges on the Cumberland River. (Vera Garner.)

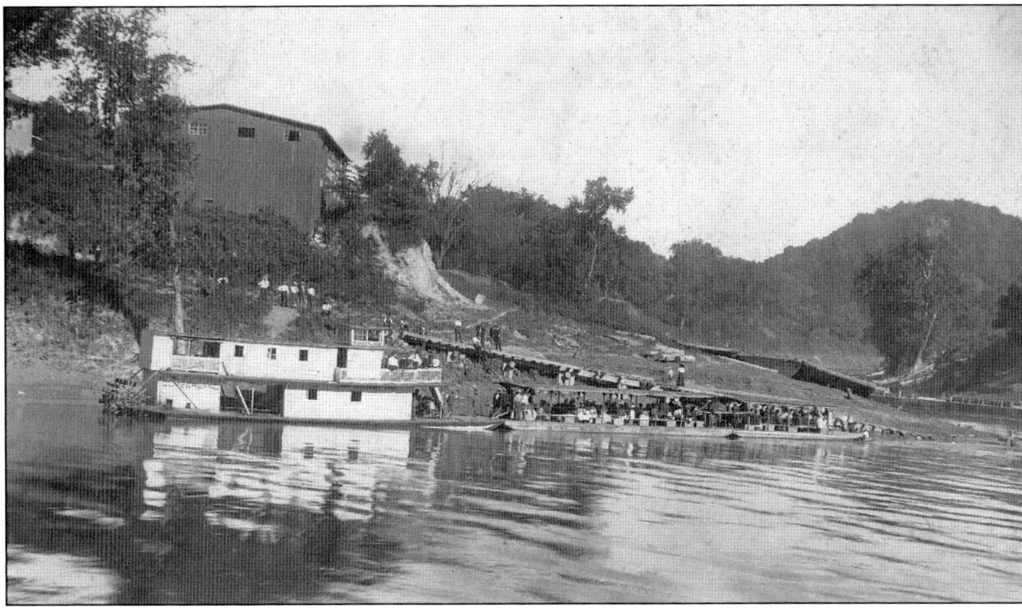

The use of steamboats on the Upper Cumberland River began about 1880 and continued until near 1930. In this photograph, the small steamboat *Cumberland* pulls a fully loaded passenger barge. (Wayne County Museum.)

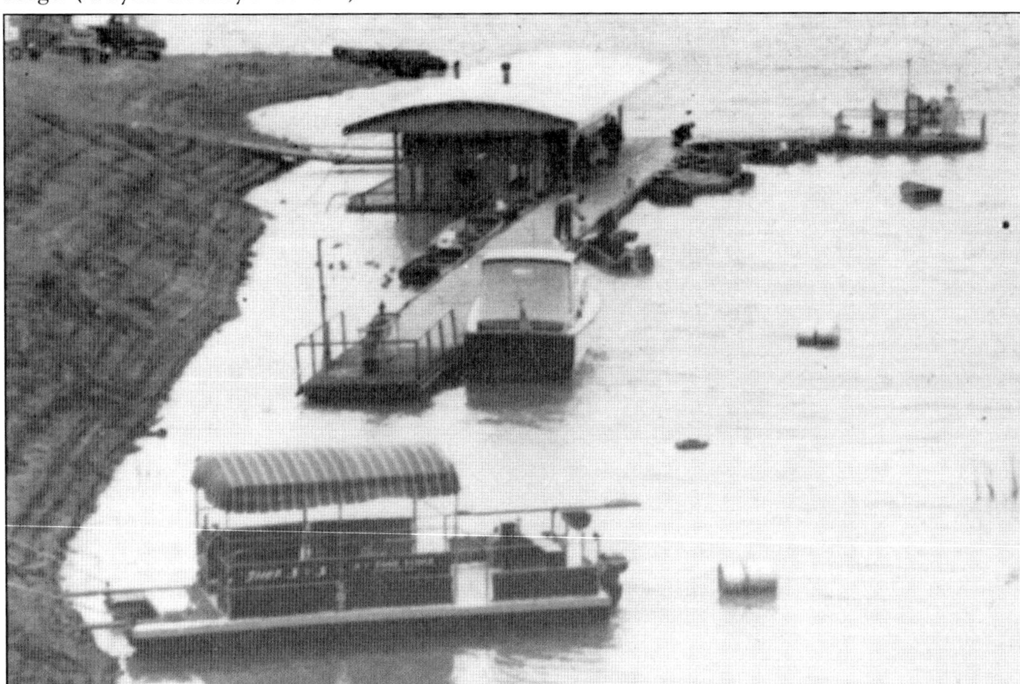

One of the most popular places on Lake Cumberland is the Conley Bottom Marina. The original Conley Bottom Dock began as the Highway 90 ferry above Cumberland Falls. Frank "Pat" Vogler had the ferry cut into three pieces and trucked to Conley Bottom, where it was reassembled. The little building seen in this image is still there. In 2010, it serves as the engine shop. (Wayne County Museum.)

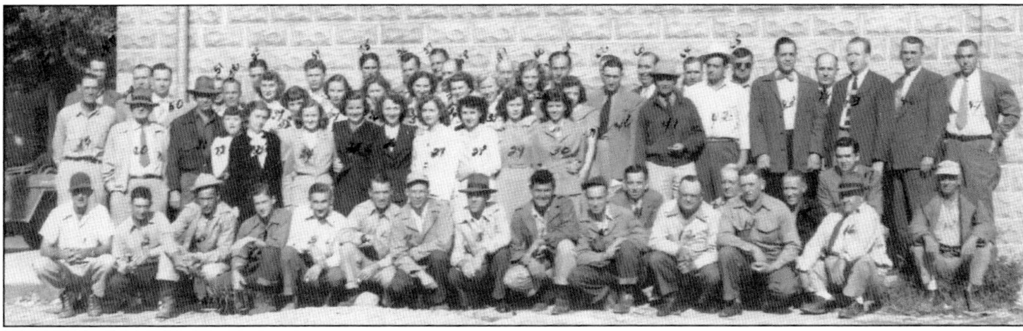

In order to create the impoundment area for Lake Cumberland, 402 parcels of land had to be purchased from Wayne County residents. The group charged with acquiring this land is shown above. In 1947, the Land Acquisitions Office of the U.S. Army Corps of Engineers set up shop on the second floor of the Ira Bell building on Columbia Avenue. Their tasks included appraising land, timber, and buildings as well as surveying, conducting title searches, and purchasing the land. Some of the people were hired locally, but the majority came from other places. The young women, mostly business college graduates, immediately earned the nickname "Dam Girls." Several of the Dam Girls married while they were here and made Wayne County their home. (Drexell Anderson.)

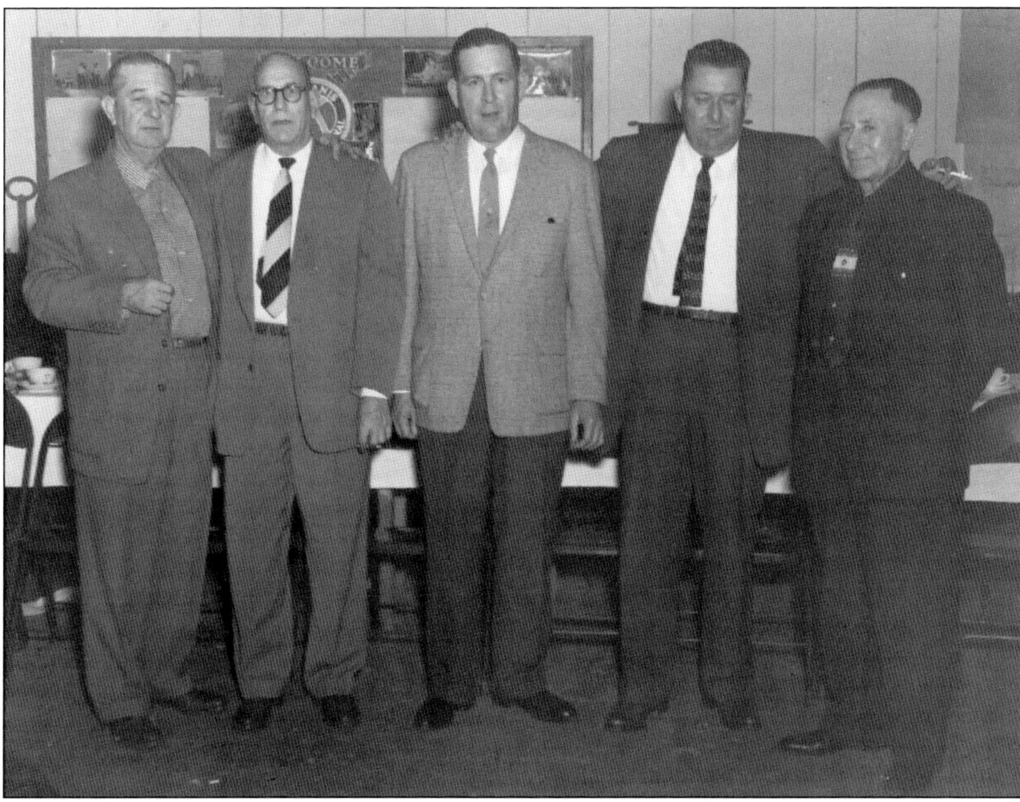

This 1957 picture was taken in the basement of Hotel Breeding. The occasion was a dinner given by Charlie Stokes in honor of Tom Ragan. Pictured from left to right are Kay Huddleston, C. B. Compton (president of Standard Oil in Kentucky), Charlie Stokes, Milford Richardson, and Tom Ragan. The local men seen here are the generation of Wayne County people who saw the tremendous changes that occurred in this area when Lake Cumberland was formed. (Katy Lou Rector.)

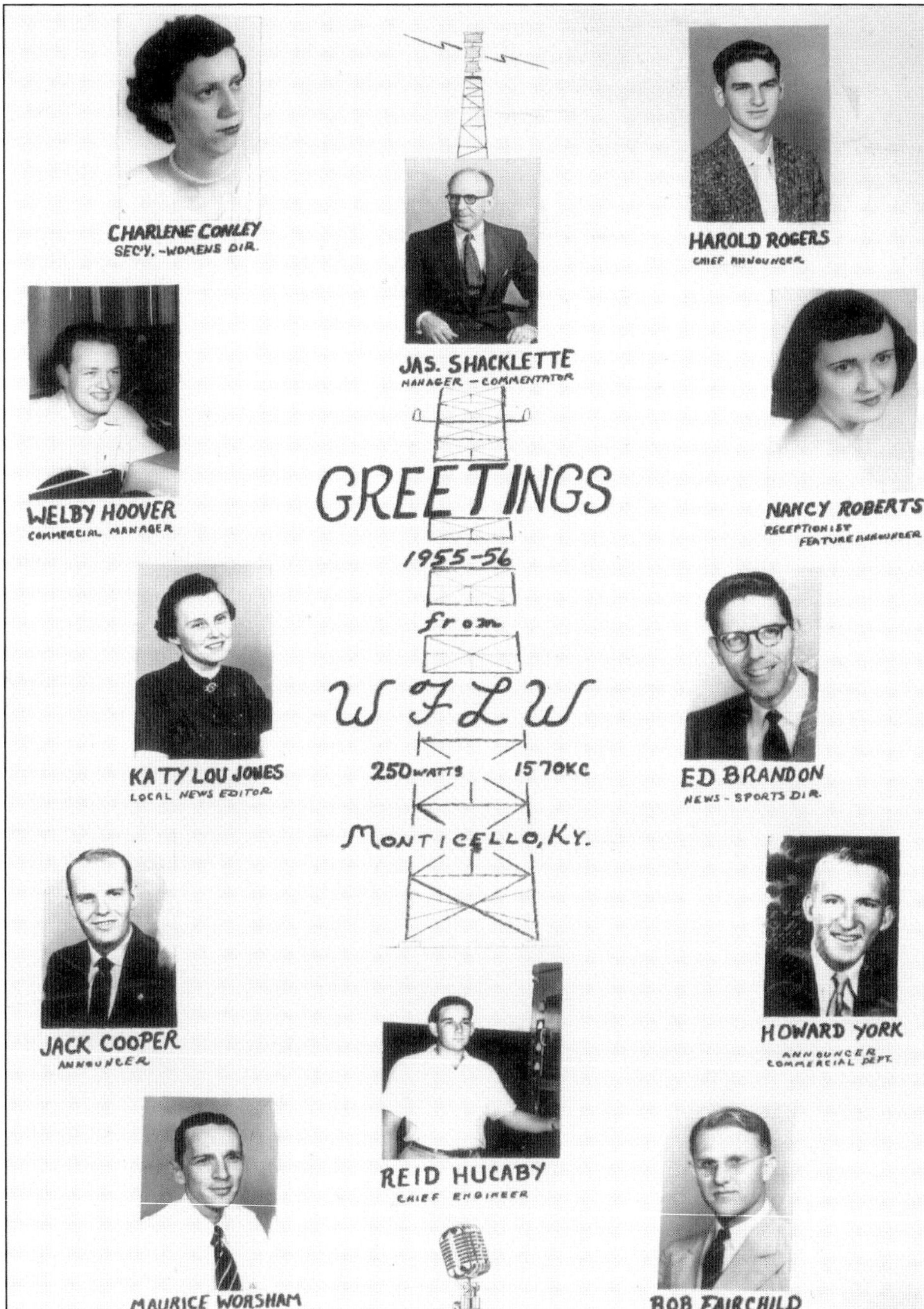

It took Campbellsville's James Shacklette more than a year to get radio station WFLW up and running. After coming to Monticello in January 1955, he remodeled the Claud Huffaker residence on Worsham Lane, installed broadcast equipment, and received permission from Washington to go on the air. Shacklette then sold the station to Fred Staples. The first staff of WFLW is shown here. From its beginning in the 1950s, WFLW has been of great service to the Lake Cumberland listening area. (Katy Lou Rector.)

Seven

People

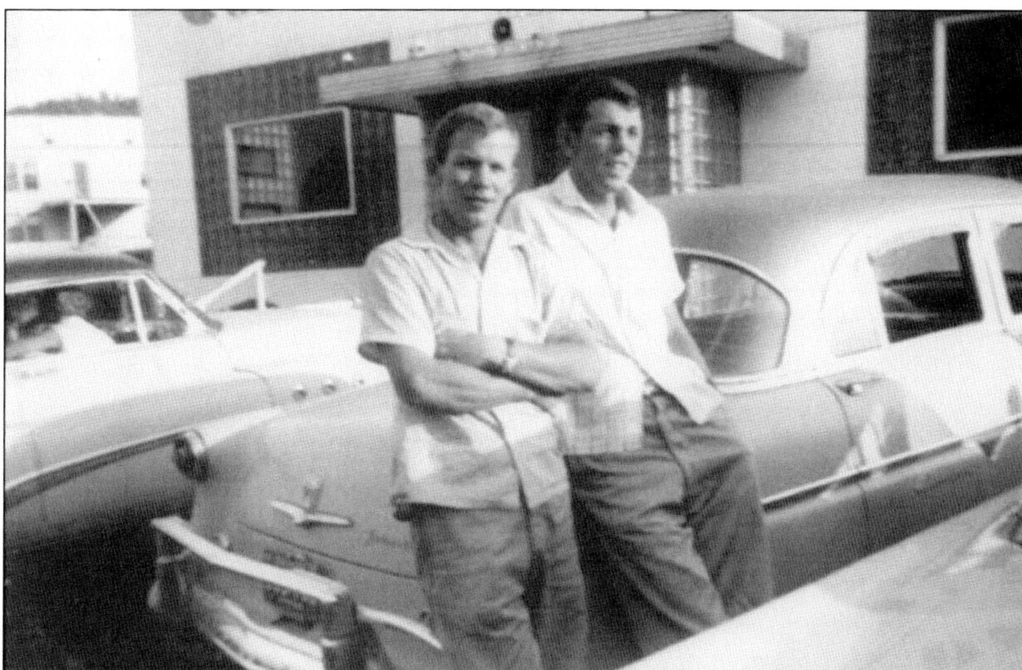

What could Wayne County teenagers do for entertainment in the 1950s? If their family owned a television set, they might have watched black-and-white television programs at home. If not, they might have gone to the Wayne Theatre to see a movie, or they might have done what most every local teenager did—check out the social scene at Cumberland Dairy. Bill Fred Twyford (left) and Roger Criswell are pictured at the dairy about 1956. (Wayne County Museum.)

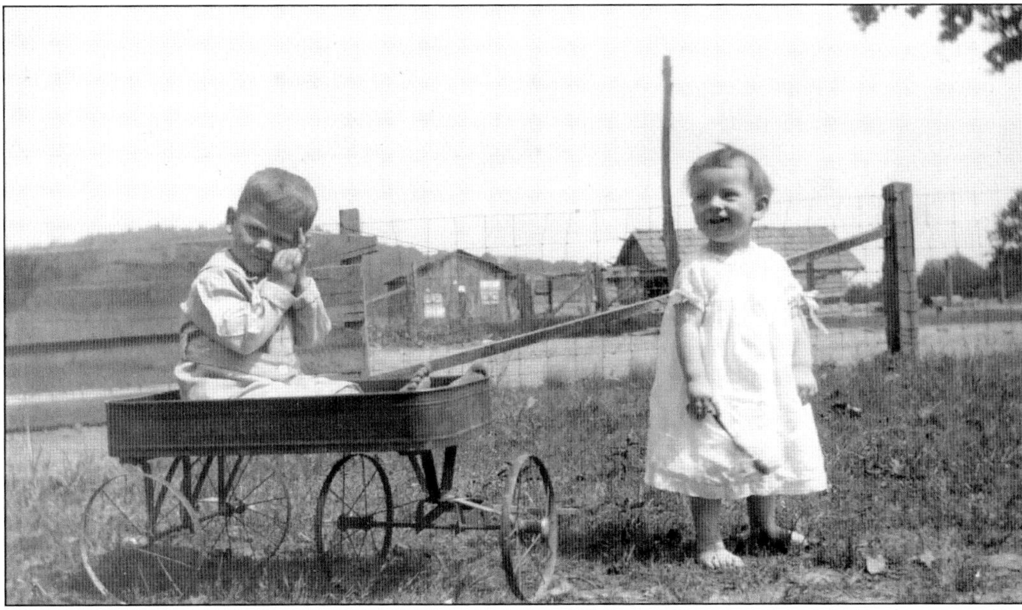

Dressed in their Sunday best, two small sons of T. R. and Ida Guffey are proud to be photographed with their up-to-date wagon. Charles Guffey is seated in the wagon, and Clarence Guffey, who was born in 1920, stands in front. (Vera Garner.)

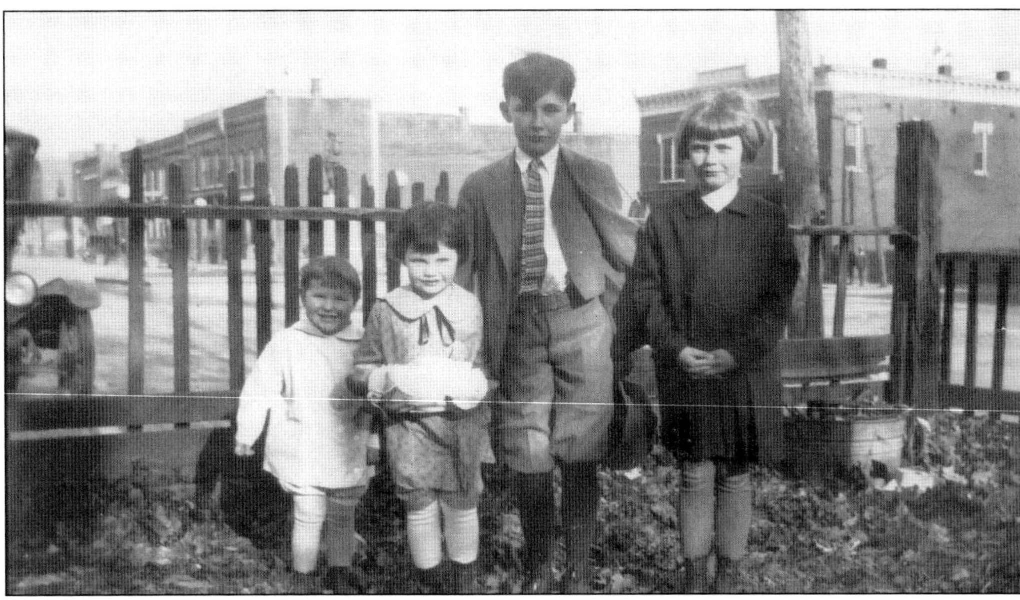

Standing just inside the fenced-in yard of the old Feuston (or Fewston) Tavern, some of the children of Ed and Nynne Lee pose for the photographer. Identified is Ed's son, Paul Lee. Both Ed Lee and a son who is not pictured here, Richard Lee, were undertakers. The backdrop for this picture is the public square of Monticello. (Sarah Dalton.)

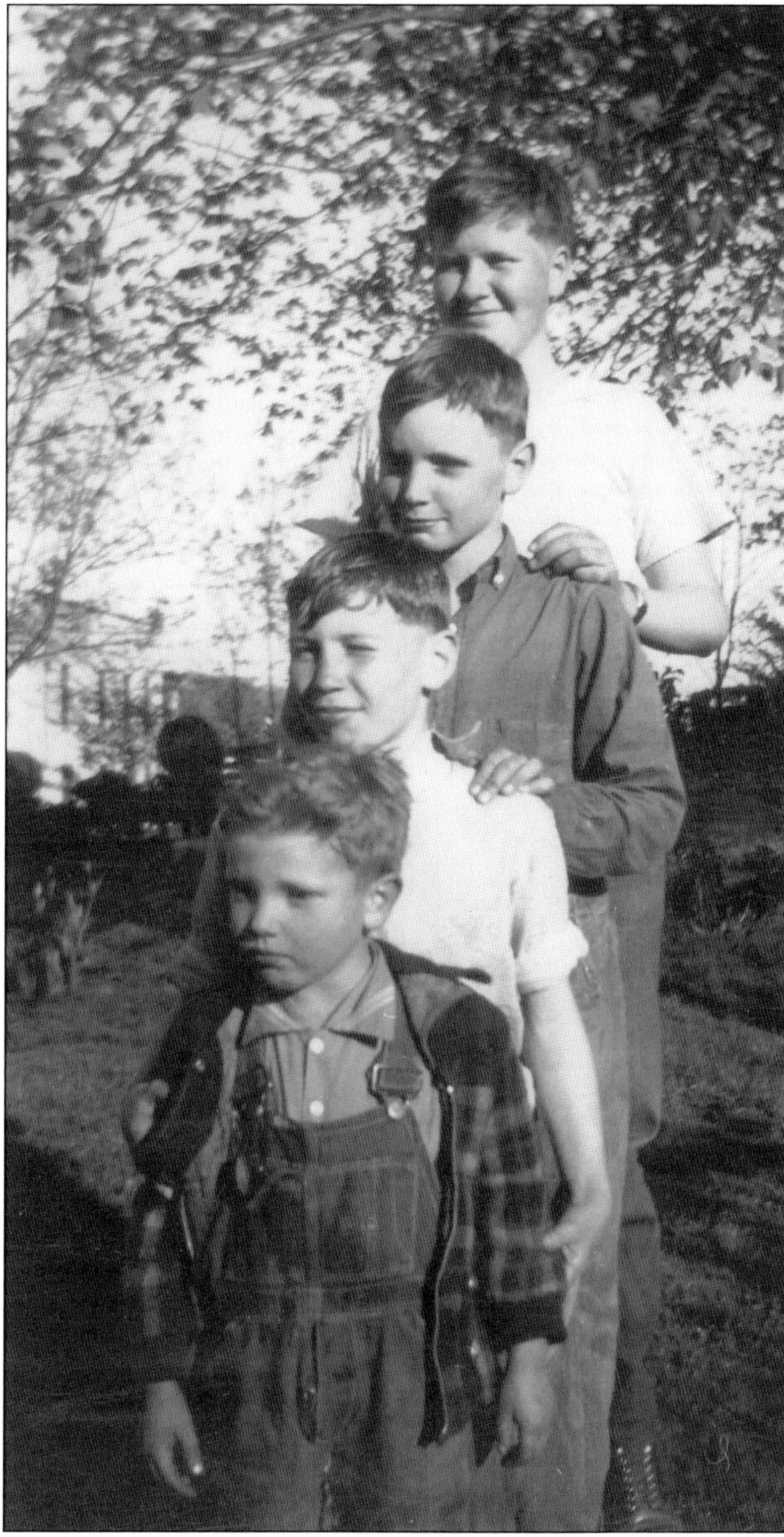

These good friends had no video games to play, but they had trees to climb, pretty rocks to find, and fields to explore. Seen here in descending order are Proctor Rankin, Roy Snyder, Bob Lee, and Roy Snyder's brother. (Bob Lee.)

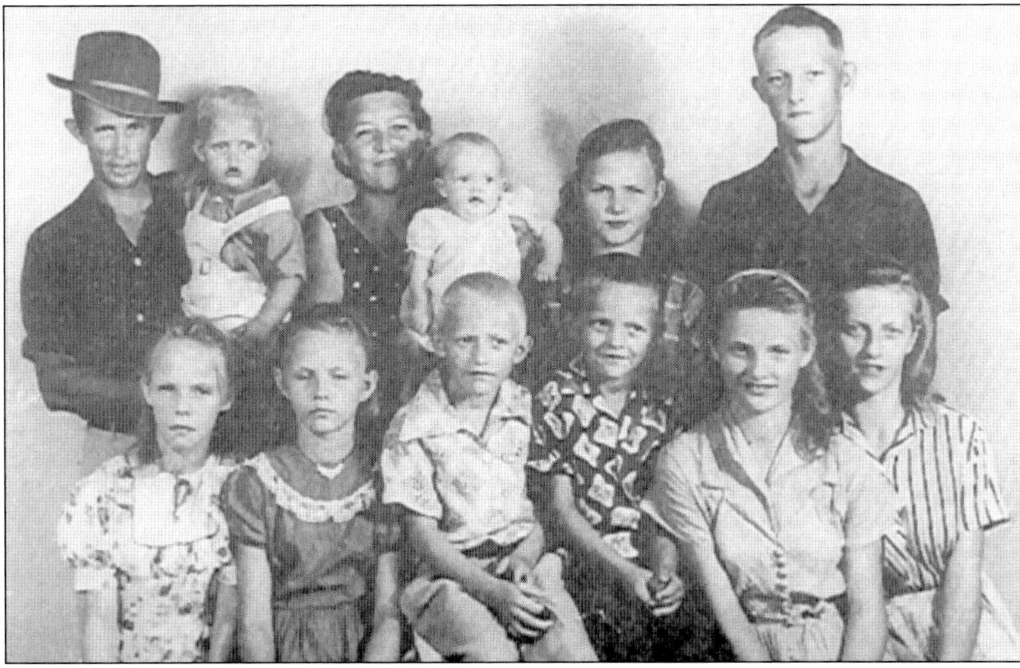

Five sets of twins and four single-birth children were born to Preston and Rosey Bell, of eastern Wayne County. Pictured from left to right are (first row) Flora and Cora, Jim and John, and Christine and Nadine; (second row) Preston holding Jessie, Rosey holding Netty, and Lena and Jack. Jessie and Netty arrived in the world unaccompanied by a twin, while twins Annie and Mary, the oldest pair, lived only a few days. Two other single-birth children died at a young age. (Wayne County Museum.)

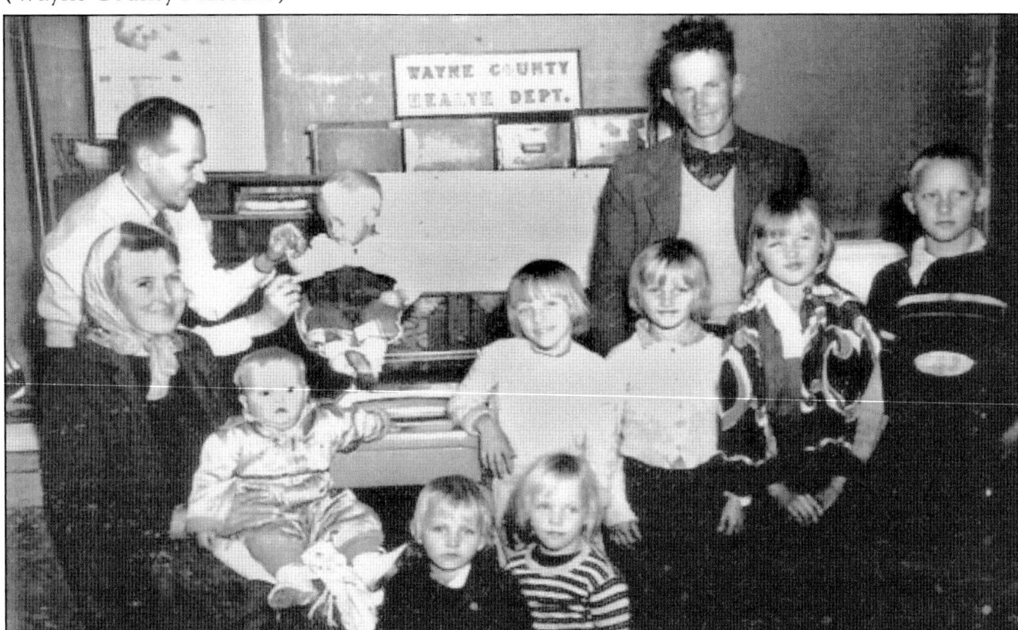

The Bell family is pictured here during a visit to the Wayne County Health Department. The children are receiving a checkup given by Dr. W. R. Kelsay. (Wayne County Museum.)

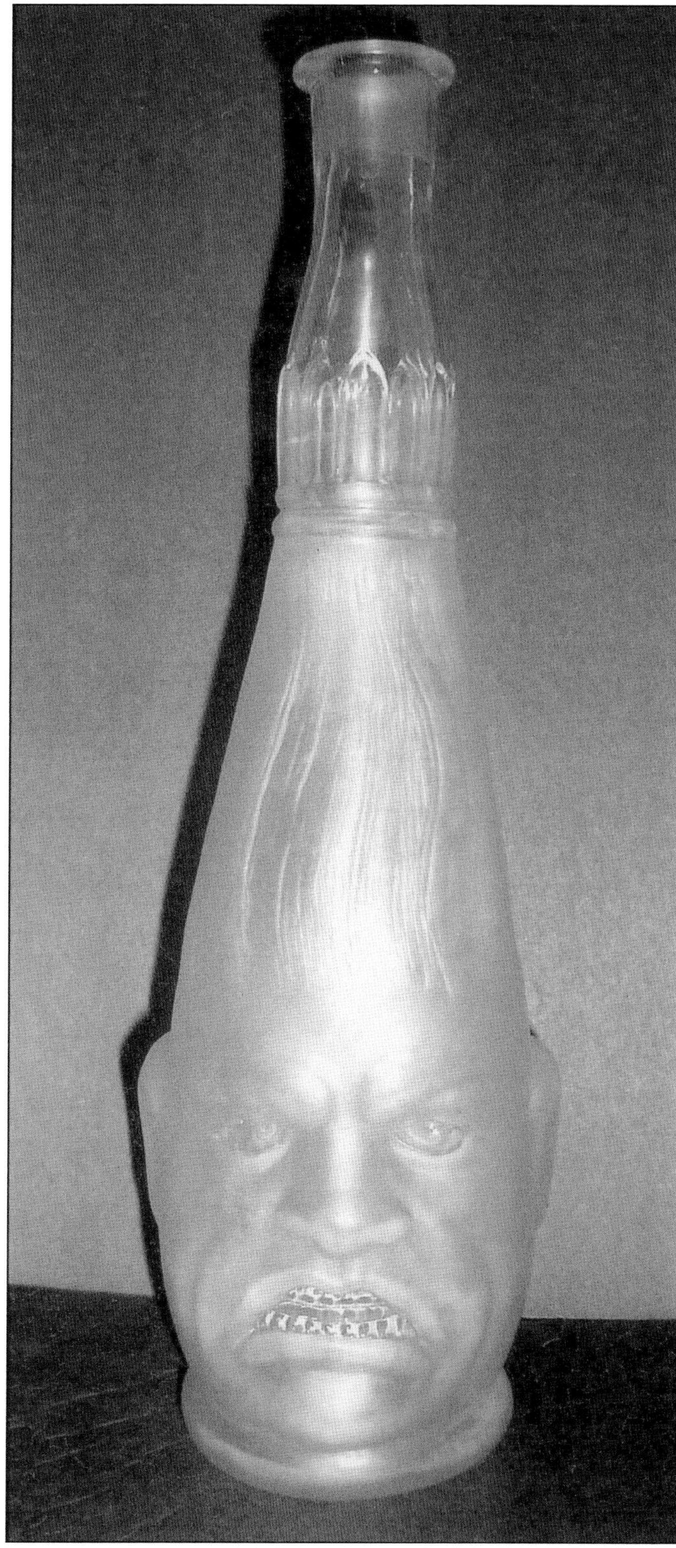

This bottle represents a special occasion in Huffaker family history. On the day George Coffey asked for Emma Huffaker's hand in marriage, he presented this bottle, filled with apricot brandy, to Emma's father, John Marion Huffaker. Consent for the marriage was given, and George and Emma were married in 1900. The Huffaker family has placed this family heirloom in the Wayne County Museum. The opposite side of the bottle features a smiling face. (Wayne County Museum.)

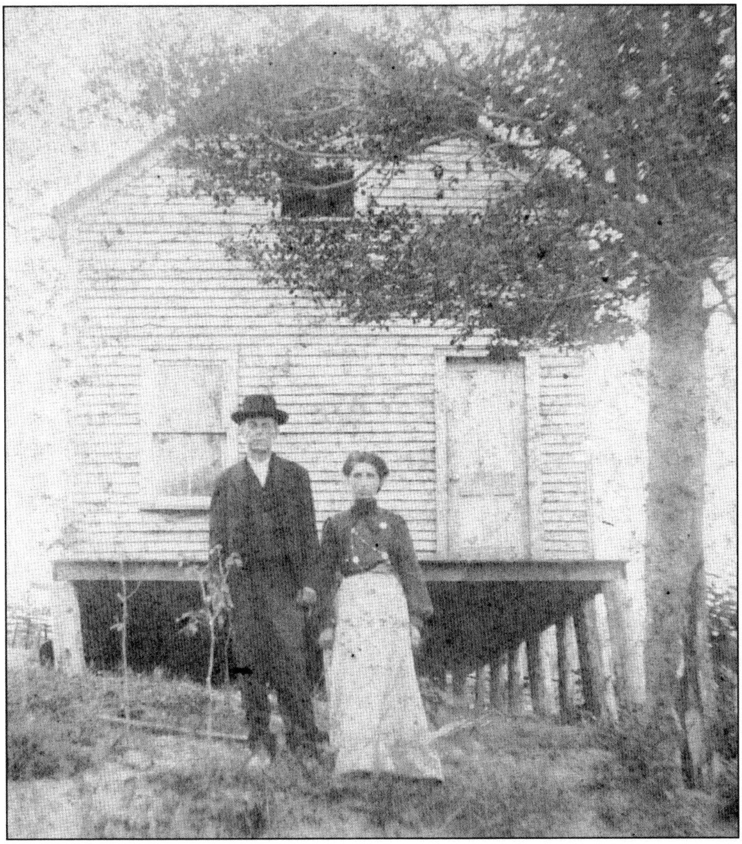

George and Emma Coffey are pictured on their wedding day in front of the old Sandusky Chapel Church in the Sumpter community. (Jacqueline Daffron.)

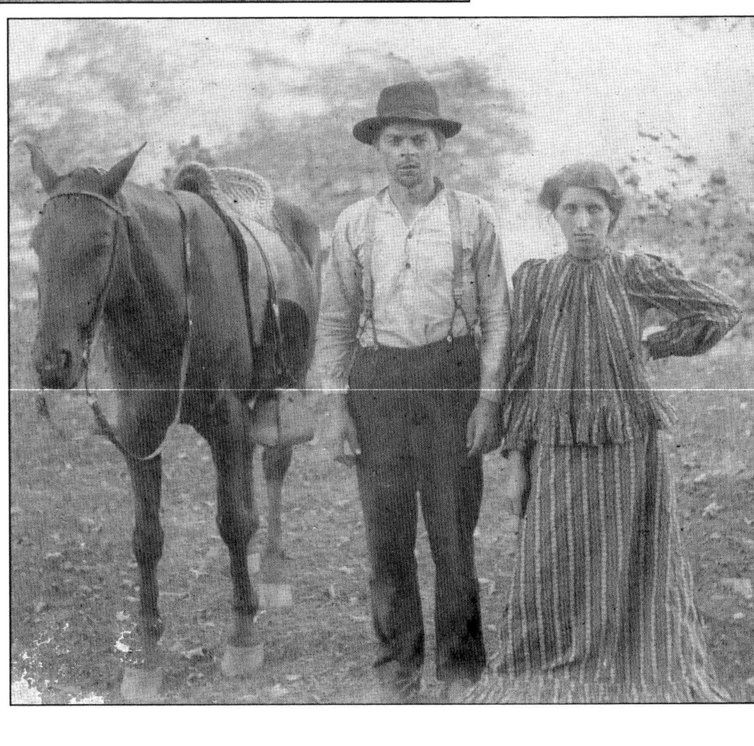

George and Emma lived in the Gibson Hollow, where George owned and operated a gasoline distillation plant. He also worked in the oil fields. (Jacqueline Daffron.)

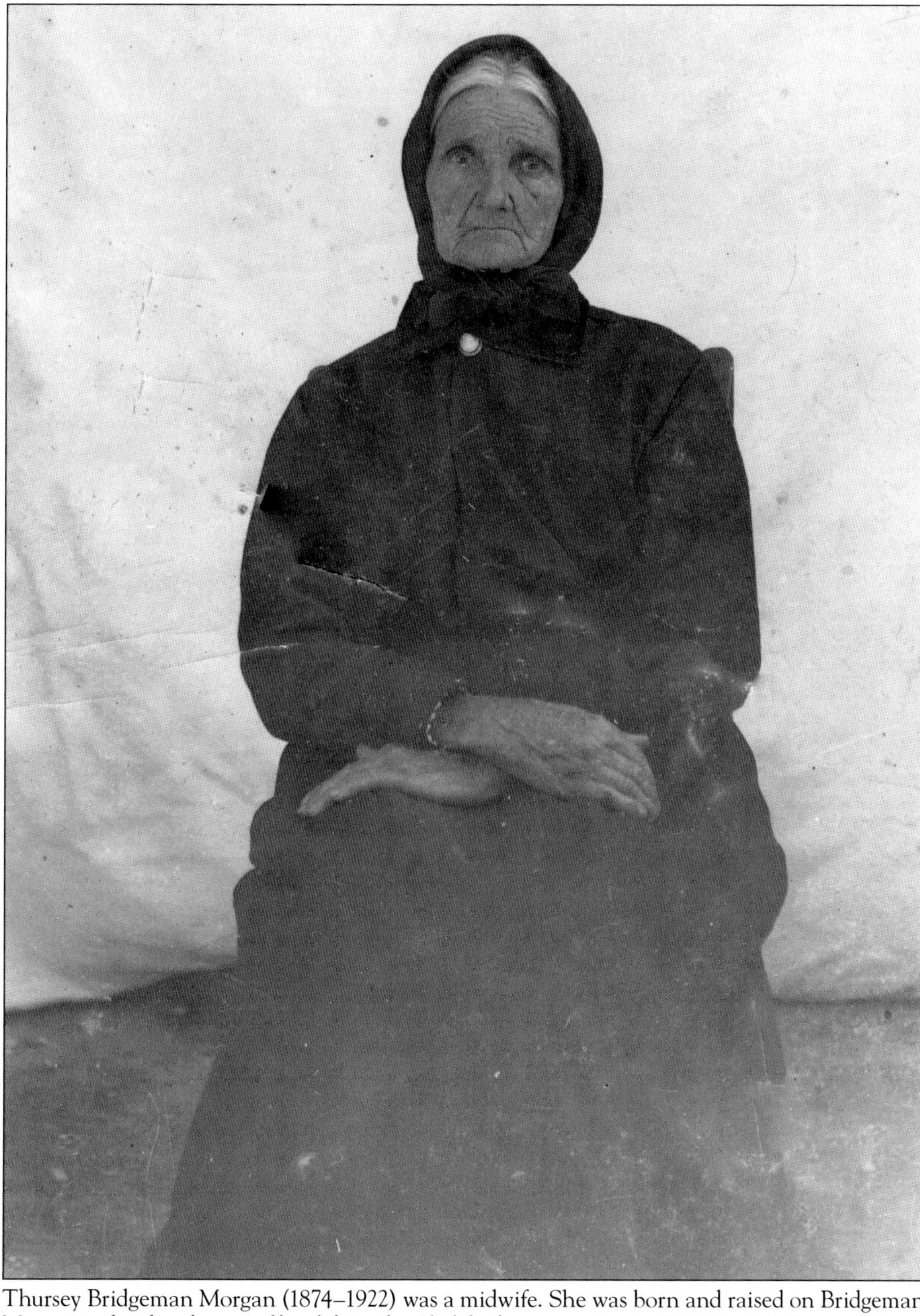

Thursey Bridgeman Morgan (1874–1922) was a midwife. She was born and raised on Bridgeman Mountain, but lived most of her life in the Slickford community. In 1917, Dr. J. F. Young, Wayne County Health Officer, reported that there were 64 midwives living and working in Wayne County who were registered in the U.S. Bureau of Vital Statistics. (Joan Abbott.)

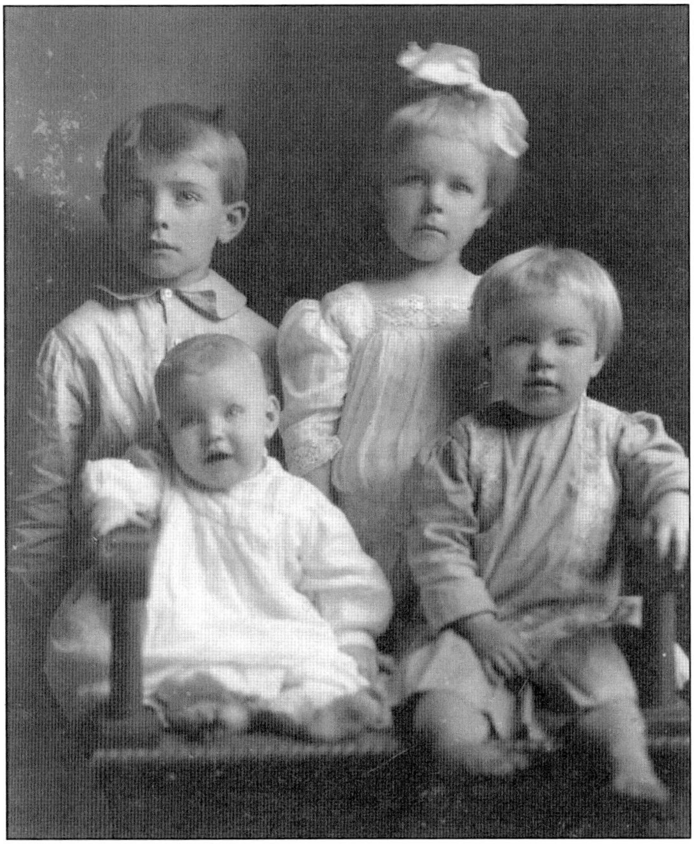

Many people came to Wayne County when the oil boom was at its height. Sterlie and Lillie K. Bertram moved here from Clinton County so that Sterlie could work as a driller. They lived in the Slickford and Mount Pisgah communities. Seen here, from left to right, are their children: (first row) Vena and Mabel; (second row) Dennis and Gladys. After Lillie's death, the family moved to the Cooper community, where Sterlie farmed and continued drilling for a time. Sterlie was later remarried to Eula Hurt, with whom he fathered eight more children. (Wade Upchurch.)

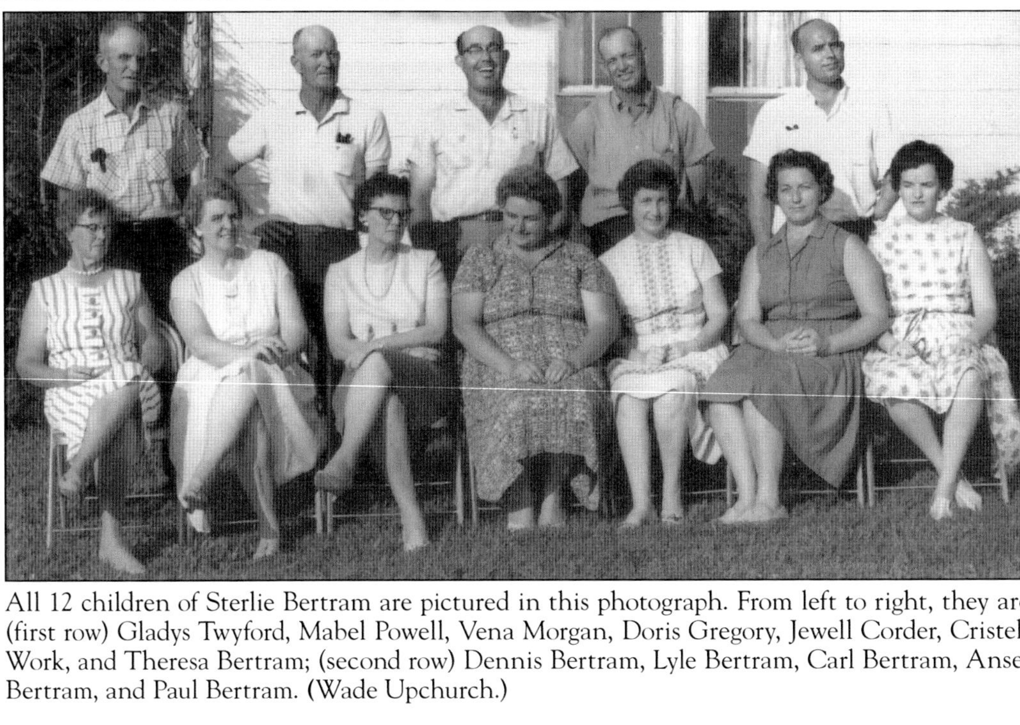

All 12 children of Sterlie Bertram are pictured in this photograph. From left to right, they are (first row) Gladys Twyford, Mabel Powell, Vena Morgan, Doris Gregory, Jewell Corder, Cristell Work, and Theresa Bertram; (second row) Dennis Bertram, Lyle Bertram, Carl Bertram, Ansel Bertram, and Paul Bertram. (Wade Upchurch.)

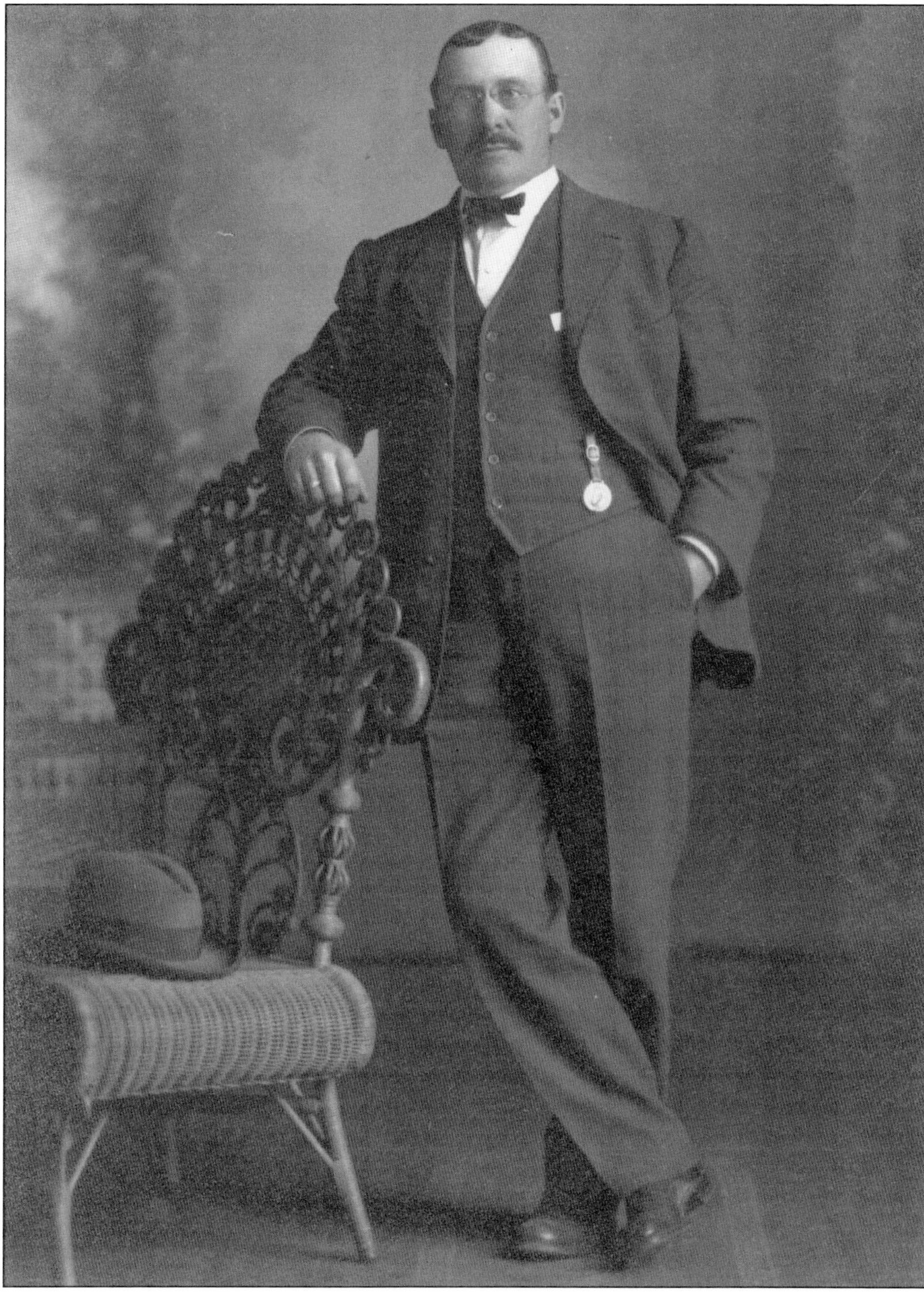

Beginning in 1919, George M. Hedrick was president of Monticello Bank for 30 years. He served during one of the toughest financial times in American history—the Great Depression. The bank withstood those years, and under Hedrick's direction, its capital skyrocketed to more than $4 million before he retired. (Bonnie Tate Carr.)

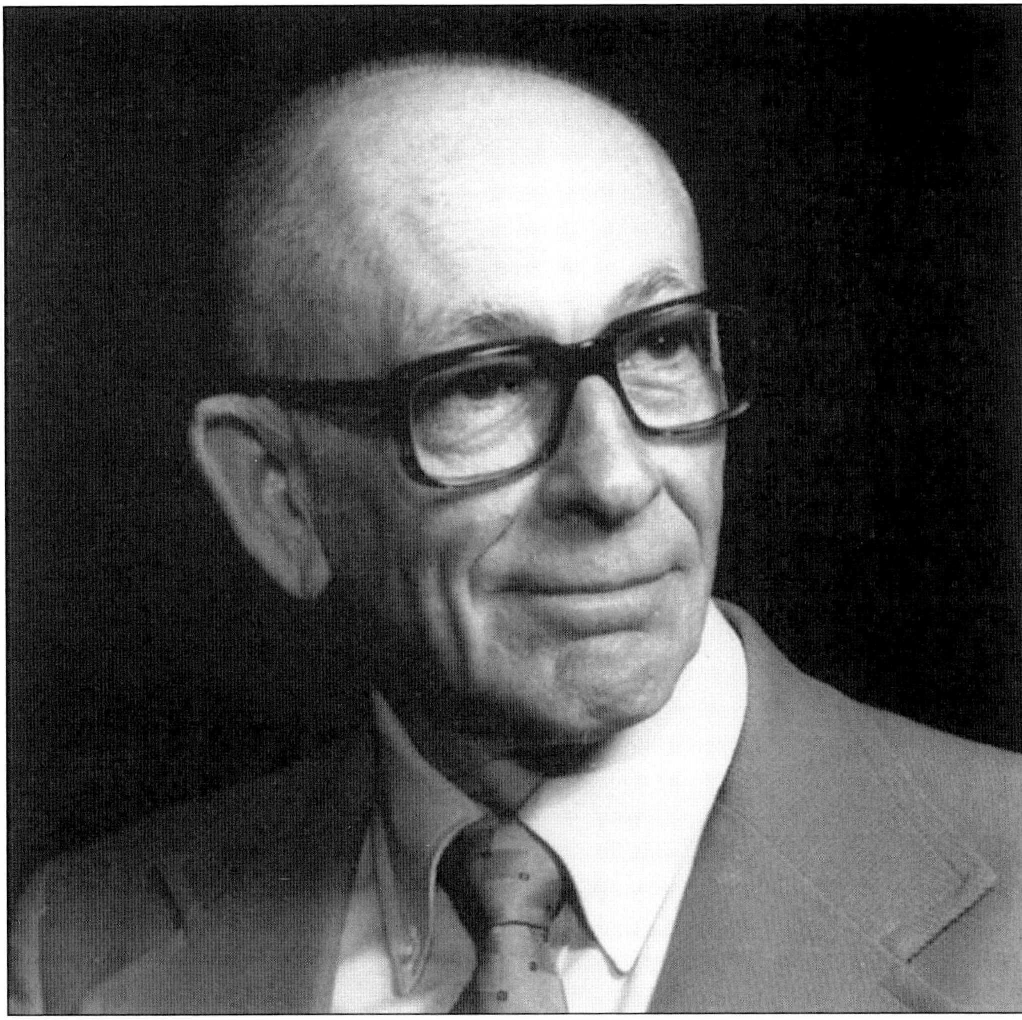

For decades, Garnett Walker (1919–2007) was a leading educator in the Wayne County School System, serving in several capacities and concluding with 17 years as the first principal of Wayne County Elementary I (the Walker Building). He was admired and respected by the children who were educated in that building, even by those who had to "sit under the dinner bell." Walker was also known for his in-depth knowledge of local history and for his ability as a Bible-study teacher. (Wayne County Museum.)

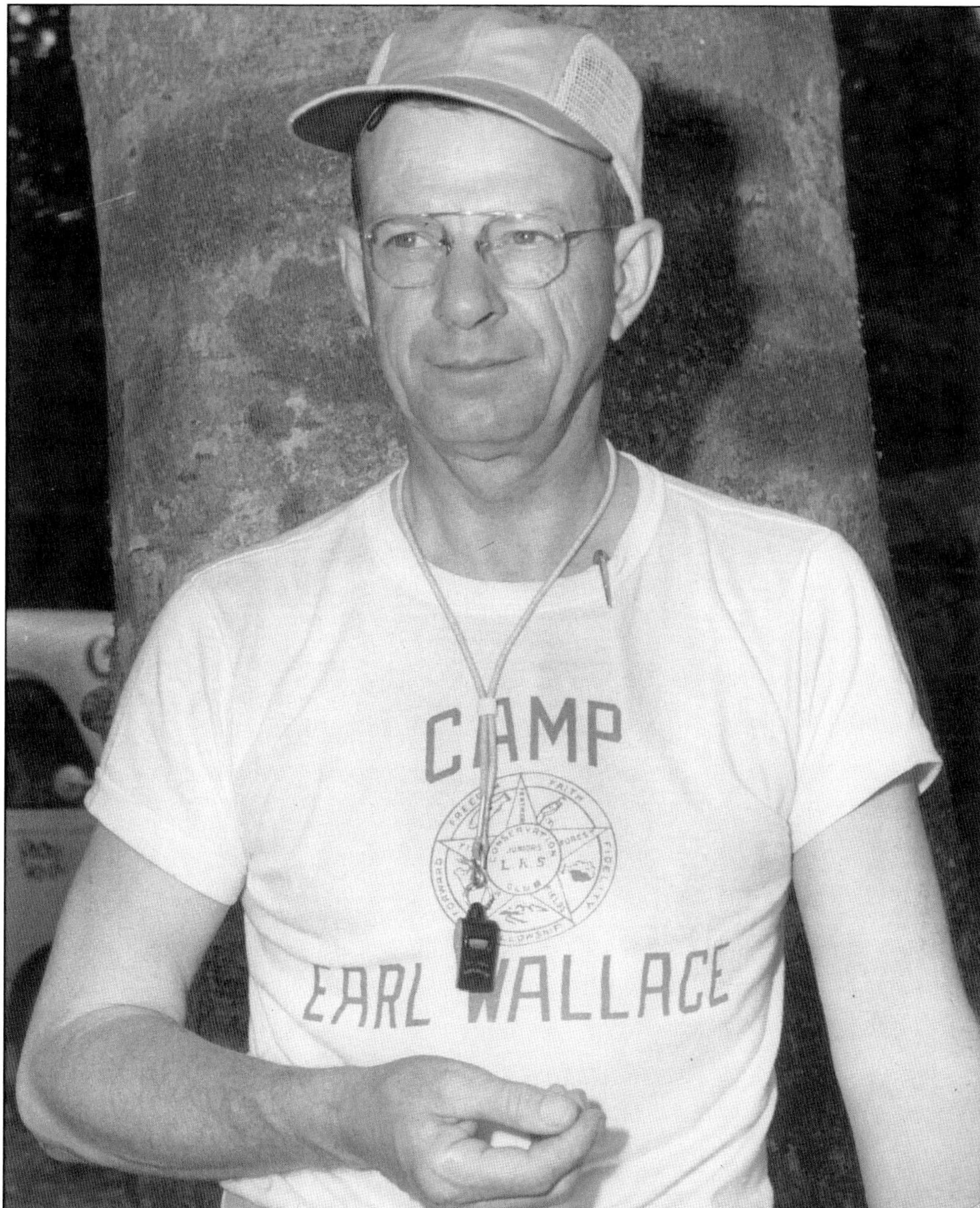

Raymond O. "Casey" Cook is remembered as a man who contributed much to community life. Because he was deeply interested in seeing young people become conservationists, he was instrumental in bringing the Junior Conservation Camp Earl Wallace to Wayne County. He was counselor at the camp for a number of years. Situated on beautiful Lake Cumberland, this camp still hums with activity every summer as boys and girls have lots of fun while learning valuable conservation lessons. (Dr. Robert B. Breeding.)

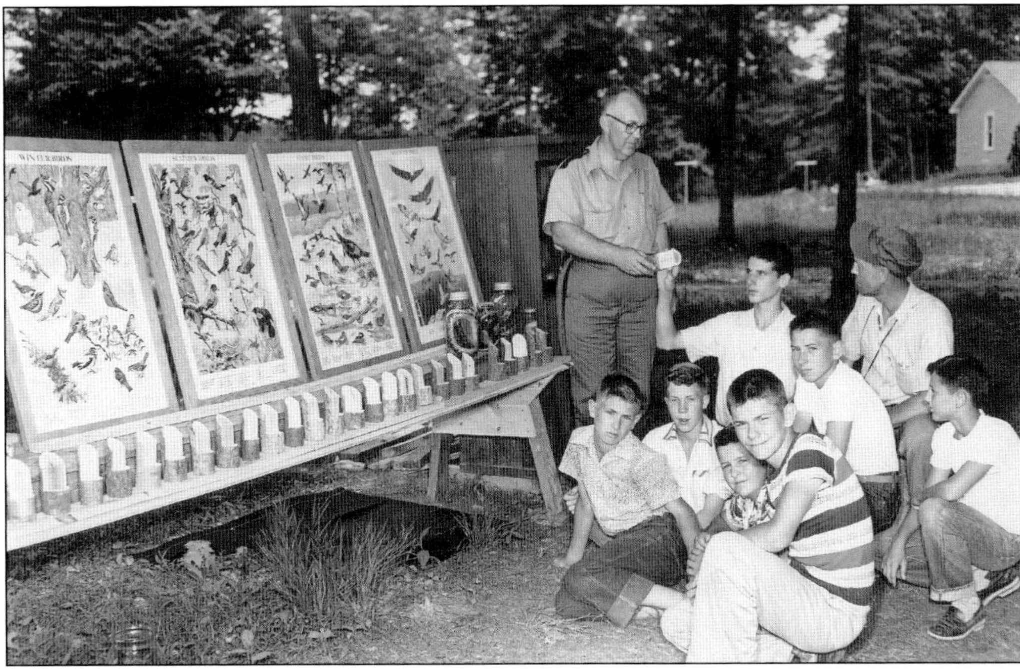

Camp Earl Wallace, which opened in 1951, is operated by the Kentucky Fish and Wildlife Agency. Wendell Dalton worked at the camp for 25 years. As camp director, he immersed himself in the program and became a fountain of knowledge about nature study, outdoor survival skills, and the many other aspects of the Junior Conservation Program. He was passionate about the lessons the youth needed to learn and had a rare ability to communicate those lessons to them. (Mildred Dalton.)

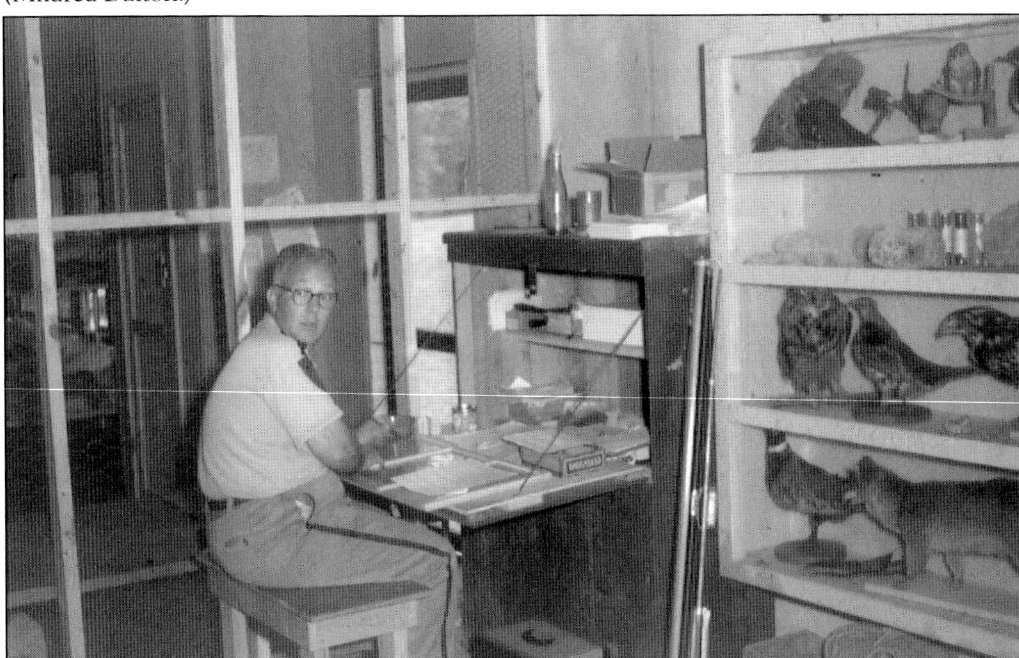

Wendell Dalton is shown here in his office at Camp Earl Wallace. (Mildred Dalton.)

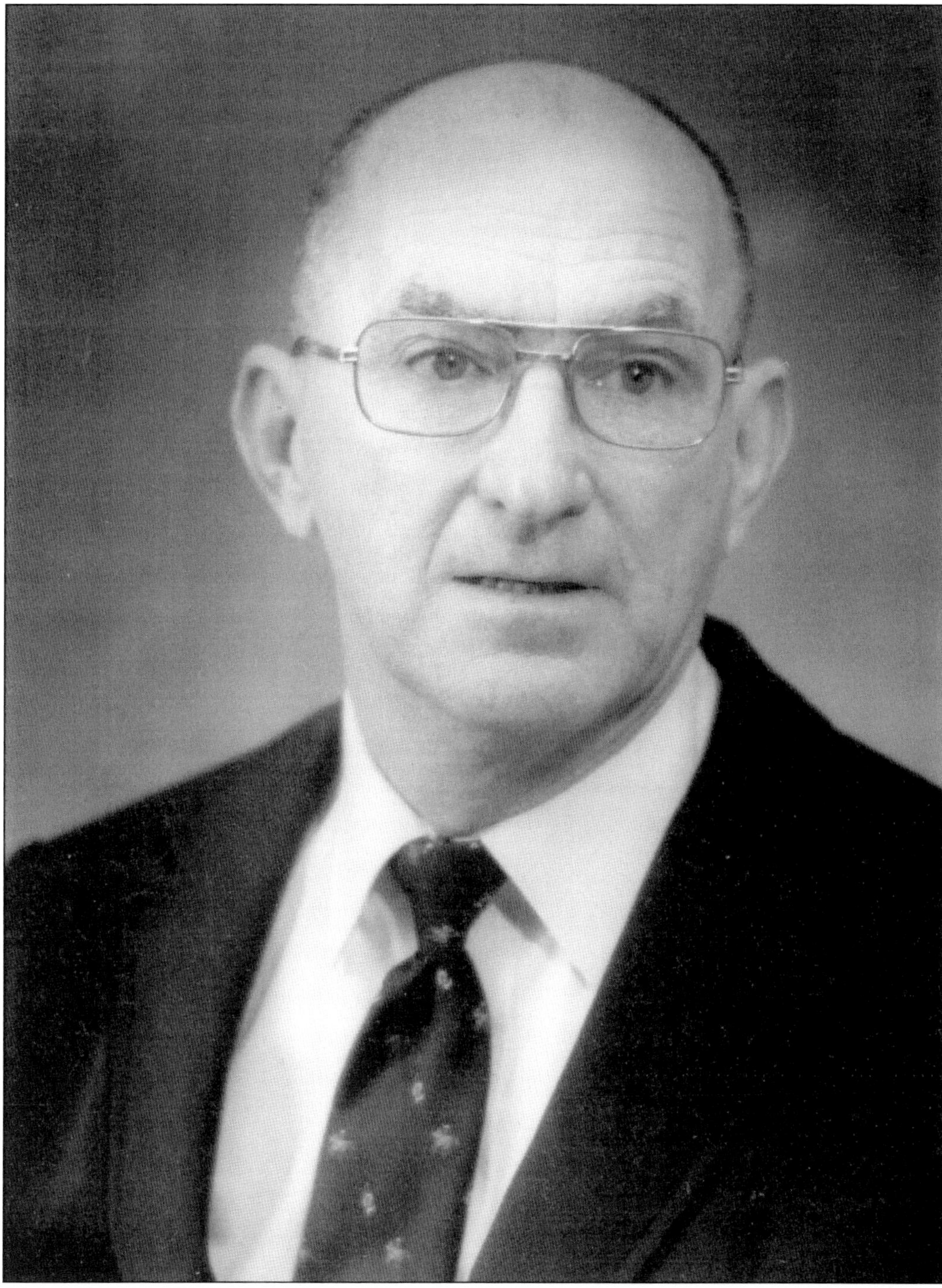

John Rickett was the Wayne County 4-H agent from 1960 until 1990. A native of Whitley County, Rickett became very involved in community life in Wayne County, giving special attention and effort to the Monticello Church of Christ, the Boy Scouts, the Library Board, the Fair Board, and, of course, the 4-H program. With his unassuming manner, Rickett has been a great influence for good in Wayne County. (Wayne County Cooperative Extension Office.)

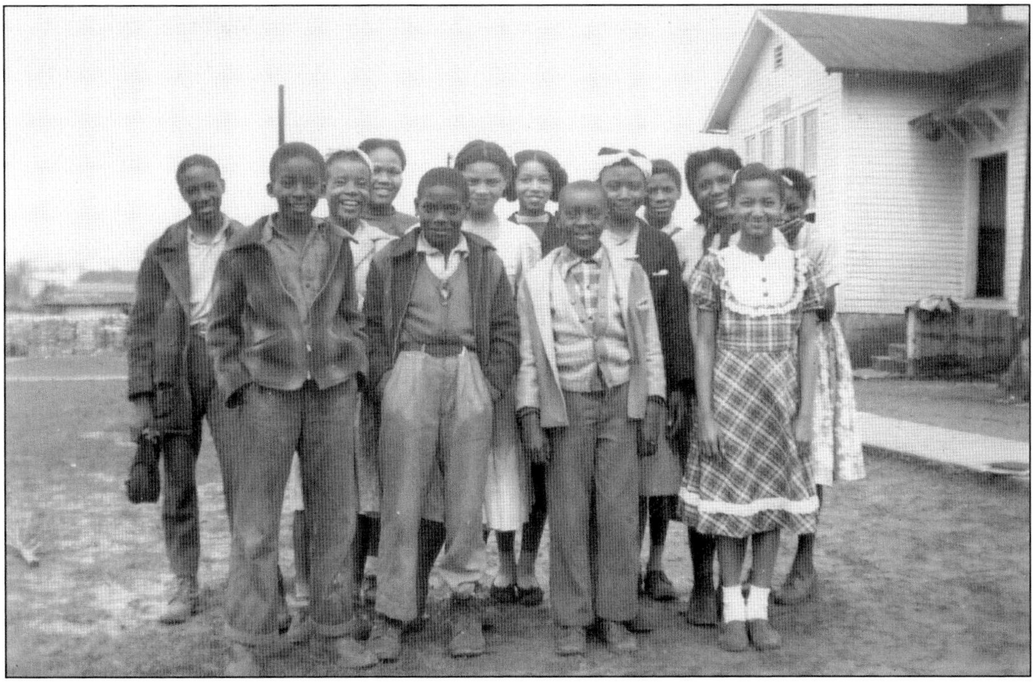

The first Wayne County 4-H clubs began in the 1920s. With their practical hands-on approach to life skills and their emphasis upon the development of good citizenship, leadership, and character, 4-H clubs have been of immense benefit to countless young people. A Travis School 4-H club is shown here. (Melvin Jones.)

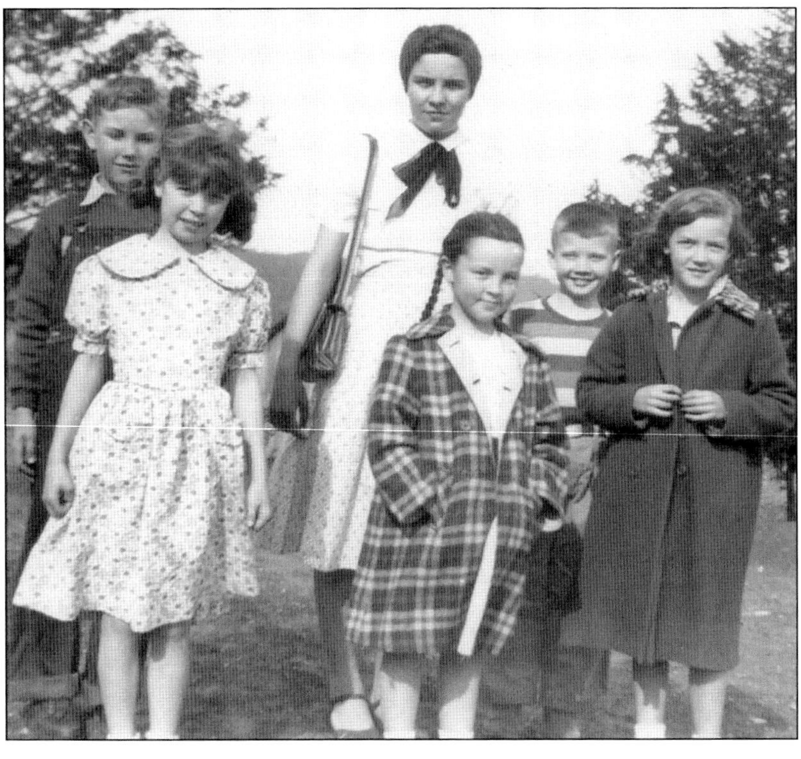

Pictured here are the members of the Oil Valley School 4-H club. From left to right, they are John Reed Keeton, Jewell Perkins, Nancy Abbott, Howard Roberts, and Joyce Keeton. The club's advisor is unidentified. (Abbott family.)

In the early 1900s, the Joseph and Amelia Marcum Shadoan family operated a major business center in the Frazer community. This consisted of a general merchandise store that also served as a post office, barbershop, and voting place. Near the store, Joseph operated a gristmill, slaughterhouse, and sawmill. The store burned in 1942, but the two-story brick house they built beside it still stands today. He also operated a store in the Bill Wray building on Main Street in Monticello and was part owner of Shadoan-Lee Undertaking Company. A leader in the community, Joseph would help a neighbor clear a field for the planting of crops, teach a good Sunday school lesson, or buy whatever mules, hides, hogs, chickens, eggs, feathers, or walnuts his neighbors needed to sell. (Wayne County Historical Society.)

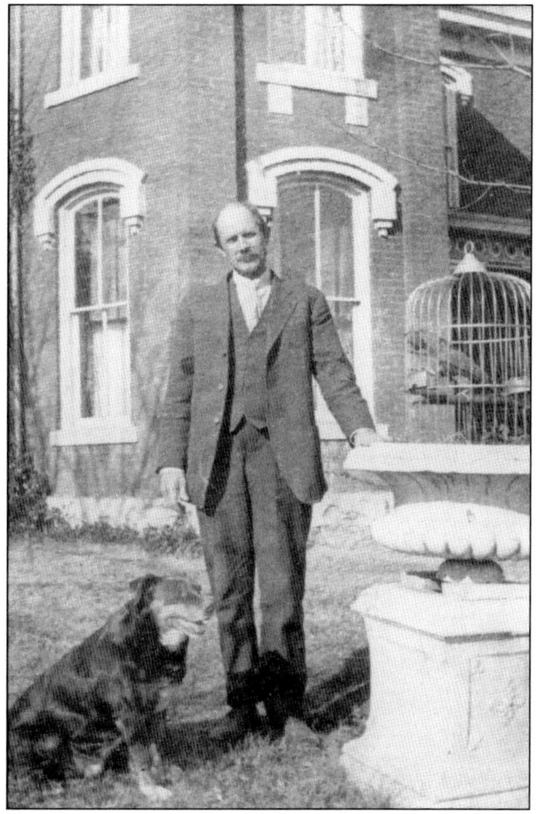

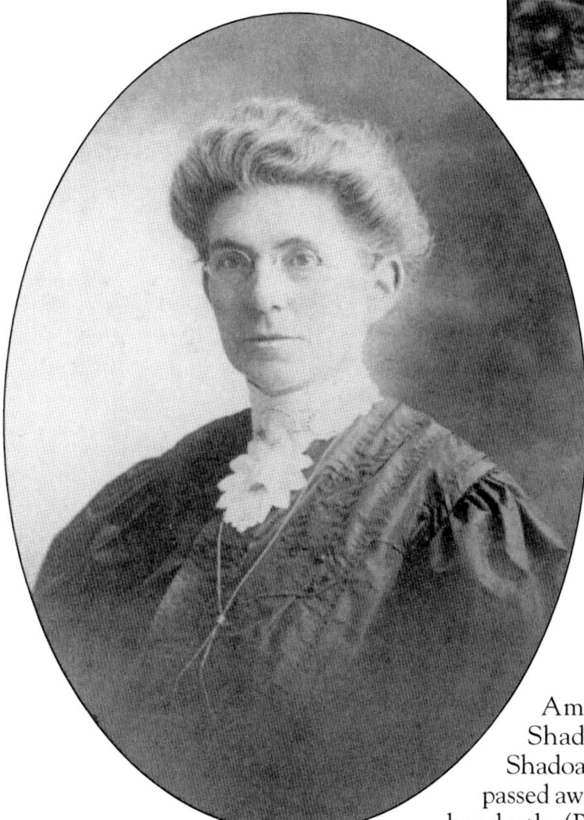

Amelia Marcum Shadoan, wife of Joseph Shadoan, continued to live in the beautiful Shadoan home for some years after her husband passed away. She proudly maintained the home until her death. (Bob Lee.)

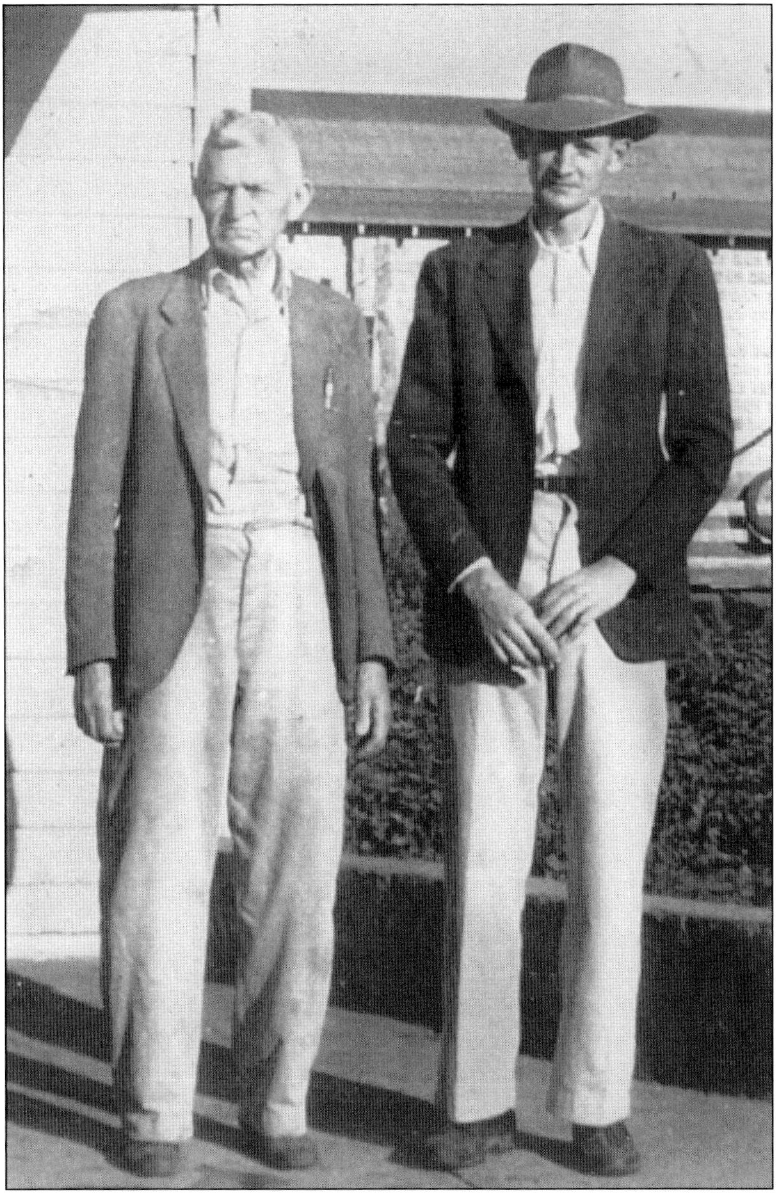

Father and son Sam Rankin and Howard Rankin were extraordinary businessmen and leading citizens of Monticello. Sam operated a number of businesses. In addition to a mill, he owned two stores and ran a freight house from which cargo was hauled back and forth to Burnside. In 1929, the 16-year-old Howard's career as a grocer began when he and friend Paul Gehring bought a pig and slaughtered it. From the corner of the freight house, they sold the meat for 20¢ a pound. This photograph was taken on South Main Street with the corner of Howard's first store building and his slaughterhouse visible in the background. In 1947, Howard built a brick building for a grocery store. This business flourished and changed with the times until it closed in 2008. Because of Howard's remarkable memory and his involvement in so many facets of community life, he was frequently sought out to answer local history questions. Always passionate about politics, he served as Wayne County judge from 1950 to 1954 and served on the Monticello City Council for 33 years. (Howard Rankin.)

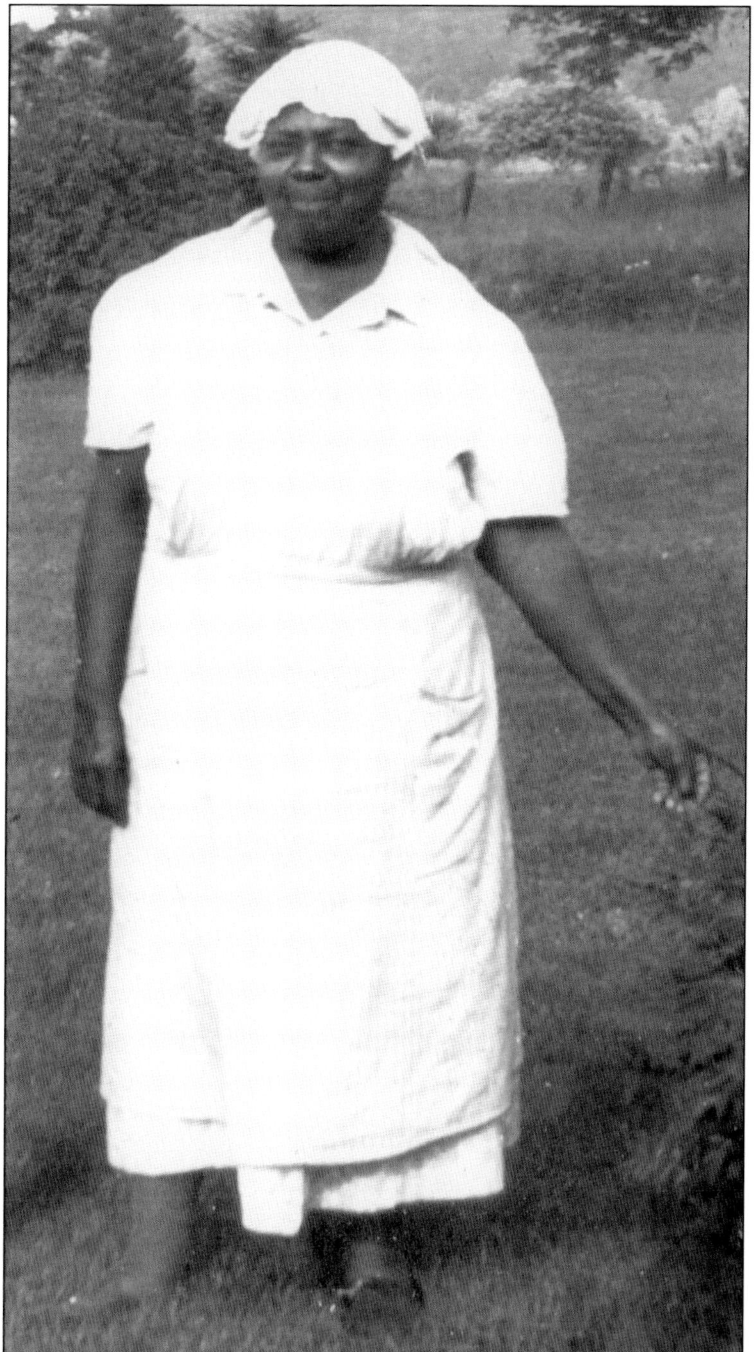

Sallie Redman (1882–1970) was part of the Burton-Breeding family for three generations. The 1910 census records indicate that the Charles H. Burton family was living on North Main Street and that Sallie Redman, a cook, was part of the household. Later, Burton's daughter, Carrie, married Robert G. Breeding, and at some point, Sallie became part of that household. She cared for the children and was very much part of the family. She lived the rest of her life with the Breedings, and they took care of her and provided for her during her declining years. (Dr. Robert G. Breeding.)

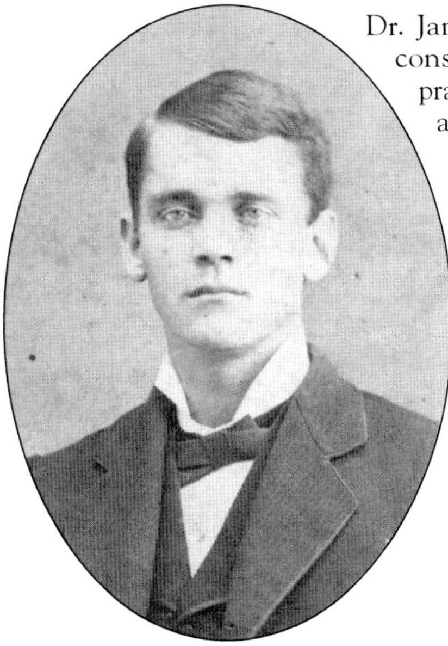

Dr. James Franklin Young (1858–1931) was for many years considered the best-educated person in the county. Young practiced medicine for 40 years in Wayne County and worked as the county's first health officer. During both the Spanish-American War and World War I, he examined men for military service. (Wayne County Museum.)

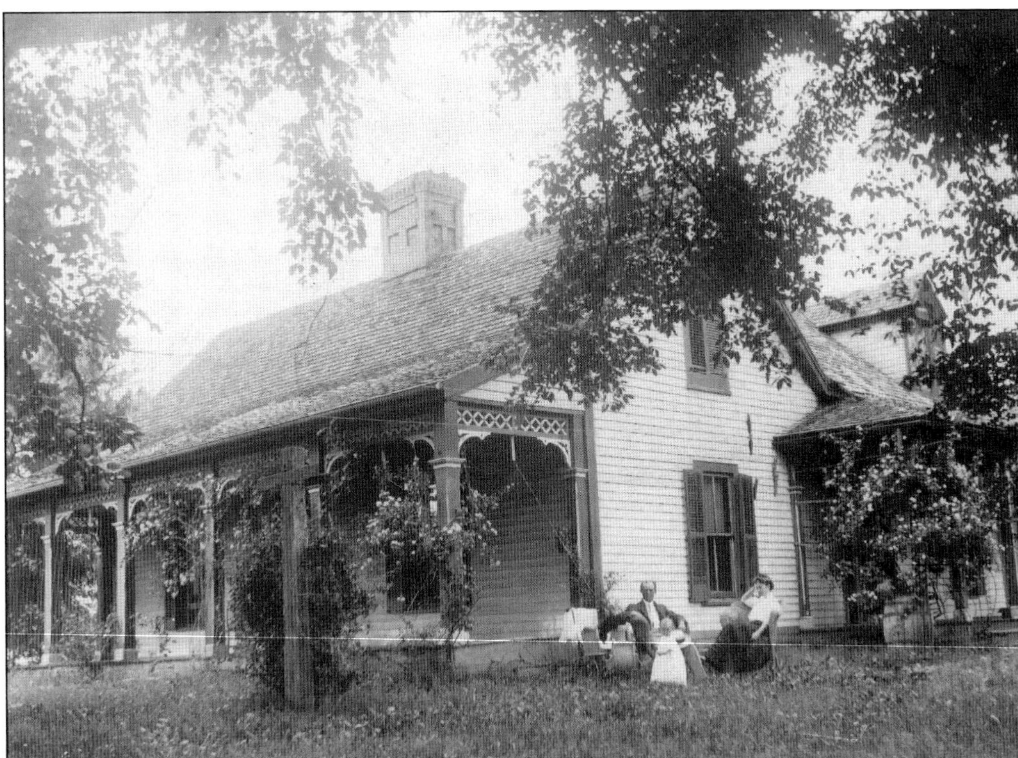

The members of the Wayne County medical profession have always distinguished themselves in the capable practice of medicine. Many qualified physicians have moved into the community and established thriving practices. Just after the Civil War, Dr. J. A. Jones moved from Lincoln County into the Mill Springs area. Two of his sons, Dr. Claude Jones and Dr. Theo Jones, also became physicians. This *c.* 1907 photograph was taken at the Jones home at Mill Springs. (Wayne County Museum.)

Lula Sandusky Duncan (1884–1978) had childhood memories of guiding a plow pulled by a team of oxen, of swinging an ax to cut firewood, and of walking 5 miles a day to attend school. Lula became a teacher. During 15 years as an educator, she taught at Frazer, Mill Springs, Monticello, Wray Hill, Dogwood, and Collett's Hill. She married John Duncan, and the couple became the parents of nine children. For eight years, without missing a day, she drove a horse and buggy to carry the U.S. Mail from Monticello to Frisby. In 1969, at the age of 73, Duncan fulfilled a dream when she graduated from the Chicago School of Nursing. For the next 10 years, she worked as a nurse. Her life was an amazing journey. (Duncan family.)

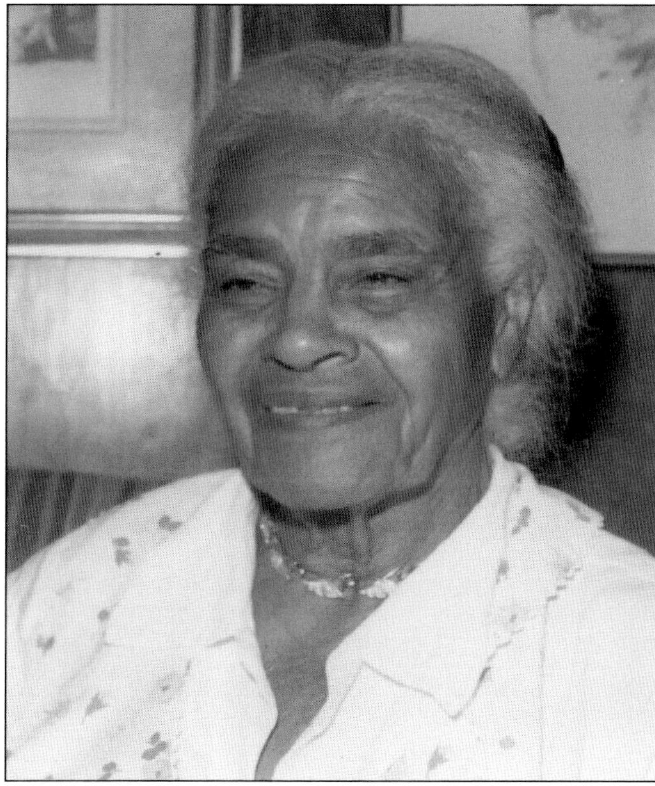

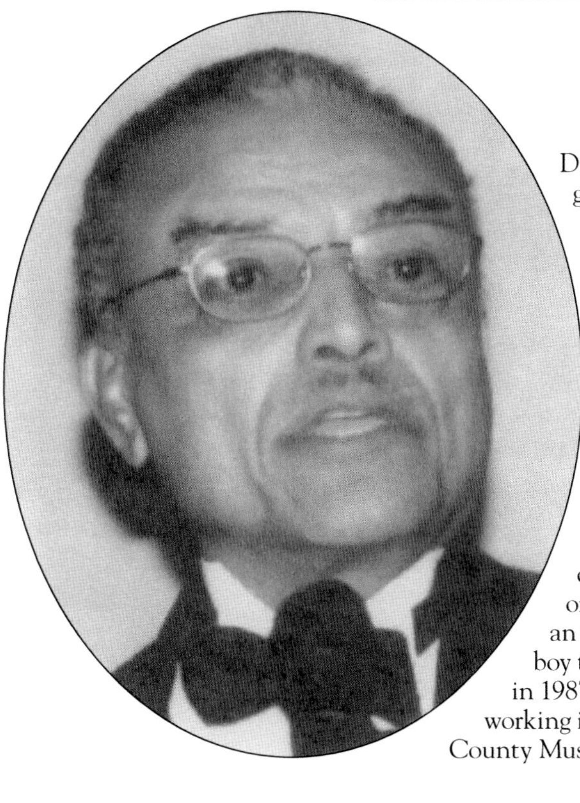

Dr. Thomas J. Craft was born in 1924 and grew up on Vine Street in Monticello. As a child, he worked hard delivering milk and milk products for the family business, the Craft Dairy. A strong work ethic combined with an insatiable desire to learn took him through all of the academic steps to the top of his chosen profession—developmental biology. He received his Ph.D. in 1963. Craft's research involved transplants, skin grafts, and the problem of graft rejection. As he worked in the laboratories, classrooms, and on administrative staffs of various colleges and universities, he also focused on helping young African Americans achieve an education. Having risen from milk delivery boy to nationally known scientist, Craft retired in 1987 and now lives in Ohio, spending his time working in a number of volunteer positions. (Wayne County Museum.)

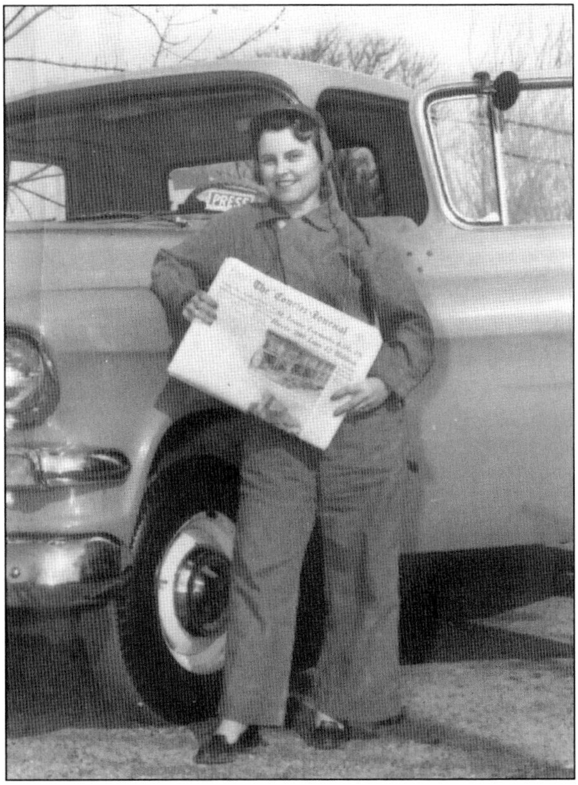

Perhaps it was the tug of adventure that led Katy Lou Rector at age 22 to become the first female "paperboy" that the *Courier Journal* ever employed, but it was a love of the job and a strong work ethic that kept her delivering papers for 41 years. (Wayne County Historical Society.)

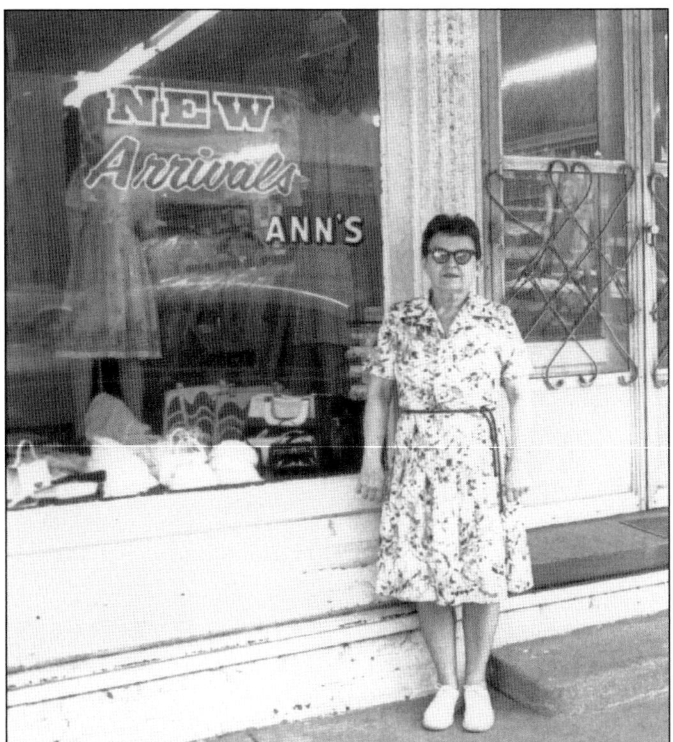

Another part of Katy Lou Rector's life revolved around Ann's Ladies' and Children's Apparel, which she owned and managed for 30 years. From 1927 until it closed in 1993, Ann's was a part of the business scene in Monticello. (Wayne County Historical Society.)

Tom Ragan became the first Standard Oil agent in Wayne County and built the Standard Oil Bulk Plant on North Main Street in Monticello around 1927. Ragan also had the Ford Dealership and built a new concrete building on Short Street (now East Columbia Avenue) for that business in 1920. At the time, it was one of the finest and largest in this part of the state. As of 2010, both structures he built for his businesses were still standing. (Katy Lou Rector.)

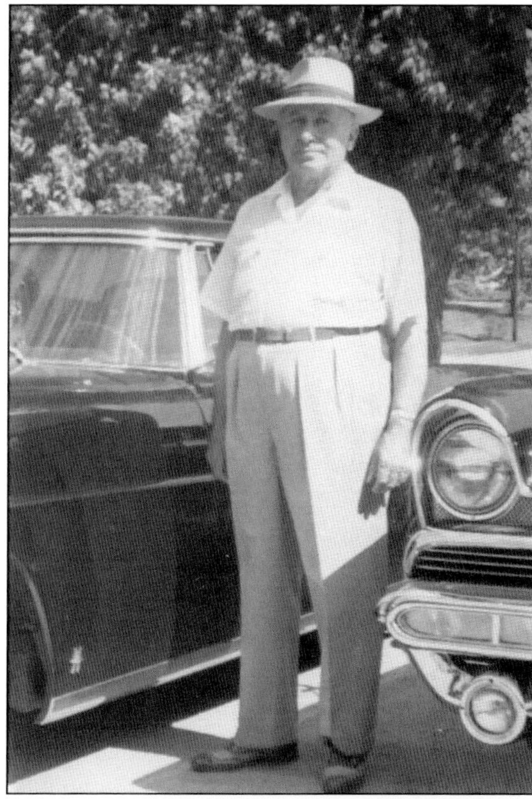

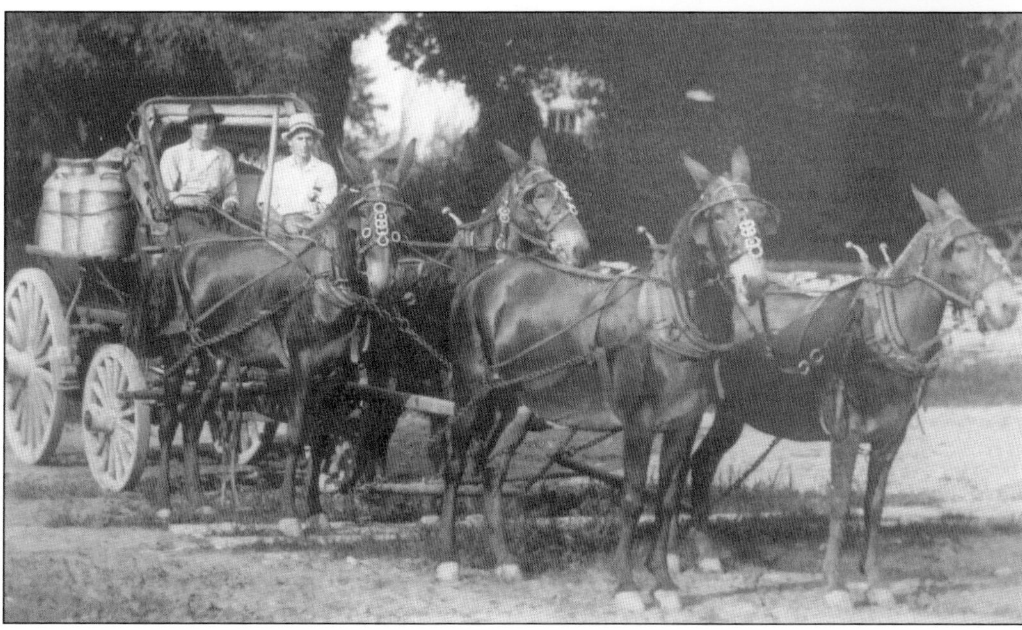

As a young man, Tom Ragan began his career with Standard Oil Company by making two-day runs to and from Burnside. The vehicle shown here, drawn by four mules, carried mostly kerosene. When the Model T Ford came on the scene, the demand for gasoline brought changes. Ragan was soon pulling a tank wagon, which held 715 gallons. (Katy Lou Rector.)

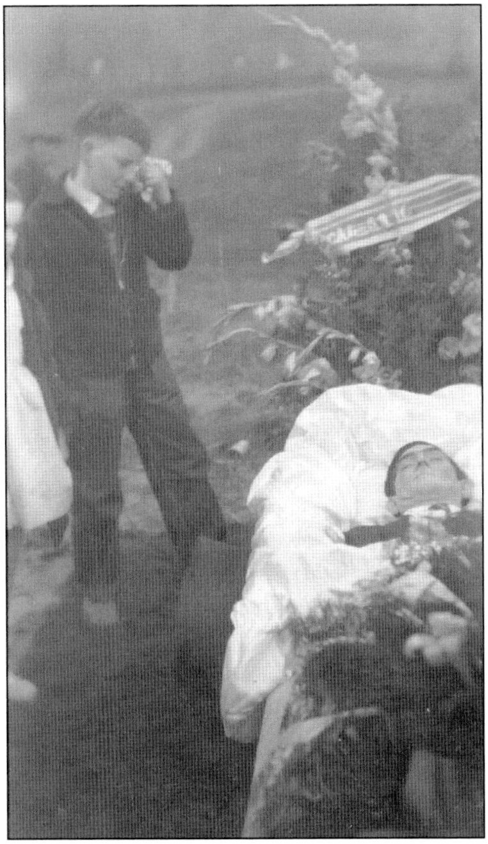

Life has always had its difficulties and hard times. The people of Wayne County certainly faced their share of hard times. Lorenzo Dow Guffey of Wayne County was working in a coal mine in Hazard and became trapped, resulting in his death. When he was buried, his family gathered around his casket and wept at their loss. In this 1941 photograph, his son, Hayden Guffey, expresses his sorrow at the grave site. (Herlan Dalton Guffey.)

When a person died, the community joined together to lend a helping hand. Food was prepared, daily chores were assumed by others, and neighbors would undertake many of the preparations for burial. This could include the making of a casket or coffin. When Kate Denney died, her body was placed in such a coffin. This photographic essay shows the honor her family had for her as they lovingly laid her to rest in one of the many cemeteries in Wayne County. (Wayne County Museum.)

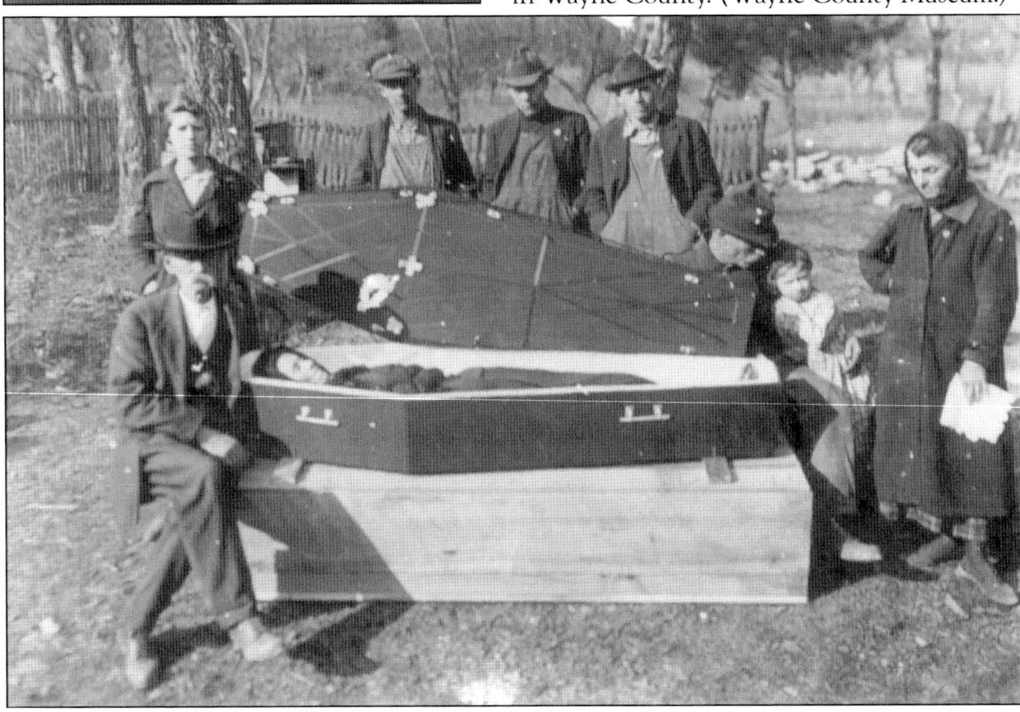

Eight

Recent Past

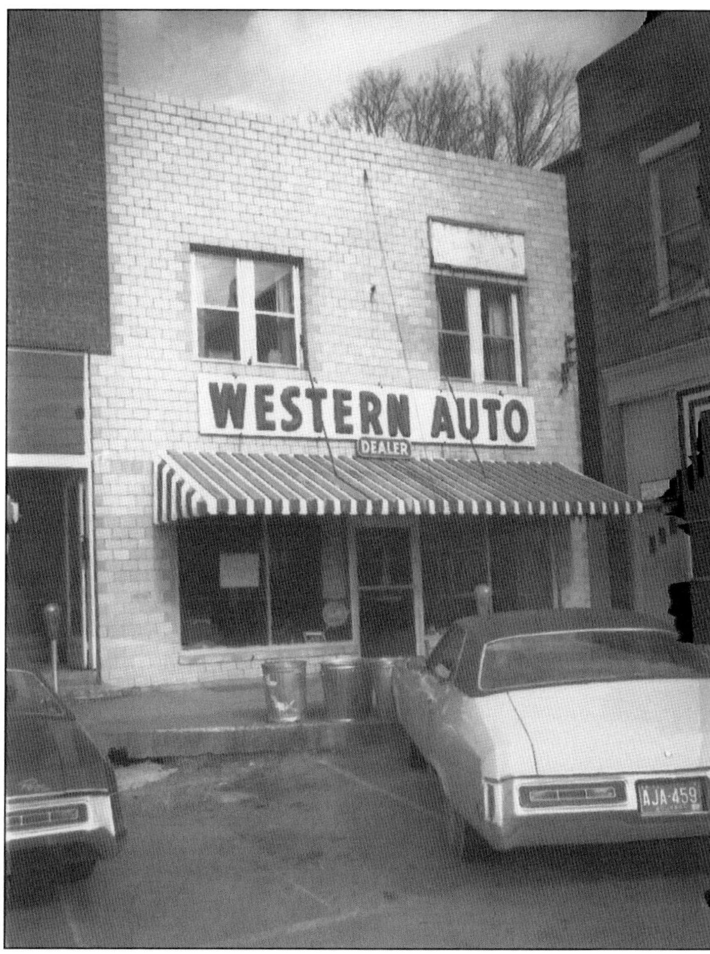

For two generations the Anderson family owned the Western Auto firm in Monticello. In 1944, when the firm was located in one of the street-level units of Hotel Breeding, Elmer Anderson took over the store. In 1946, he built the structure shown here on the public square, and for 29 years, this building housed Western Auto. Elmer's son, Drexell, worked with him in the store, and his daughter, Jo Ann, ran a beauty shop on the second floor. In 1975, Drexell built a new building for Western Auto on Kendrick Avenue. In 2010, the Monticello Police Department is located in this building. (J. D. Rogers.)

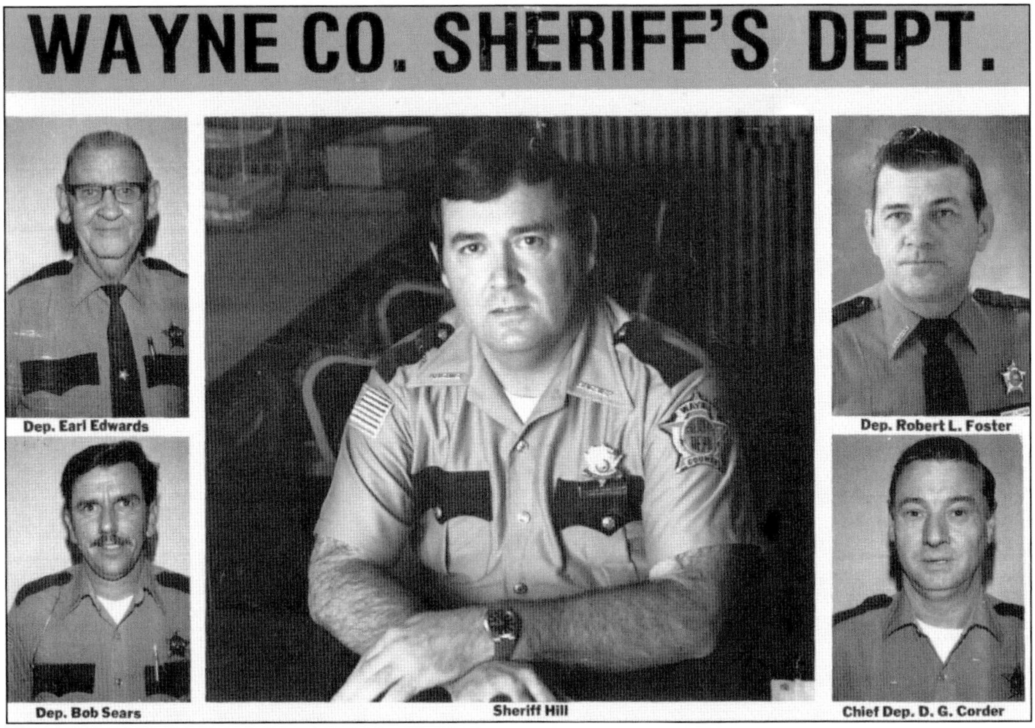

Sheriff Hill holds a special place in the history of law enforcement in Wayne County. His common sense, his determination to do what was right, his courage in the face of attempts on his life, and his dedication to the safety and welfare of Wayne County residents endeared him to local people. Wayne County citizens elected him five times to office. Sheriff Hill's bullet-riddled uniform, his picture, and newspaper articles are on display at Carbo's Police Museum in Pigeon Forge, Tennessee. (Wayne County Museum.)

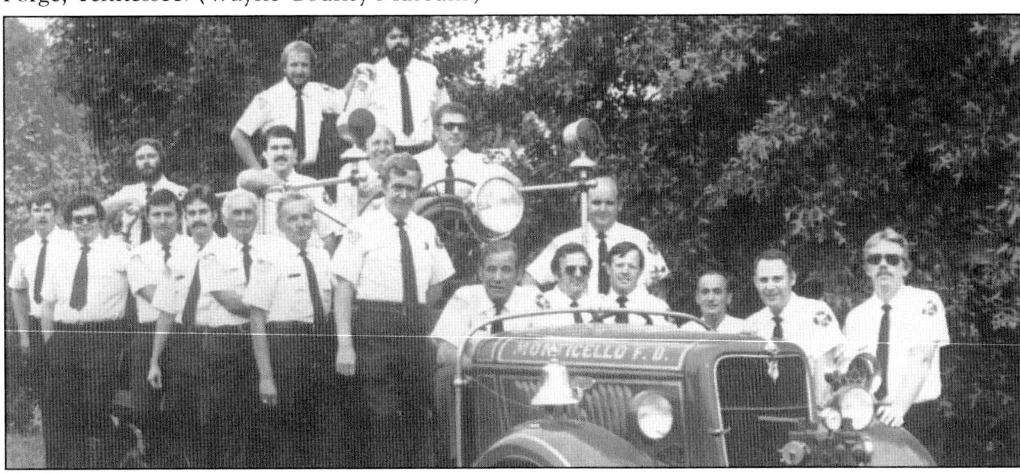

Pictured in this 1983 Monticello Fire Department image are Mike Anderson, Ray Chesney Dellard Duvall, Henderson Eads Jr., Steve Ferrell (fire chief in 2010), Joe Gibson, Dana Gibson, James Gibson, Glen Hickey, Forrest Hicks, Danny Guffey, Jack Lair, John McAlpin, Alan Richardson, Aaron Stringer, Bruce Turner, and Bill Upchurch. Also pictured are four men who joined the department in 1951: Brook Gibson (became fire chief that year), Drexell Anderson, Earl Sexton, and Maurice Worsham. (Wayne County Museum.)

Dr. Eben Bayard Rice lived on North Main Street and maintained a small hospital behind his home. He was mayor of Monticello from 1934 to 1937. He owned and operated Monticello's first airport, a 65-acre facility with a 2,000-foot runway. This was considered one of the best privately owned airports in the state. The day it was dedicated in 1934 was a big day for Wayne County. About 6,000 people thronged the streets of Monticello and gathered at the airport to watch a parade, take $2 plane rides, see airplanes perform intricate loops, and witness more parachute jumps than they had ever seen. (Wayne County Historical Society.)

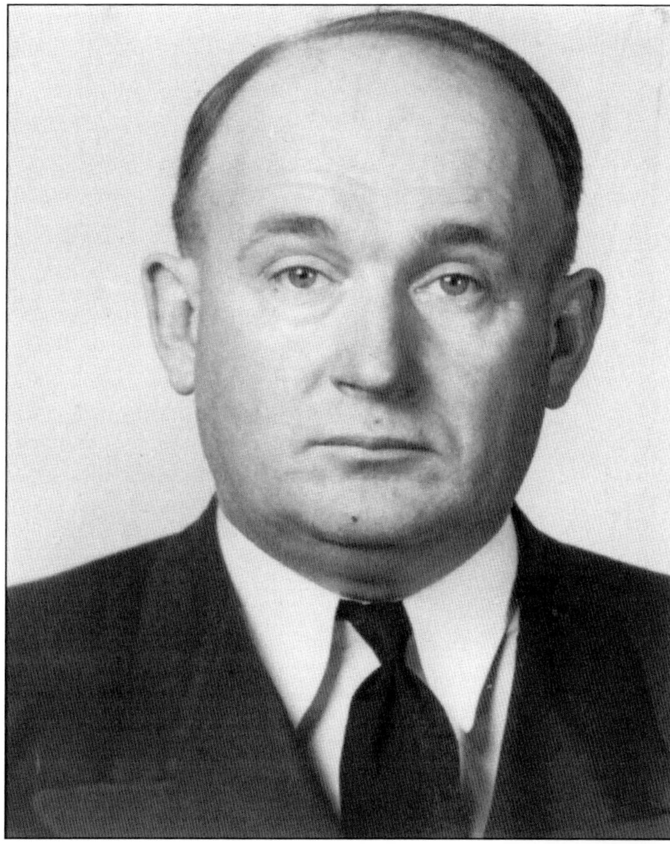

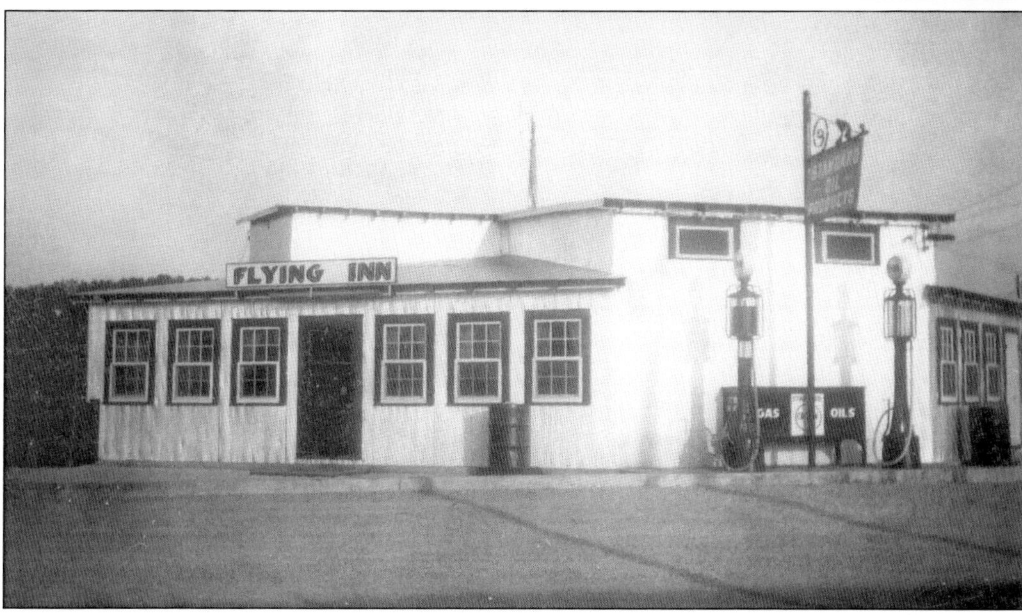

The Flying Inn once stood at the edge of the E. B. Rice Airport. Over the years this building at the first airport was used as an airplane hangar, a restaurant, a nightclub, and a meeting place for countless groups. In 1990, it was destroyed by fire. (Wayne County Historical Society.)

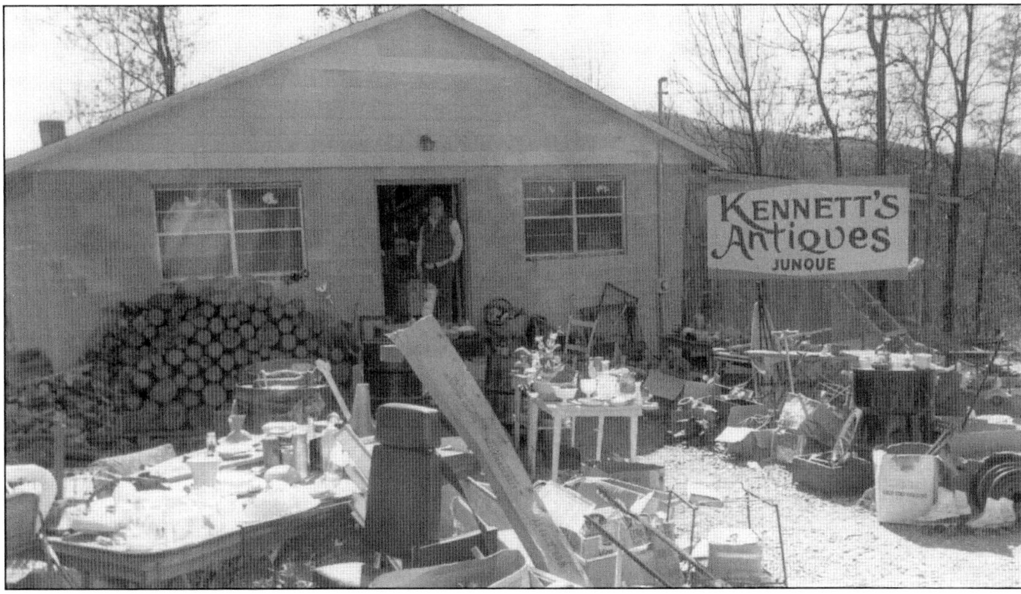

Since 1968, Kennett's Antiques and Junque has been an institution in Monticello. Calvin Kennett operates his store south of Monticello on Pump Station Hill. Along with his business, this knowledgeable and experienced antique dealer has had another career: For 33 years he taught history at Wayne County High School. Kennett's enthusiasm for his subject matter and his unique teaching style are remembered by hundreds of people who sat in his classroom as teenagers. (Wayne County Historical Society.)

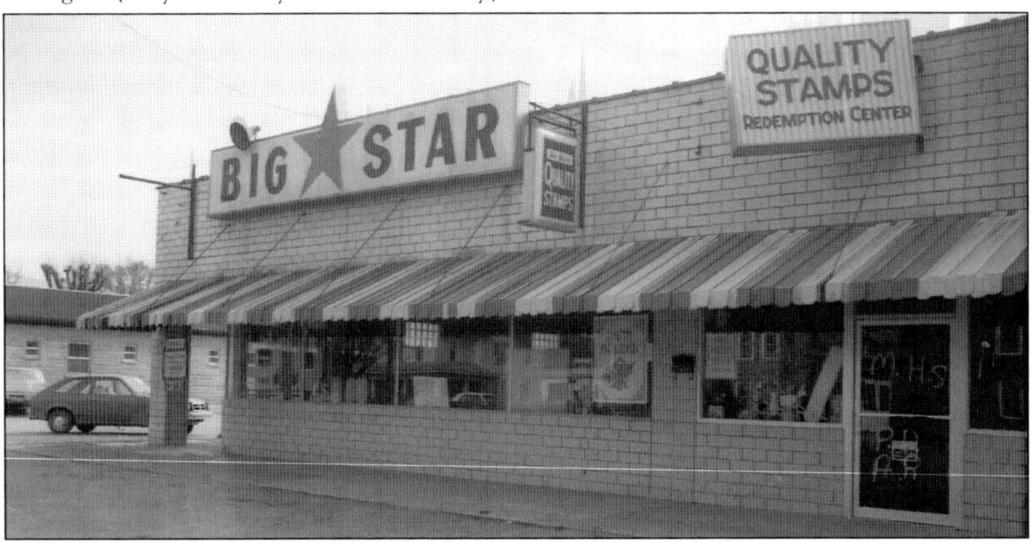

This building on North Main Street was built by Jess and Jim Chesney in 1951. It was operated until 1969 as the J and J Kentucky Food Store. Milton Roberts, the next owner, operated a grocery store called Big Star in the building. Other businesses housed there were the WPM Manufacturing Company and a cabinet shop. The smaller unit on the right was the location of at least three businesses. Wayne Auto Parts began there in 1955 and continued until 1971. At another time Cooper Jewelry was located there, and as shown in this 1976 picture, the unit housed a stamp store at one point. For many years now, the entire building has been the office of Dr. James Sawyer. (J. D. Rogers.)

Nine

Hotel Breeding and the Wayne County Museum

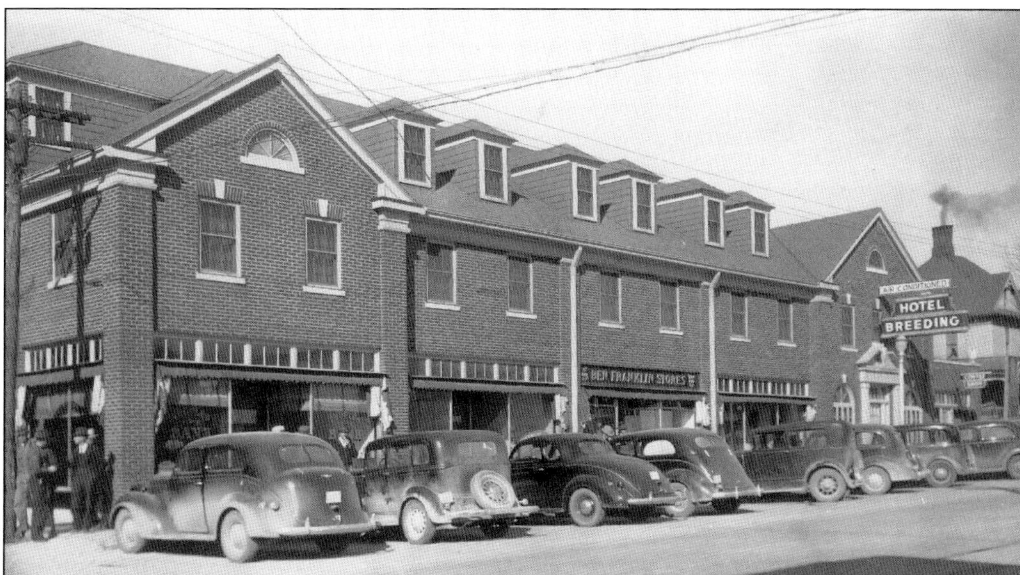

Hotel Breeding was built in 1936 by Robert G. Breeding. The six large street-level rooms housed the hotel lobby and a number of businesses. Peoples State Bank occupied the southern room, and the northern room was the coffee shop. Guest rooms were on second and third floor, and a full-sized basement contained a large dining room where various social functions were held and civic clubs conducted their meetings. In 2010, the old Hotel Breeding building serves as a real "front porch" for Wayne County history. It houses the William Crenshaw Kennedy Jr. Memorial Museum (Wayne County Museum) as well as the Elizabeth Furr Duncan Library, a much-used genealogy library. (Dr. Robert B. Breeding.)

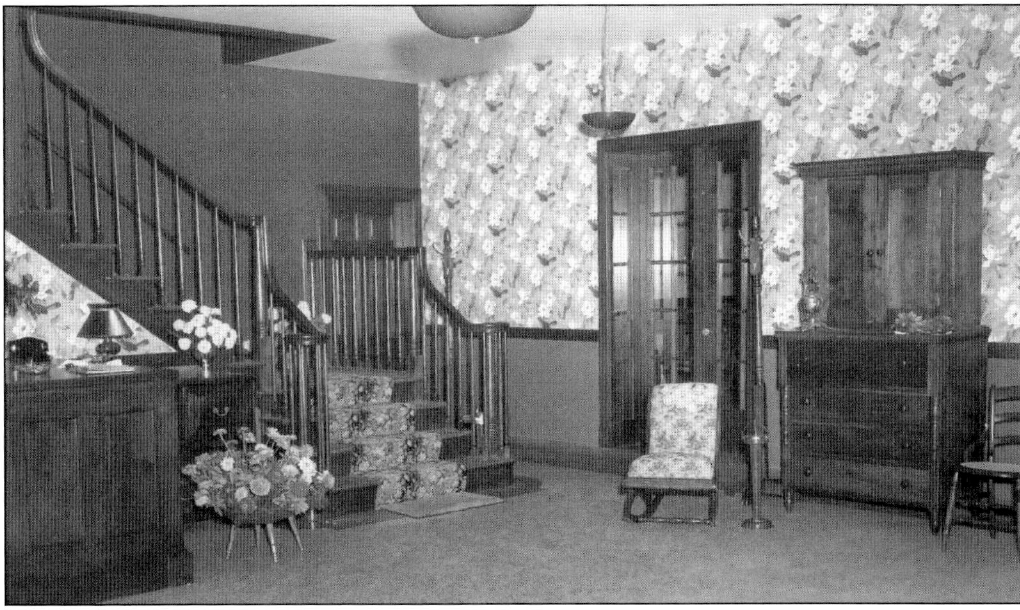

The ambiance of the lobby of Hotel Breeding bespoke fine accommodations. In 2010, the lobby serves as the gift shop for the Wayne County Museum. The glass doors that once opened to the hotel's coffee shop, the terrazzo floors, the hotel desk, and the stairway are original to the building. The old hotel lobby serves as a fine entrance for a trip into history. (Dr. Robert B. Breeding.)

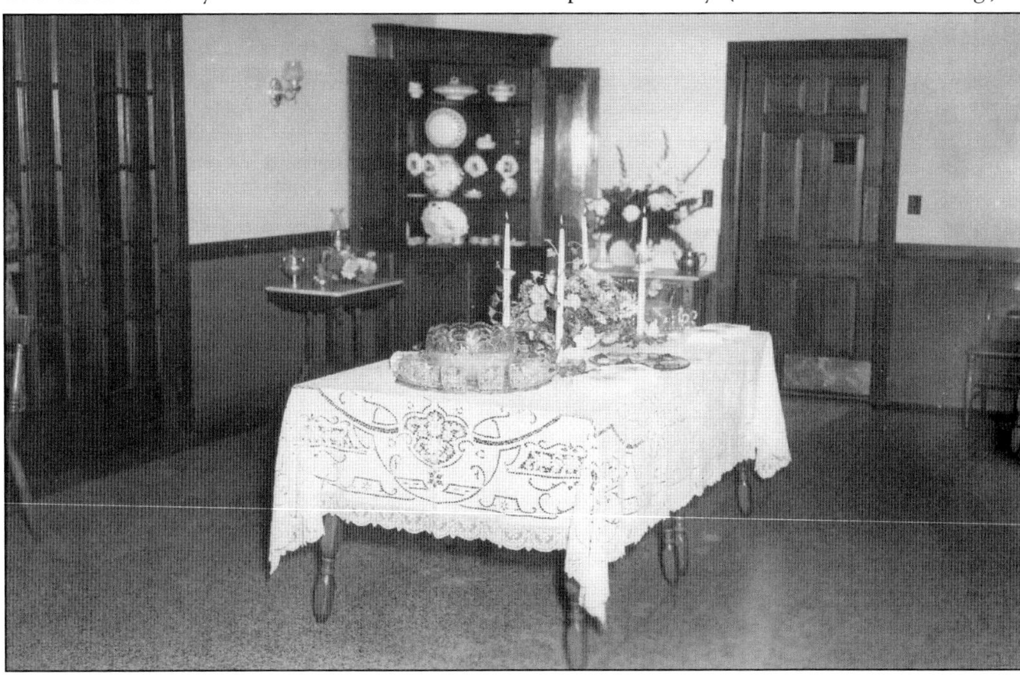

Around Monticello there was no better place to dine than at the coffee shop in Hotel Breeding. For more than two decades, the food and the service in this small dining room were unsurpassed. Black-bottom pie, always on the menu, is mentioned by nearly everyone who remembers eating there. In this picture, the restaurant appears to be set up for a special occasion. As of 2010, this room was serving as an office for the Wayne County Museum. (Dr. Robert B. Breeding.)

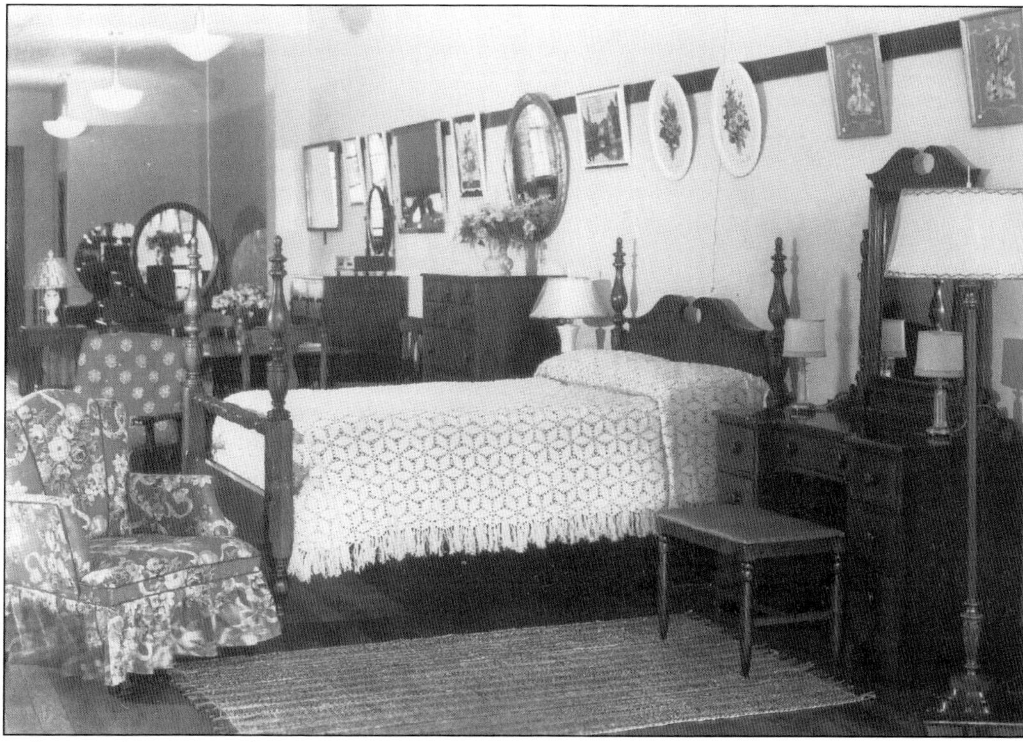

Billy Breeding opened Breeding's Furniture Store in 1945. Quality furniture and beautiful arrangements were givens at this store. At first the business occupied only one unit in the Hotel Breeding building, but it soon expanded to two units, and appliances were added. In all, the business operated almost 35 years under the same roof. (Dr. Robert B. Breeding.)

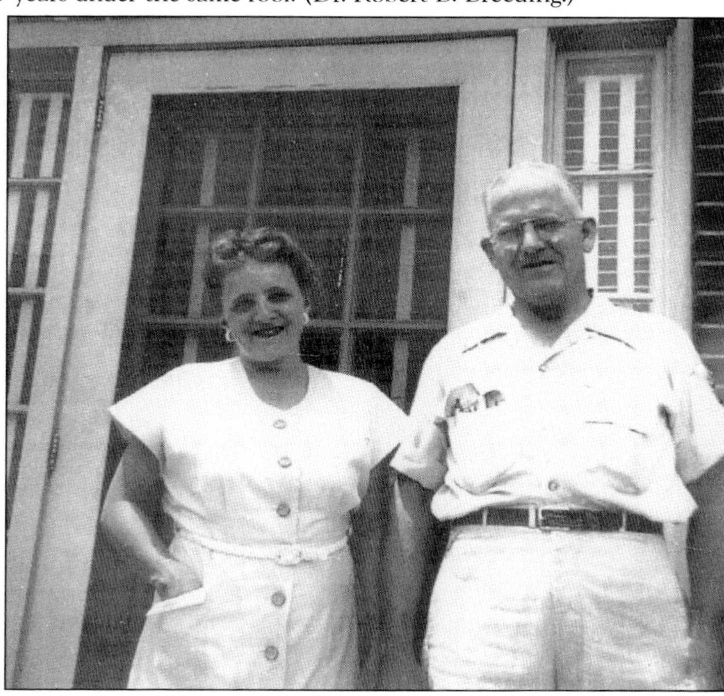

The Ed and Katy Roberts family operated Hotel Breeding from 1949 until 1959. Business flourished during those years: The hotel's coffee shop was known as a fine place to dine, guest rooms were often filled to capacity, and the large basement meeting room was much in demand. (Wayne County Museum.)